LORI-A...

Things I

Only

Tell My
Friends

The
"And Then It Happened"
events that formed my life

Tellwell Talent
www.tellwell.ca

ISBN
978-0-2288-0227-3 (Hardcover)
978-0-2288-0226-6 (Paperback)
978-0-2288-0228-0 (eBook)

To my humble, courageous and loving husband "Ralph".
You are the wisest and strongest person I know.
Thanks for all the laughs and tears that we have shared.
Your love of life and compassion for others inspires me.
It is frustrating to be proven wrong when we bet,
but at least the money stays in the family!

TABLE OF CONTENTS

My Purpose

"When writing the story of your life, don't let anyone else hold the pen."
—Harley Davidson

While my husband and I were in the stressful process of selling our multimillion dollar business, an award winning private language school, I had gone to a different psychic every month for two years. My friends laughed at me because when I didn't get the exact answer I wanted, I just went to another one. The psychics said that the sale of my company would go through and I would be happy with the deal. The business eventually sold and their accuracy was spot on. But while I was expecting the deal to close for months and months, I just wanted someone to tell me that everything was going to be ok. (I was not born with patience... I blame that on my mother.)

During all these sessions, just about every psychic told me that I should be writing a book. Many were surprised that I hadn't started already. I have compiled two books, one was stories of my puppy Elvis. The other was when the school we owned celebrated its 20th year in business. But those were collaborations of other people's stories.

I was not sure what I should be writing about, so I asked my closest friends. Every single person came up with a different topic, so thanks to them, I decided I would write about each of their suggestions.

Most who know me are shocked when I tell them I used to be a major procrastinator, because I am one of those people who have their Christmas presents wrapped by August. But I remember in school, I would wait to the last day to study or to finish a paper, I would do laundry only when there were no clean clothes left.

I would spend every last dollar of a paycheck, and only pay the minimum balance on my credit cards.

All this created a lot of anxiety and my insides hurt with worry. I spent more time thinking about what I had to do, than the actual amount of time that it would take me to do it. ***And then it happened!*** I was in my early twenties, when I finally went to a doctor after months of stomach pains. After seeing not one, but five doctors, I was diagnosed with ovarian cancer and was given a death sentence. First, I was in shock and then in denial, and then I just got angry. I didn't want anyone to know I was sick and I ended up going for surgery all by myself. The hospital wouldn't release me unless someone could pick me up. So, I called a taxi and asked him to say he was my friend. I went home not knowing if I would live or die. The doctor told me that if I ever did survive and tried to get pregnant, I would probably die while giving birth! That is far from the way doctors would handle a patient today. There is now a human papilloma virus (HPV) vaccine that all girls can take around the age of eleven to thirteen years or before intercourse, that prevents this cancer, so please look into it if you have young girls in your life. Somehow I did survive, so I promised the universe and my spirit guides that I would never procrastinate again.

One thing I have learned, is that very few of us end up in the place we imagined when we were young. Apparently, I told my family when I was very young, that I wanted a small house with a white picket fence and three kids. I have no memory of ever thinking of that. Now, I treasure the freedom of not having to worry about children of my own.

I do remember in my twenties thinking I would never marry, or if I did, that I would have been divorced a few times. Turns out, I married the most wonderful man on earth. I know we will be together forever, as long as we are both growing together and always making sure the other person feels loved. I thought I would be working 60-hour weeks for someone else, as the vice president of a major company (I don't know why I thought vice president instead of president). Turns out I have had quite a few careers, a night club manager, costume designer, a private investigator, and a restaurant general manager. And then became an entrepreneur at the age of twenty-four.

When others ask if I know my purpose in life, I tell them I do! Some seem surprised I already know mine, as it seems to take others a lifetime to find theirs.

I truly believe I've found my purpose in life: *"To celebrate life as often as possible and to remind others to."*

In this book I show you step by step, how to put on a stress-free small dinner party or a large celebration for 300. I take you through the importance and steps for meditating and visualizing. Being a medium, I explain how to hone your intuitive skills to use in all aspects of life. I share stories about having a successful business, how I motivated my staff and why we won many customer service awards. I share key factors in keeping my 27-year marriage happy and strong. Stories and suggestions on traveling to over 100 countries around the world. The lessons in each chapter are to help others avoid the mistakes I made and suggestions on how to make your life, business and relationships more enjoyable.

We all only have a number of life-defining moments that can change our lives. I am hoping this may inspire those who need a little bit of courage or push to live their life to the fullest. To take chances, trust your own instincts, do not listen to the naysayers and most importantly, to celebrate each and every step in your life.

So, Universe, here are my life lessons, stories and wisdom that I would only tell my friends. These are from my point of view. Names and dates may have changed to protect the innocent, or because my menopausal memory of these events may be different from theirs! These stories are not to air dirty laundry except my own. (Okay, there may be a few dirty bits here and there.)

Let me share my *"And then it happened..."* moments, so that when yours come along, it may help you recognize them, and have the courage to take those opportunities to change your destiny.

"Go through life like a duck: majestic on top, kicking like hell underneath."

—Anonymous

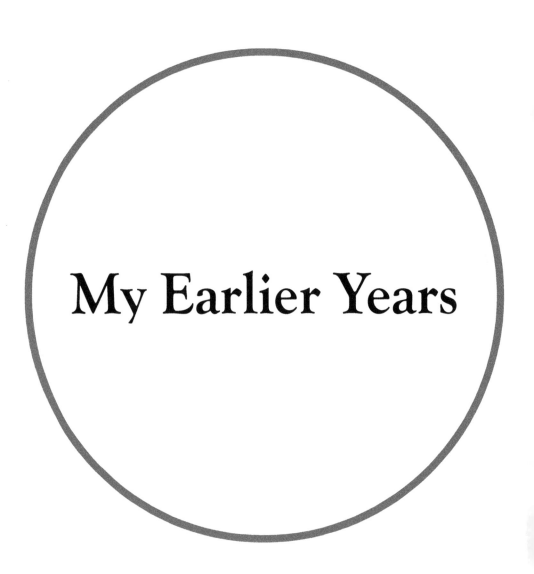

My Earlier Years

FROM THE GET GO

"If you don't do wild things while you are young, you'll have nothing to smile about when you are old."

—*Anonymous*

I was born and raised in Saskatoon, Saskatchewan, Canada by my teenaged mother. Mom tells me that I never spoke one word until my second birthday. Then I came out with full sentences. Growing up, my nickname was Skinny-Mini-Miller-Motor-Mouth. I was super skinny (aka anorexic) and I would talk to anyone and everyone. I bet my mom misses those first quieter years.

She tells me that I was always a free spirit and that I had extreme focus on whatever I was doing. I didn't let anything get in my way. She divorced my father when I was four years old. He moved to Vancouver, where my older brother and I were shipped out to see him in the summers.

I seriously have no idea how my mother did it. I don't remember a day that we didn't feel loved and cared for and somehow we always had everything we needed. Well, I would have liked more candy and pop growing up, like our neighbor's kids had, but Halloween candy can be eaten over many months (but not candy corn… whoever invented that should be made to eat it every day).

As kids, we would be out playing on the street, until Mom yelled for us to come home. My brother and I were latch-key kids from the time we were very young. We came home by ourselves from school for lunch, made a baloney sandwich, watched "The Flintstones" and then headed back to school.

Being raised in a humble home, I was taught the importance of being thrifty and creative. I was setting goals as far back as I can remember. I saved for years just to buy my own 12 inch black and white TV for my bedroom. It had three channels and I loved it! Selling fruit and lemonade as kids is probably something a lot of us did. (Did you hear you need a permit for that in some cities now?) It's a great way to supplement an allowance. I remember one summer when we neighborhood kids decided to put on a play. We worked hard to learn our lines and my mom provided the costumes. I remember not sleeping the night before, worried about forgetting my lines. I don't know if the "box office" take was divided equally as my brother was in charge of the cash, but I do remember having a lot of fun.

I remember being fiercely protective of those close to me, as I am today. One situation as kids, my brother was getting picked on by three boys. I jumped in and started wailing on them. When I got home, my brother screamed at me saying he was humiliated that his little sister had to protect him.

I loved any and all holidays growing up and would have the house decorated for Valentine's Day, St Patrick's Day (no one I knew was even Irish) and every other celebration of the year. I started cooking at a very early age, so it came easy to me as I got older. The only reason my brother and I kept up piano lessons was because our instructor's mother would teach us baking while the other one was getting the piano lesson.

When I was about ten years old, I wanted to surprise my family by cooking dinner. I found a recipe that looked perfect. I went to the grocery store with my allowance to buy the ingredients, but I couldn't find the exact ones, so I just substituted a few. I went home and made the dish. My family came home and I very proudly presented my fabulous seven-layer meat and potato dish. When I scooped up a big bowl for everyone, they just started laughing.

Crushed by their laughter, I *begged "What's wrong? I followed the recipe!"* Unfortunately, the layer I substituted was the problem. The maraschino cherries looked like the crushed tomatoes in my mind. Our dog, Kojak wouldn't even eat it!

And then it happened! At the age of thirteen, my mother was rushed to the hospital with a ruptured ulcer! The extended family was to come for Christmas and so I got at it. I made the turkey, potatoes, veggies and more. I am not sure how I knew how to make them, my mom probably taught me as she cooked. The big family meal might not have tasted perfect, but everyone was just happy we were all together and that Mom was going to be okay. I know this day changed me in many ways, but I have never been afraid to cook anything after the success of that meal.

I had part-time jobs since I was ten, and loved the idea that I could make my own money and decide what to do with it. I may have always had an entrepreneurial spirit as I was the one who organized our after-grad party for my high school. I booked the buses, and arranged the venue, food and music. I sold tickets every break time and kept account of the money coming in, while allowing for all the expenses I needed to pay. When people ask me if I have any regrets in life, I say only one. We had a student in our graduating class named Johnny. I kept reminding him to bring his $20 for the after-grad party. Every day he assured me he would bring it tomorrow. Grad came and went and I ended up clearing over $500 profit, which was a fortune back then. It was a hoot and I think everyone had a great time. Later that summer, it hit me that Johnny never ended up coming to the after-grad celebration. I could not believe I had forgotten about him. Our public high school was just an average school, but we did know who the less fortunate kids were. I was so busy organizing everything I never once thought that maybe he couldn't afford the $20 ticket price. The realization that I walked away with a nice profit while not just giving him a ticket, left me feeling crushed. So, if by chance you read this book Johnny, I am truly sorry for being a selfish teenager. These days, I try to make sure that whenever I am in a position to help others, I take it.

My first memory of falling for a boy was in kindergarten. There was a boy in my class named Stanley. Apparently, one day the teacher had to call our parents in, because we wouldn't stop kissing in the cloakroom.

I had plenty of boyfriends growing up. But in my mind, I almost always asked them out. I do remember one boy in high school that I tried asking out over and over again, and was turned down every time. I heard years later that he was gay, which somehow at the time, made me feel better.

I had one horrible boyfriend in high school who was a complete jerk. I have no idea what I saw in him and over the course of the relationship we had huge fights. When I had finally had enough of his behavior and told him we were done permanently, he came over to my house and put his fists in several of our walls. I am not sure how my family got him out of the house, but we threatened him by calling the police and he left. Thankfully, I rarely ran into him again. I have asked a lot of my girlfriends later in life if they dated abusive men and a surprising amount had a guy physically or mentally abuse them.

As I got older, most of the men I dated were much older than me, and therefore my mom was the same age or younger than my dates. Sometimes, when they came to pick me up, they would see her, and lose all interest in me. She was one hot mama!

Early Travels

I got the travel bug early. I believe traveling helped define who I am and who I wanted to become. I would work hard at my jobs, just so I could travel. I don't know how my mom didn't die from worry. Every trip was an adventure, every situation was a chance to learn.

At the age of nineteen, when the local radio station advertised a big singles trip to Hawaii, I signed up right away. It sounded perfect to be traveling with a group of like-minded people, except only four people showed up at the airport! It wasn't the type or number of people I expected at all. We had fun individually, but rarely saw each other for the whole week away. This was one of my first lessons traveling: ask more specific questions. *"How many are going? What ages are they? How many men versus women?"*

It was a blast meeting tons of people in Hawaii as I have never had a challenge meeting people or going out on my own. I went to a male strip show one night, and a bunch of the performers and a few of us gals in the audience ended up going out for dinner after the show. It was a hoot. They were all great people and we ate and laughed until the wee hours.

Being young, naïve and from the Canadian Prairies, I was taught to be very polite to everyone I met. One night I was sitting alone at a lovely restaurant on Waikiki Beach, when this man walked up to my table and asked if he could join me. I said okay. He kind of gave me the creeps, so I finished dinner and told him I was going back to my hotel. He insisted he walk me back to my hotel. I told him no thanks, but he wasn't backing off, so I quickly jumped in a cab and told the driver to just drive away. The next night while walking down the same beach the same guy came up to me again.

I was trying everything I could do to get away from him. ***And then it happened!*** He jumped me and threw me into the bushes. I don't need to tell you what happened. I was in so much shock, I just got up after and ran away. It took me years to tell anyone. I was embarrassed and thought I should have been smarter. It did make me grow up quickly and from that day on I had no problem telling men to get lost.

Please learn from this painful lesson. You do not have to be polite to people you feel uncomfortable with. You can scream and get other people's attention. Being a little embarrassed is a lot better than the alternative.

My passion while in school in Saskatchewan was psychology with the desire to become a counselor. I volunteered to help in Alcoholics Anonymous and Narcotics Anonymous. But shortly found this sapped much of my energy and I realized I couldn't spend my life doing this. I had no idea of what I wanted to be at that point.

At this time I was working at the city's largest nightclub. I loved this job, I made great tips, with lots of dancing and fun times. I worked very hard and learned much about managing staff. It never got out that I was actually under the legal drinking age when hired, and ended up being promoted to manager. This was my first time interviewing and hiring. It was very interesting learning how I could ask the same question different ways to get the information needed from an applicant.

On another adventure when single, I was at the airport catching a plane to Hawaii. There was a very long line at check-in, so I went to the bar for a drink and thought I would check in later. I sat beside a young couple who just got married and were on my flight for their honeymoon. We were chatting for a while, and I must have lost track of time. The bride said we should head to the gate. I ran to the check-in desk to find the flight was now full. I proclaimed, *"But I have a ticket!"* The airline agent offered me a seat on any other Air Canada flight that left that night. When I protested a little more, she offered to pay for a hotel at any destination I chose for four nights. So that is how I ended up at the West Edmonton Mall and Hotel instead of Hawaii. FYI, it is the biggest mall in North America. I called my

mom from Edmonton and told her the story. We decided that she should
get on a flight and come shopping with me. She arrived the next day. We
hit every store in the mall as well as the comedy club where she kept being
singled out by the comedians.

We didn't need to ever leave the mall as everything we wanted was there.
By the way, this hotel has themed rooms, and is great for the kids or a bit
of romance. The mall has a water and amusement park, and can be a fun
vacation in the middle of winter for you and your family.

On the last day, Mom was packing up our things in our hotel room.
Her flight was leaving early in the morning and mine was later that day.
She offered to take home all the items we bought, so I could just go with
a carry-on bag. She kissed me goodbye and left. I went back to sleep for a
while, then got up and showered. I looked around the room and discovered
there were no clothes anywhere. My mom had taken every bit of clothing
home with her! I ended up calling the manager of a clothing store in the
mall, and after telling her my story, begged her to come up to my room
with my sizes. After trying the clothes on, I went down with her to pay the
bill. We all had a good laugh about that. Another lesson learned is to always
check you have clothes to wear when someone offers to pack up for you.

On a vacation to California, I met a guy who ended up taking me to
Disneyland. He paid, and about ten minutes after we entered, a security
guard asked to speak privately to him. My date returned and told me we
had to leave. I was confused. My first thought was this guy was a crook or
something. Nope! The security guard asked us to leave because I was dressed
"inappropriately." I was very young and skinny and was wearing cut-off
jeans. Apparently I cut my "cut offs" a wee-bit too short, because my bottom
was on full display. Note to self for my next life: no short-short shorts at
a family destination. But man, what I wouldn't do to have that butt now!

Club Med Days

My next trip, a year later, was a two-week holiday to Club Med in the
Caribbean. I loved every second of it. Every night there was a performance
by the staff (the Gentils Organisateurs, or G.Os.) The activities and the
food were excellent and everyone had a fabulous time.

Most of the wardrobe I took with me were clothes I had sewn myself.
I always liked unique clothes, not off-the-rack or the trend that everyone

else wore. I got many compliments on my clothes that week. ***And then it happened!*** The Chief of Village came up to me as I was basking by the pool on my last day. He had heard that I was a seamstress and asked if I would be interested in a job there. As it turned out, the previous costume designer quit in a huff and they needed someone immediately.

I asked him about three questions and said yes! I phoned the guy I had been living with back home and told him I was not coming back. (It really should have been a sign for both of us, when one of us goes on a two-week vacation to a party place without the other.) I called my job at the nightclub and quit. I called my friends and my mom to ask them to pack up my personal things from my apartment, and never looked back. If I had not decided on the spot to take the opportunity, I would not have had the path of adventures that were in store for me.

I worked in several locations at Club Med, the standard contract was for six months. So work was every day for the six months, food, wine and accommodation were free and I was paid $400 USD a month. I had a great time learning new languages. Most of the staff that worked in my department came from France where the head office was located. And they didn't want to mix with you unless you spoke French, so I had to learn quickly. The next resort I was sent to was in Mexico, so I learned Spanish very quickly. I studied Ukrainian in school, but never really used what I was taught, except when I was around my Ukrainian grandparents at Christmas. Nowadays the only Ukrainian words I remember are, *"Hi, do you want a beer?"* I can't remember if my teachers taught me that or my grandfather.

I loved being creative all day long designing and sewing. Looking back on all my jobs, the best were the ones that I could be artistically creative. I did a lot of traveling to different Club Med locations, as they also sent me on many buying trips to New York for the fabric and accessories for the costumes I made for shows. The reason I ended up not wanting to go back to New York was that I had to stay in some cheap and nasty hotels while on these buying trips. I saw too many weird people there in the '80s.

As I traveled the world, I met and dated many men. I remember thinking that I would never settle down, as there are too many interesting ones. I dated a few guys who were guests at Club Med, including a local drug dealer (I didn't know that until we ended our relationship). I rarely dated the same guy for any length of time, but I did fall for a few. One proposed to me after only four months together. He claimed he was a distant nephew of the King of Jordan, but didn't want to live in the Middle East anymore. He was a very nice guy, but what he really wanted was his Canadian immigration papers. When we broke up, he married another woman within a few months and got them.

I took up many new activities in my time off at the resorts. Since they were all free for staff, I went horseback riding every morning, riding bareback. We would take the horses swimming in the ocean so they could cool off. The only time I got hurt was when I was riding in the desert in Mexico and got thrown into an eight-foot cactus when a snake spooked the horse. I did not know what I was more upset about, the blood everywhere, or the fact the snake was still there when I stood up, with what I am sure, was a smirk on its face.

While stationed in the Bahamas, a massive hurricane strength storm blew in, taking down trees and damaging villas. The next morning, while on my usual run, I came across a small clearing and stopped dead in my tracks. An eight-foot snake was lying there sunning himself. I was paralyzed with fear. The snake rose up and we locked eyes. We both seemed to realize just how scared we were of each other, and a few moments later we both relaxed, then he slithered away. Unfortunately, someone else from the village must have had a similar experience, because later that night we saw the dead snake being paraded around by a local. I cried that night for the snake.

I still ask myself, *"Am I afraid of snakes, or am I in awe of them?"*, and *"Why do I see them everywhere I go?"*

I also acquired my PADI scuba diving certificate and dove as much as I could, quickly getting my Assistant Instructor's qualification. My deepest dive was over 100 feet. I swear I could live underwater. It is always so peaceful. And then I started playing tennis, which I still love, but still suck at. In my next life, I am coming back as a better tennis player! And a saxophonist.

The last posting with Club Med was in Sonora Bay, on the west coast of Mexico. When I had a break from sewing, Bob, the Head Animator, and I would spend a lot of time doing gags for the guests. Every week we would pretend to be getting married on the beach. Then during the fake wedding, we would pretend to fight and throw each other into the ocean. We did countless other gags like this. He was one of the most talented and fun co-workers that I had ever worked with, and we have remained friends till this day.

A regular at that village was one of Willie Nelson's sons. He often invited the staff to come to his dad's house. The house was a just a normal rancher style with a big pool. The atmosphere was always casual and yes, weed was a regular thing there. Willie felt more like an uncle than a celebrity.

The first place overseas where my mom came to visit, was when I was working at that Club Med Guaymas. She was very excited to be there. I took a couple of days off to go for an adventure with her. I don't remember why we didn't pack water, but Mom overheated one day and was desperate to get back to air-conditioning and a cold drink. I was used to the heat, but she found out quickly how it can get to her.

The end of that era in my life came as quickly as it began. As a costume designer, I would design all the outfits for all nightly shows. I designed and sewed anything from tuxedos and gowns, to Broadway show costumes. That week was Halloween, and as you would guess, every guest (Gentil Membre or GM) came to my office to ask for a costume. I had worked 18 hour days all that week trying to please everyone. When the Chief of Village burst into my office at midnight of Halloween night and yelled at me to get to the disco to join the guests (part of the duties that everyone in the animation department were required to do), I tried to explain I was utterly exhausted. He cursed something back in French.

And then it happened! I grabbed a pair of scissors and flung them as hard as I could across the room at him. Luckily, I missed his 4'8" slimy head. I was fired on the spot and sent home the next morning.

More and More Life Lessons

I flew to Vancouver after Club Med and asked my father and his wife if I could stay with them. I was not close to them as my stepmother hadn't shown much patience during our summer visits as kids.

I was offered three jobs the first day I applied, and worked my butt off for a few months. The relationship with my father ended when he accused me of being a prostitute and a drug user. I have no idea where that came from. I was always working and never at home, except to sleep. I knew friends would call the house asking for me and was way more sociable than they were, but to be accused by a parent of being something so far from the truth was just horrible. I wouldn't wish that on anyone, so that was basically the end of our relationship. I spent years in therapy and a bad attempt at trying to kill myself by downing a bottle of pain killers over that. Now, I just feel sorry for them.

After my short stay in Vancouver working every day, I went back out to travel the world, with a new friend, Anne, on a European backpacking trip across the continent.

We had a blast traveling on $25 a day, starting in London. We loved the old buildings and spent time in museums and galleries. ***And then it happened!*** My claim to "15 minutes of fame" was when I was asked to help with the costumes for the London production of *Cats* by one of the guests I had met at Club Med. I was thrilled to see my name on the program in London. If I had hesitated by thinking I was not good enough to work on a major production, I would have missed out on a life-changing path. It stretched my comfort zone to the moon.

I did a few sewing gigs after that great experience, but my favorite was when a director asked me to design clothes for a porno movie he was making. Let's just say a lot of Velcro was involved! Sorry Mom, I never told you. But it was interesting being on set and seeing how these movies were made.

After earning some more money with that job, Anne and I headed for France, where we lived off cheap red wine, cheese and baguettes. In Spain, we slept on the beach and had the best paella. We usually tried to catch the night train to our next destination to save on hotel costs. We woke up one night on the train with the ticket collector's hand down Anne's shirt. Despite his protests, I doubt that he was actually looking for tickets there!

Then we headed north to Denmark, where I met some of my distant relatives. We drank Aquavit with every meal (90 proof). It was a very expensive country so we didn't stay long.

We tried 'special brownies' in Amsterdam. Oh, come on…… I am sure many of you would had tried it too if you were there.

I was lucky to be in the smallest country on Earth (based on land mass), Vatican City, just as the Pope was making a speech from his balcony. I had no idea what he was saying, but the crowd was mesmerized. It was not a long speech but the audience roared with excitement and applauded when it was over. Check the Pope's schedule online and plan your trip around his appearances as it is a fascinating thing to see. To see thousands show up for his words of wisdom and then disappear back to their daily life is amazing.

We almost got robbed in Rome by begging ladies carrying fake babies, whose ploy was to drop one so unsuspecting tourists would rush to help. I grabbed my friend's bag just in time as one of these robbers was lunging for it.

In Italy, we quickly learned that if you sat down for a coffee at an outdoor café, you would be charged a lot more than just standing drinking it. Another thing, if you are traveling to Italy on a budget, be aware of bread basket scam in restaurants. In the first restaurant we went to, after sitting together and ordering soup, they placed a bread basket on our table. In Canada, we were always given bread baskets for free in restaurants, so we dove in. When the bill came, we discovered they charged us individually for the same amount of bread as one person. The next time we entered separately, ordered a salad and when done, we just put the extra bread in our bags and paid the bill. We had enough bread for the next meal. I was also shocked that things like jam and ketchup would cost extra in Europe.

I got really sick in Venice while we were there. I remember not being able to find accommodation on our budget, so I spent most of my time sleeping in a park feeling terrible.

From Italy, we took the overnight boat to Greece with dozens of other backpackers. We all slept outside on the deck sharing stories about our adventures. Looking up at the stars with a warm wind keeping us cozy. We saw the Acropolis in Athens and drank the local inexpensive wine, Retsina, which had been made the same way for 2000 years. We both agreed they really should change the recipe ASAP. Anne and I made many friends, had so many laughs and adventures. I treasured every moment and knew that this experience had changed me for the better.

I was literally down to my last $20 after traveling across Europe in our last stop in Greece. I went for a morning hike in Athens, then sat on a hill meditating. I flipped a drachma to decide if I would go to Toronto or Vancouver with my airline ticket. It landed heads for Vancouver, so I flew back and at the airport, I picked up a newspaper to look for rooms for rent. There was no Craigslist back then, but I saw an advertisement for a room for $200 a month in a house in North Vancouver. I called the house and confessed I had no money, but offered to clean the house while I looked for work. There were five guys sharing the house and they agreed. I took the bus over and moved into the smallest bedroom/closet that there ever was. The house was a pig-pen, so I started cleaning that night. The next day, I got a job before 10am working for a women's retail chain. I saved up and moved out in a couple of months to my own place.

I found I liked sales and discovered I was great at it, first working in a family company. A few months later I applied for their supervisor position but was not successful. The lady they hired was not nearly as good as I thought I was and it started eating at me. I did things that I shouldn't have and got fired, which I completely deserved! The lesson I learned was to not be counter-productive just because you don't get your way at work. It can come back and bite you in the butt, or hurt your reputation!

All I ever had in my mind was to save up as much money as I could, so I could to go traveling again. The more I traveled, the more I learned about myself and about life. I believe you cannot really, truly know your real character without being around total strangers and situations that you have no one to rely on except yourself.

Africa Was Calling Me

For as long as I can remember I always wanted to go to Africa. I was still in my early twenties and had recovered from my ovarian surgery, when I finally bought a one-way ticket and went on my way.

Cairo: Being a young, white, blond girl back in those days was fascinating to the locals. On my arrival in Cairo, a couple of men working at the airport figured out that I was traveling by myself and an easy mark. They insisted on accompanying me through immigration, saying, *"You won't understand the language."* As I told the immigration officer where I was staying and the men overheard. I told them to get lost but they were not taking no for an answer, following my cab to my hotel. I told the reception person that I was not with them, and to not give them any information about me. An hour after entering my room, the phone starting ringing and after not picking up, there was knocking on my door. I kept the lights off for another hour before heading down to the dining room. They were not there, thankfully. After dinner, I called for the hotel manager and told him what happened. He moved me to an upgraded room and promised they will not be allowed back in the hotel. Not a good start to this adventure. I only came to Cairo to see the pyramids but turns out they were all under maintenance, so I only saw them from a distance. Two more lessons learned. One: to check to see if the things you want to see are actually available, and two: never let a stranger know where you are staying. Big mistake! I did pick up a cheap wedding band in the market there, wearing it helped keep aggressive men at bay.

Mombasa, Kenya: After checking-in to my hotel on the waterfront, I took a long walk on the beach with my new flip flop rubber sandals. It was almost 100F outside, I didn't mind as I have always loved the heat. After my three hour walk, I returned to the lounge at my hotel downing a gin and tonic when I looked down at my sandals. They had literally melted down to the sole.

The best thing I had packed for that kind of heat was baby oil and tin foil, brought all the way from Canada so as to get a deep tan. Needless to say, I have spent the last 30 years of my life trying to get rid of the sun damage.

Mombasa was everything I hoped for. I loved giving the local kids pencils, paper and candy. All the kids wanted to touch my blond hair and my fair skin. They would come right up to my face and were fascinated with my green eyes. I would teach the children English songs and we would sit under trees together for hours. I always figured that if I ever adopted a child, he or she would be Kenyan.

Before leaving for Africa, I had received all my shots, including taking my malaria pills. But, one night I woke up shivering, turned off the air conditioner and opened the window. The next morning, I knew I was in a bad way because the chair in my room grew feet and started dancing. I quite liked watching it dance around the room but at some point I must have clued-in that this is not just a ghost playing with me. I called for a doctor and he took me directly to the hospital. After spending a night there re-hydrating, I felt much better.

Don't even think about going on these adventures without getting all your vaccines. The doctor said getting mine saved me from a far worse outcome.

After a few weeks in Mombasa, I found a recommended travel agent in town and booked a ten-day, five-star safari leaving the next day. It was so cheap compared to the prices I saw back in Vancouver. I headed off with four others to the great Maasai Mara National Reserve. We saw every animal in the book and loved every second of it. One night when we were all in our huts, a lion took down another animal right outside our fenced-off area, so loud it sounded like it was **in** my hut.

It was both exciting and scary. Funny when you first get there, you are so excited to see your first giraffe or elephant, but after day one it becomes common place. You then search for the elusive ones. We went up in a hot air balloon for an early morning ride. When the burner was low, we could get so close to the big animals, and we could hear them breathe. So cool! The thing I learned being there, is that animals need to be protected, but they also need space to roam.

Africa was my first introduction to many different species of monkey. While on safari we came across a truck driver that had his window open as he was driving on the highway. Somehow a baboon jumped onto the truck, reached in one window and took a chunk out of the driver's arm. And we thought they were all cuddly little fellows! The small monkeys at the hotels were an amusement for guests, but a huge pain for staff as most hotels offered breakfast buffets. The first day I was in Kenya, I walked in and chose a table. I left my hat on the table then went to get food, but when I came back, my hat was gone. The waiter warned me to not leave anything at the table, and fortunately retrieved my hat from the monkey. I was entertained every morning as new guests would make the same mistake of leaving food and belongings unattended.

After the safari, I headed to Nairobi for some big city adventures. And boy were there many! The very first night at my (so-so) hotel, I didn't leave the room as there was a lot of commotion right outside my window. The next morning, I headed out early to get something to eat. ***And then it happened!*** Two rival street gangs used me as a human shield, thinking the other wouldn't dare hurt a white, female foreigner. Both sides started throwing rocks at the other group with me in the middle. I have never run away faster than then, knowing I could have been killed. Bruised and bleeding, I locked myself in my bathroom and stayed close to my hotel for the next day. The hotel manager heard about my incident and the police were called in. They advised me I should never go out alone and should always take a taxi if I do. At this time in history, any locals who hurt or stole from any foreigner would serve severe jail time. The sad part of this story is that the kids in these gangs were as young as four or five years old and homeless. When their father dies or divorces, their mother often needs to remarry, sometimes with the new husband insisting the wife gets rid of her children. Unfortunately, many mothers, out of desperation, comply.

There was this one legendary restaurant in Nairobi that all the travel books insist you go. It was a impressive place with a massive tree in the middle of it. Tourists and expats would attach notes to this tree sending messages to fellow tourists they have met along the way in Africa.

In that restaurant later that week, I started chatting with two young, blond Irish gals who came on a modeling contract to Kenya. As soon as they arrived they found out it was bogus! (Remember, this was before the Internet). They were down to their last few dollars, so I offered them to stay with me at my hotel for a couple nights before their flight home. We were out for dinner at a small restaurant the next night, having a great time chatting up others and everyone was very relaxed. The two got up to go to the bathroom together (as tourist books said we should), when a Middle Eastern man approached my table and offered me one hundred dollars to say nothing if the girls disappear. I yelled for help and the staff came a runnin'. The guy fled and I ran to the restroom to see if the girls were okay. They were fine, but we were freaked out. We heard stories about how young foreign girls would be drugged and shipped off for sex slaves, we just never imagined it could happen to us. We all went back to our hotel room and downed a bottle of wine to calm our nerves. After the shock was over, I joked to them, *"What am I, chopped liver? He didn't offer any money for me!"* We burst into laughter. We all agreed if you are traveling on your own, especially as a woman, make sure someone knows where you are at all times. And to scream in a dangerous situation, as it may save your life.

The girls left and I decided to climb Mount Kilimanjaro, in Tanzania. I flew down and was met by my tour guide and we went directly to base camp. I had never climbed before, but I felt I was in pretty good shape to be able to do this. We started up the next day with a group of tourists from all over the world, working on doing the mountain in about seven or eight days. Unfortunately, one of the ladies that was with us turned very ill and we had to head back down on day five. The rest of us were offered another chance to go back up, but I had had enough and was happy to check that off my bucket list.

And that was the last major trip I had by myself.

Vancouver is My Home

After returning from six months in Africa, I was walking by a restaurant in the West End that was under construction. I popped in and met the owner. I offered if he needed help hiring or training staff to call me. The next day he did and asked if I wanted the job as General Manager. I took it and we opened the restaurant the following week. We had live jazz on the weekends and built up a following pretty quickly. It was an interesting experience to meet all the local, upcoming artists. Most of the talent were lovely people, a few were real jerks. I won't name names, as one went on to become quite successful, but my advice if you are an up-and-coming artist, is to be on time for your gigs and don't arrive stoned or drunk. A great part of that job was the hairdressers next door. Every day before I started work, they did my hair any way they wanted, and in return I bought them lunch. I showed up in the most amazing hair styles.

Our chef was a nice guy, as was the pastry chef. Then one night, around 11pm and just as I was about to close, and after the chefs had gone home, a group of ten came in for drinks and dessert. I was working my butt off trying to make the restaurant successful, so I sat them, made their drinks and then prepared and served dessert. I had watched the pastry chef prepare them, knowing it wasn't brain science to make a swirl on a plate and add the sweets on top. The next day though, the pastry chef lost it on me, yelling that it was his reputation on the line. I tried to reassure him that I prepared them as he did, even the busboy agreed. My boss stood up for me and the pastry chef walked out the door. Chefs can be very challenging to work with! A lesson learned that day.

Weeks later on a Friday night, as I was working the room at the restaurant, I approached the table of one of the more recognizable Italian restaurant owners in Vancouver. ***And then it happened!*** He asked if I liked my job and I replied I loved it. He asked me to come work for him and he would double my salary, but he wanted an answer immediately, needing me Monday morning. I looked him right in the eye and said, *"Deal, see you Monday."* I came in the next morning to give my boss two days' notice. He was very understanding. Looking back on that situation, I realize that was not fair to the owners. I was paid back many times over the years by staff who just never showed up for work, or quit on the spot. I really don't suggest doing that to anyone. Karma can be a bitch!

A few weeks later, the owners of that jazz restaurant I had left, were on the front page of the newspaper being charged with money laundering and the restaurant was shut down immediately. I guess the universe must have given me a nudge to take the risk of changing employers.

For all you restaurant managers out there, the one big thing that I was taught was that you should be working the room. Know your return customers by name. Welcome them back, know their usual drink, and introduce yourself to new customers. I eat out a lot, and I am constantly shocked by the lack of awareness hosts have about their regular customers. I still don't think any of our favorite restaurants know our names, though some know us by sight, but very rarely do they say, *"Welcome back!"* It's a small thing that holds a lot of weight.

My new job was going well except for the fact that my new Italian boss would come in, start yelling at my staff because the espresso was not made right, or that they were pouring the wine wrong. Anything he would see that wasn't right, he would yell at them in front of customers. I spent half my time dealing with upset staff and dealing with a very difficult chef. I learned very important lessons through him on how to keep staff satisfied and motivated. I just did the opposite of everything he did!

Months later, on a nice spring day, I went to work to find my boss and the other three general managers of his restaurants gathered in my office. **And then it happened!** The bottom had fallen out of the restaurant industry and all of his GMs were let go that day. I walked home, stunned. A bottle of wine later, I decided I will never work for anyone again. And I never looked back!

> *"Sam walks into his boss's office. "Sir, I'll be straight with you, I know the economy isn't great, but I have three companies after me, and I would like to respectfully ask for a raise." After a few minutes of haggling the boss finally agrees to a 5% raise, and Sam happily gets up to leave.*
> *"By the way", asks the boss as Sam is getting up, "which three companies are after you?" "The electric company, the water company and the phone company", Sam replied!"*
> —Anonymous

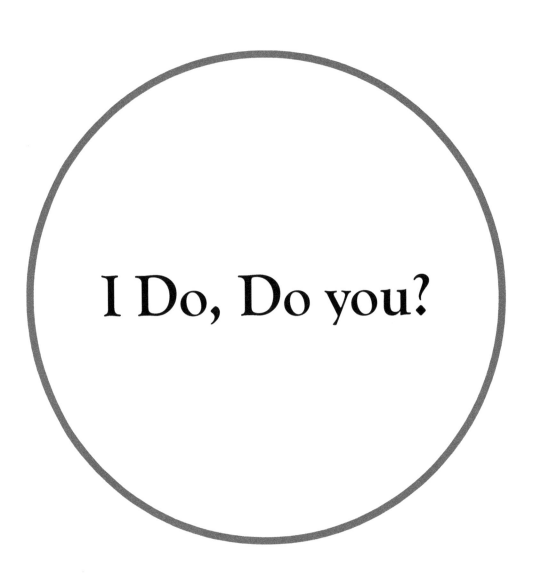

I Do, Do you?

LOVE AND MARRIAGE

*"The difference between an ordinary marriage and an
extraordinary marriage is in giving just a little 'extra' every
day, as often as possible, for as long as we both shall live."*
—*Fawn Weaver*

My Ukrainian grandmother was engaged to a young man when she was just a spring chicken. Then my grandfather came over to buy something from her farm. The two of them instantly fell in love. My grandmother broke off her engagement to the other guy and married my grandfather three weeks later. Their love lasted throughout their entire lives.

Love at first sight never happened to me. My brother claimed it did to him. The reason I feel I picked the perfect man in the end, was that I had dated a lot of different types of men. I knew what I wanted and what I didn't want.

The Ralph and Lori-Ann Love Story

It was not love at first sight for my husband or me in 1990. Ralph came to one of my Toastmaster club meetings in Vancouver. I was President of the club "Kismet" (which means "destiny") at the time he joined, looking to meet people and to improve his public speaking. I was giving a speech that day, and he told me later he thought I was full of myself. He had an accent, a nice New Zealand one, but I thought he was another one of those guys looking for someone to marry so as to stay in Canada.

At the time, I was seeing a guy who just gave up his dental practice in Vancouver and who decided to move to Australia. He phoned me from Sydney saying how much he missed me, calls that mostly came late at night, his time. I was out with Ralph casually by then and revealed to him my plans to go to Australia to see this other guy. By this time, Ralph had developed strong feelings for me and was crushed. He made a mixed tape of his favorite music (Sting, I think) and gave it to me that day at Granville Island Market. (Don't laugh, that was a very romantic thing back then.) I thought it was so sweet, but thought Ralph would have no idea how to handle a woman like me.

I bought a ticket to Australia and told the ex-dentist I was on my way. When I landed, I was shocked that he was not there to pick me up. I waited for 45 minutes with still no sign of him. I called his apartment and no one picked up (those were the days way before cell phones). After renting a car and booking a hotel, and just as I was leaving the airport, he walked in. He said the wrong thing, *"Oh, I didn't really think you would come!"* I walked out without answering him and did a two-week tour around the Gold Coast by myself. I never saw him again.

The Indy car race was on during my time there. I walked into a bar for happy hour and saw Mario Andretti sitting by himself at a table. I walked over to him to wish him good luck with the race. He asked me to join him and we chatted about how he got interested in racing and how he hadn't had any major crashes. We talked about the jerk that I came to Australia for. A few years later he had his big crash and I was relieved to hear he survived.

When I returned to Canada, I ended up calling Ralph to go for a run. We had hung out a couple times so I just guessed he was still single, not knowing that he had met another woman and was happy. He didn't know if I had married my guy or what. I assumed, because I was back in Vancouver, that he would have known that it hadn't worked out. And you know what they say about "ass-u-m-ing".

We had become jogging friends, and we enjoyed each other's company. One weekend, he was away visiting friends and I was with another man on a dinner date. I was sipping my cocktail at a restaurant with this guy and all I could think about was Ralph. ***And then it happened!*** It hit me like lightning: *"Oh my God, I am in love with Ralph!"* I dramatically threw a $20 bill down on the table and told my date I had to leave.

As soon as I arrived home I called Ralph (still before cell phones) and left a message for him at his friend's home on Vancouver Island to urgently call me back. When he finally did, I asked him to come back to the city as soon as he could, but didn't tell him why. When he entered my apartment, I ran to him and declared, *"I am in love with you, please move in with me!!!"* He looked at me calmly and said, *"I am sorry, I can't."* I was crushed! I threw him out of my apartment.

Refusing his phone calls for the next few days, I felt it was a mistake to have fallen for him. Then the doorbell rang with a delivery for me. It was a single red rose with Ralph's resume wrapped around it. On a future date on his revised resume to me, he added *"Got married in 1992."* I was very confused. I called him and he said, *"If you had any patience, I was trying to tell you I couldn't move in with you because you said you never wanted to get married, and I did!"* I apologized profusely, saying I would love to be his wife one day. He moved in with me a few weeks later. On a future date on his revised resume to me, he added *"Got married in 1992."*

Do you remember those first few months of a new relationship? They are exciting and passionate. We would always be playing pranks on each other. Many times, I hid in a closet when I heard him come home and scare the life out of him when he came near. He would hang small buckets of water over the front door, so when I opened it I got soaked. Do you remember the old American TV sitcom with Ralph and Alice, *The Honeymooners?* That's how our "Ralph" nicknames began.

And the other one would reply. *"Whatever you say Ralph!"*

Ralph and I have done many self-development courses with Tony Robbins, including fire walking. One relationship exercise was to fully describe your ideal mate, to write down what you wanted from a partner and what you didn't want. Six months after moving in, he found this long forgotten list from a program he had done much earlier. It was surprisingly accurate description of me. Included were details like my eye color, hair, heritage, height, interests, place of birth, education, personality and much more, all before meeting me. This shows the power of visualization and the subconscious. If you have the chance to listen to Tony or join his course, do so. We have introduced many people to his programs and everyone has discovered something valuable from it.

Pick a Partner Who Has Different Interests

I am constantly amazed at the knowledge Ralph stores in his head. We were playing a board game and he was asked who the Women's NCAA champions were five years before. And he knew! He can talk to anyone about their national, state or city sports team, or political situations from around the world. When we travel, he always has a conversation starter and tells me historical or interesting facts about each place. I truly believe he is the smartest man I have ever met, and that is why I keep getting amazed by him year after year. But God forbid he remembers his phone or keys when he leaves the house!

We both have many different interests and friends we individually spend time with. We work with different charities. For all you single people out there, if you are looking for a mate that has the same interests as you, go for it. But I find that we have learned a lot from each other having such different interests. I can now give stats about soccer or rugby. (Actually, I love rugby sevens now; it's the best spectator sport out there). We have been to many World Cup events around the world. Ralph now knows the rules of hockey and how to spot where the puck is. I can now tell you about gold stock prices and where it is heading. He now knows who is on *Dancing with the Stars*, and I can now tell you what's going on in politics… well, the short version anyway. I love languages while he can barely say *"Hola!"* Ralph can now tell you which movie is being shot in Vancouver or what the new colors of the season are. He is the romantic one. I am the practical one. He keeps every card I ever gave him, while I think those just take up closet space. I love getting dressed up and going to galas, while he would be happy to never wear another tie in his life.

The Last Days of Being Carnivores

Shortly after Ralph and I met, we picked up a large bucket of Kentucky Fried Chicken and headed to Stanley Park for a picnic. I used to love KFC. Ahh… those heavenly eleven herbs and spices! We both had decided that we wouldn't eat meat anymore, so this would be our last. For me, it was because a doctor pointed out that my body doesn't process meat very well, and I would lose weight if I stopped. For him it was the animal cruelty issue, and environmental reasons. We were licking our lips, smelling the KFC in the car as we drove to the park.

We ate the entire family-sized bucket. ***And then it happened!*** Within thirty minutes we were both sick to our stomach and that was that. We've not had meat since (at least not on purpose), although still eat seafood. An occasional piece of crispy bacon may find its way into my mouth, but more often than not, I will chew a piece to enjoy the flavor and then spit it out. (They say nine out of ten people love bacon and the other one is lying). Sorry Colonel, I can't stand the smell of your chicken anymore.

The Engagement

Several months after he moved in, we headed up to Whistler on a warm, sunny June day. We were having a nice, relaxing morning and he suggested we take a ride, *"I know a guy who works at the heliport up here."* We pulled up at a small airport and Ralph asked me to stay in the car. He came out a few minutes later and said, *"Guess what? He can take us up on a free flight."* We were both excited. I got in first, strapped up and readied my camera to take some shots. Ralph and two pilots got in and we took off. It was a beautiful day and we could see for miles. Then the pilot landed up on a secluded mountain covered with snow. We got out and Ralph went to the back of the helicopter. He pulled out our stereo and my picnic basket from home.

I thought *"What the....?"*

The pilot said he had to go fly somewhere else and he would be back to pick us up in an hour. Ralph explained to me he brought the gear just in case his friend would take us up. We blasted some great tunes, opened the basket and had some wine, and an amazing picnic. Later, he asked me to get dessert from the bottom of the picnic basket. I reached in and pulled out a ring box. ***And then it happened!*** I turned around and he was on one knee asking me to marry him. I have no memory of what he actually said. All I remember was him saying, *"I can't wait to have memories with you."* I was blown away, which takes a lot. He put in a music tape and played our song from *Phantom of the Opera*, and we danced. When he turned me quickly from something and I looked back to see a cameraman a few hundred feet away taking pictures. It was the second "pilot" from the helicopter. He had hired a professional photographer to capture the whole event. Ralph likes to tell this story by saying, *"If she said no, I would have left her on the top of the mountain"*. There is a big lesson here. We were totally broke when we got engaged, but Ralph used whatever connections he had to make the moment a lifelong cherished memory.

So please put the effort in for the "Big Ask". Most partners would love to have an engagement story that they will always remember. And when the topic comes up, and it does, yours would like to be able to share an eventful engagement.

Meeting the Family

My Ukrainian grandmother and I had a very deep connection, and I couldn't wait for her to meet my new love. ***And then it happened!*** I received a call saying she was sick and we should come as soon as possible. Ralph and I both felt the same way and we literally jumped in the car and drove twenty hours to Saskatchewan to see her. We had just got engaged and I was hoping he would have a chance to meet her. We arrived at the hospital, hugged her and I introduced him. Then she sent me away so she could talk to him. When I returned a while later my grandmother had tears in her eyes, saying, *"I am 90 years old, and I finally meet the perfect guy!"* She died hours later. I was blessed to have been there for that. If we hadn't jumped into that car that very minute, we would have missed this great moment.

Ralph is from a large family who are mostly living in New Zealand. On my first trip there, I spent the 24-hour flight studying all his siblings', their spouses', and kids' names. The challenge was our plane was delayed for a couple of hours on the tarmac in Vancouver. My husband had bought a large bottle of Baileys at duty free to bring to NZ, so he decided to crack open the bottle and watch the hockey game that was showing on the screen. Eight hours later we landed in Hawaii to transfer planes. Ralph had made it through the whole bottle of Baileys by then and was in fine form. We nearly missed our connecting flight as getting an intoxicated man to walk fast is not easy. You can't do this anymore, as drinking your duty free alcohol on a flight is illegal.

We landed in Auckland, took a taxi to one of his old college friend's home for the night. The guy didn't even get up out of his chair to greet us, as the game he was watching was obviously more important. The Kiwis are very serious about their sports.

A few days later, after we moved to a little hotel, I headed down the street to a little bakery to surprise my husband with breakfast. I walked in and asked if I could get something to go. She stared at me like I was a crazy person.

I smiled and spoke slowly and clearly, thinking she could not understand my accent. She still just stared at me. So, I tried to act it out, as many of my friends like Janet and Jan know (I am the queen of charades). The lady finally got what I was saying. We laughed and she explained that what I wanted was "takeaway", and not something to help me "to go" to the bathroom.

My next phrasal confusion was when we were in downtown Wellington having dinner at a nice hotel. I needed to relieve myself, so I asked the concierge, *"Where is the bathroom?"* He sent me up the elevator to the third floor, which I thought was odd. After looking up and down the hallway and not finding a washroom, I came back down and explained I couldn't find it, *"Don't you have one in the lobby?"*

He barked, *"Why would we put one in the lobby?"* So, I reverted back to good old fashion charades and acted out what I was looking for. He burst into laughter and said *"Oh the toilet! It's just over there!"* So, another lesson learned. Even though you think you are speaking the same language, you may still need to act out what you mean. And for all the Kiwis reading this: it is not "beetroot," it's just "beets." And when you weigh something, you do it with a "scale"… just the one… not "scales". Oh, and "beer" is not pronounced the same way as "bear".

Choosing to take Ralph's last name didn't require a second thought, I was honored to take his. But it did surprise many people in my life, and I had a unique family name from my father that only a few direct Danish family members have. Also, I had been the only girl born on my father's side of the family in generations. Up to then, parents would name their first-born boy after the grandfather and the second-born boy was named after the father. When my brother had his son, our Danish grandfather was shocked to find out he did not name him after our father.

When a few of my Danish family came over to visit one year, I asked them if they had heard how we got the spelling of our unique last name. Everyone had a different version of how it came to be. I told them the story of what my Danish grandfather had told me, over and over. He proclaimed proudly that my great-great grandfather was playing chess with the King of Denmark one day. It was common knowledge that you should never win when you played the king.

But, as our blood lines up and down the family tree have proven, we can be very stubborn, competitive and hot headed. My great great grandfather ended up winning the match. So according to my grandfather, in retribution, the king changed the spelling of our family name to one that no one had ever heard of.

After hearing this, my relatives looked at me for a few seconds in stunned silence, then fell off their chairs laughing. We all agreed that this would be the story that we would stick to for generations going forward.

The Wedding is about the Two of You

Our first private ceremony was a week before our big wedding. We went to Stanley Park and shared our vows with each other privately. We felt that this was really the first day of our marriage

The big wedding was held Easter weekend at a place in Vancouver called Fantasy Gardens. This place had a large garden and atrium. It was a perfect April day, the tulips and blossoms were all in bloom. I had stayed at my brother's place the night before. In the morning, the girls and I had our hair styled and then brunched at my mom's. It was so warm that I was sitting naked on the balcony, getting some rays before we had to prepare. The boys decided to play a round of golf in their tuxedos. I had reconciled briefly with my father, so I asked him to walk me down the aisle. If I had a re-do on this day, it would be to have my mother walk me, as she was the one who raised me. We drove to the gardens but it was a fairly long walk to meet where everyone had gathered for the ceremony. The flower girl and the ring bearer were young cousins of mine. As we were all walking, I kept saying to my bridesmaids, *"Go faster… okay, and slow down…okay, now faster."* Finally, one of them turned to me and threatened if I didn't shut up, she would throw me in the pond.

Our wedding was lovely and even though we were flat broke at the time, I wouldn't change a thing. Ladies, most men don't care about the little details of the wedding. Most would be very happy for you to decide the details. Sometimes it is just easier to make the decisions yourself. Because my husband is from New Zealand, the ceremony concluded with the guys performing a traditional Maori haka dance. We got married on the 18th and every month we celebrate our monthly anniversary on that date. Ralph says, as the husband, it is easier than remembering a yearly anniversary. Whoever wakes up first on every 18th, sings our Happy Anniversary song to the other. Three hundred plus months later, we still celebrate it.

I remember there was a time around year two that I looked at him, and for the first time in my life, I actually knew that I was truly in love. I knew I would take a bullet for him. Some people think that kind of love should be felt before you get married. But I believe that true, deep love happens slowly over time.

Deciding if to Have Children

My husband has a lot of nieces and nephews, so when I met him, I asked him if he wanted kids. He said someday he might and I told him I might be open to adopting one day.

We were married for a few years and on a holiday in Hawaii, sitting and enjoying the sunset. ***And then it happened!***

I looked at him and started tearing up. I told him, *"I think we should get a divorce. I know one day you may want kids, but I have decided that that is not in the cards for me. I never want you to wake up one day regretting not having kids."* I left him with that dramatic little speech and took off down the beach. I was sobbing, thinking of losing him, but I would feel even worse taking the experience of having children away from him. I spent the night on the beach and came back in the early morning hours to our hotel. Ralph had also been up all night.

When he saw me, he was angry and said to me *"I never said I wanted kids for sure, I just wanted the option of having them. And now I have decided I don't!"* I laughed, because if you knew Ralph, you would know that he always wants to keep his options open. Virgos!!! We hugged each other for dear life, and we knew we were both happy with that decision. I tried to convince him to store some sperm in case he had a change of heart, but he opted for the no-scalpel vasectomy instead.

I have loads of friends who have kids and I love kids, and I am godmother to a few. I especially love newborns. The feeling when they fall asleep in my arms is pure heaven. Teenagers are a whole different story. I think countries should have a secluded island to put the unruly teenagers on and when they hit eighteen, they can rejoin society!

Occasionally someone will ask if I want children. My standard answer is *"No thanks."*

My husband once asked me if I thought parents really know what they are in for, when they decide to have kids. I replied *"If they did, do you think anyone would have a baby?"*

I jokingly call another friend's family "the nuthouse" because they had four children in five years and it was always chaos! They also had two dogs and two cats. Their son was the youngest. One day, before they even tried to potty train him, they ran out of diapers. Jennifer, the mother, simply looked at her little boy and said, *"We are out of diapers, so you have to use the toilet from now on like your sisters!"* He agreed, and that was that.

Babysitters ("renters" as my husband calls them) don't at first know what their temp children can or can't do. One day when I was feeding a friend's baby, I just propped up the bottle using his hands and he began feeding himself. When the mother saw this, she was blown away as she hadn't tried that yet.

One Mother's Day, I took my cousin's little boy out for a stroll in his carriage so his mom could go to the spa, and his dad could do some errands. I adore this baby, he has the greatest laugh. I also am proud of his parents, as they didn't hover over him, and are just calm, laid-back parents. Every time I saw their baby, he was in a good mood. I ventured out to the park with him, where we quickly came across a bunch of baby ducks. I took him out of the carriage to show him and he squealed with delight. I tried to put him back in the carriage but there was not a chance he was going back in. He screamed and cried and there was nothing I could do to get that kid back in. We were a good 45-minute walk back to my place on a gravel path. Pushing the carriage and holding him in my arms was a real workout. Every time my arms got tired, I tried to put him back in, but he would scream. Many were out walking in the park on this Mother's Day and some commented to me about how they don't miss those days. I explained what I did, and was advised, *"Oh, you shouldn't have taken him out!"* Thanks for telling me that now! The second I got back to the salon where his mother was, he happily went back in the carriage! Big thanks to Connor for teaching me this important babysitting lesson.

One of my godchildren, Braxton, has always had lipstick kisses from me. Ever since he was born, I would put on brightly colored lipstick and kiss him all over. One summer we were meeting for lunch and somehow, he went from a little boy to a teenager since the last time I saw him. He had gel in the hair and the collar of his shirt turned up. And he was wearing cologne! He came over to the table and I kissed him all over his face with bright pink lipstick.

Now, normally he would have cringed and wiped it off quickly. But not that day. He sat all through lunch with all the kisses on display. At the end of lunch, I did it again and he just smiled and walked out of the restaurant. I am sure he was hoping that the chicks would see him and think he is a real ladies' man. It's amusing, when I ask my friends if their child has a boyfriend or girlfriend yet, they strongly deny it. As if they could stop their wee one's hearts from fluttering over some cutey at school!

From my perspective, to all you brave parents out there, please do not put so much pressure on yourselves. You are doing great! Thank you for all you do to keep the world revolving. Thank you for giving up so much, so your kids have a better life. Thanks to the mother on our flight for handing out ear plugs to all the seats around them when she had her first flight with her screaming baby. Thanks for all the hours you volunteered and fund-raised at school. Thanks for not inviting us to all the school plays, sports tournaments or recitals. Thanks for listening to your kids complain about everything and not losing your temper. And thanks for finding a babysitter when I invite you to our parties.

Adopting Our Puppy

We had moved into a big house up in West Vancouver and I felt that I would feel safer to have a dog around. I didn't want to buy a bred puppy, I wanted a rescue dog. (There are so many animals in shelters that need forever homes, so please, don't buy from a puppy mill.) I contacted all the shelters and asked them to let me know if they found any Huskies, as we lived in the winter snowline, perfect conditions for them. And I love their blue eyes! When the first shelter called to say they had one, we drove out there only to find the puppy had been adopted twenty minutes before. The next call came a month later after a puppy's owners died in a car accident. We raced out to the pound, but this time the puppy was adopted by the brother of the couple who passed away. I now know how adoptive parents must feel with all these false alarms.

We had been away for a few days and came home on a Friday night of a long weekend. There was a message from a rescue shelter saying they had a ten-week-old Husky. They had actually had it for a couple of weeks, but he was so young and malnourished, they had to nurse him to get stronger. I called the lady back immediately but unfortunately the shelter was closing for the long weekend.

When I asked her who took care of the animals over the weekend, she told me her 16-year-old daughter did, so I proposed a deal. If she could deliver him to our home, I would pay the daughter a week's wages and if we had a good connection with the puppy, I would give a big donation to the shelter. I think if we lived in other places in the city, she may have been suspicious, but we lived in a safe neighborhood. An hour later the rescue shelter called back to say the puppy was on its way. When our delivery arrived, we were waiting on the street. ***And then it happened!*** This tiny puppy jumped out of their truck, ran over to me and jumped up to greet me. Then he went over to my husband and sat down regally at his feet. I laughed so hard because it couldn't have been a better introduction. I had not been a believer of love at first site until that moment. Both of us just fell in love with him. I paid the shelter's daughter and we instantly became parents.

My brother was visiting that day and puppy-sat, as Ralph and I went to the pet store. We had spent all of our energy trying to get a dog and we didn't have a thing ready for him when he arrived. We spent a fortune buying everything in sight, including an igloo dog house (where he never slept), an automatic programmable dog food dispenser (that he never ate from), tons of food, toys and a cage. When we came back to the house, my brother suggested we call him "Pay Dirt" as he went from the streets in the valley to the richest area of the city. We settled on the name Elvis, because he really was as regal as a king.

We signed up for a training course because we really didn't know how to train a dog. We all graduated grade two and we learned more than Elvis did. He was our everything. He had full-time babysitters when we were out of town. He had a dog walker daily, so he could mix with other dogs (not that he gave many dogs the time of day). After he was attacked by three other dogs, he had a massage once a week, something that really helped him as he aged.

Elvis was never a fan of children, so I always had to keep kids away or ask them to bring bacon when they came around. (Thanks Muir kids!) He and I knew each other so well, that we understood what the other one needed instinctively. He was a very smart dog (of course), and he would fetch his toys by the name of the toy we called out. Elvis would love to sit on my lap, all 85 pounds of him. (If you start putting your puppy on your lap, he will be on your lap dog forever).

He always wanted to be touching me somehow. In bed, he started off sleeping at our feet, but as he got older, he wanted to be in the middle of the two of us. If Ralph was away, he would sleep on daddy's pillow on our bed.

Living on the last row of houses by a forest, we knew we were in bear territory. From spring to late fall, adventures with bears were a weekly, if not daily, occurrence. We asked our neighbors not to put their garbage out the night before pickup, and even if you did wait until the morning, the bears would come a-visiting. One time when Ralph put the garbage out on the curb at 7am and returned a minute later with more, a bear was already going through our bins. Our friend Rita, across the street were just standing there taking pictures, safely from their balcony. Ralph made loud noises as he approached and scared the bear away, while Elvis was barking his head off from behind our gate.

Our house was built on a steep lot and the trees grew tall around us. Elvis was going nuts barking in the living room one morning, so I went to see what was making him upset. Right outside the main living room window were two baby black bears who had climbed up a tree. They must have headed up for safety after being spooked, and were now looking right into our living room. The mother bear was down below on the lawn, yelling at the kids to come down. If she could, she would have had her hands on her hips in frustration. Elvis was still barking like crazy, so they clung to the tree. They were up there for over an hour before their mom decided she'd had enough. She climbed up the huge tree and one-by-one, gripped the babies by the scruff of the neck and brought them down.

Another early morning, Elvis and I went for a run down the street and as we turned a sharp corner, we physically , ran into a black bear. Elvis was off his leash, and as I was the first to realize what was happening, lunged for Elvis's collar and pulled him away. The bear figured it out last, looked in disbelief at me and then Elvis, and then took off.

One summer we rented an RV and were heading out for an early camping adventure. I had stocked the camper up with all our supplies but it was too big for our closed garage, so we just parked it in our driveway. Around 6am, when we opened our gate to head out, we saw a huge black bear on top of the camper about to use his huge paw to tear open the skylight. We, Elvis included, screamed at him to get off, which he reluctantly relented, jumped down and went on his way.

Elvis loved the snow in the winter. He would eat it and roll around in it. Even when he was older, we would bring him up the mountain to play in the snow and he acted like a puppy again. On hot days, I would sit with him in my car and run the air-conditioning on high so he could cool down. Huskies do not like the heat.

When we bought our penthouse downtown, I wasn't ready to move there, thinking Elvis wouldn't like life in the city. But as it turned out, it was great for him. He could be outside on our three huge decks all year round. We couldn't let him outside at night in West Van due to the bears, skunks and other wildlife.

The only thing Elvis didn't like about living downtown was the fake grass we had on all the balconies. At the house, he would cool down on hot days (and to drive his daddy nuts) by digging up the grass and lying in the cool dirt underneath it. He tried and tried to dig up the fake grass on our penthouse balconies. Sometimes he would try and dig for ten minutes and then just start barking at it, or me, in frustration. It was always comical.

How many of you think your pet needs a pet? Well, my husband thought Elvis would like one. So, one Christmas, he just showed up with Gerry the gerbil. He put the cage and a year's supply of food in our den. Elvis would just sit by the cage, stare and just shake. I knew without a shadow of a doubt that if we took Gerry out, Elvis would have a go at him. Gerry stayed with us for a week but I just couldn't take it anymore. I wanted to let Gerry out of his cage as I am not a fan of caging animals. Ralph thought they would get along fine, just like the time he and my mom thought Elvis and her cat Goldie, would love each other. (How are the scratches healing Mom?) The next week, he posted Gerry on Craigslist for free. Within minutes he had people begging to adopt him. He went to a family whose son's gerbil had just died. When Ralph left with Gerry to give him away, Elvis went into the den and lifted his leg, and peed on the table that Gerry's cage had been on. He had never done anything like that before. I let Ralph clean up that mess!

Stretching Comfort Zones

Years ago, there was show on TV called *The Decorating Challenge* where you swapped houses with a friend to do a room makeover in each. My friend, Jennifer and I applied, and were selected. We then had to talk our husbands into it.

The budget the show gave us was $1000 for each room. We worked with a designer and a contractor as we prepared our West Vancouver homes. My husband and I upgraded their dining room while they revamped our master bedroom. Luckily, being a seamstress helped, as the sewing project they wanted me to complete ended up taking me half the night. The show gave us 48 hours to finish, after which they brought us back blindfolded to our own home, and into our made-over room for the big reveal. The director told us they would only be shooting this in one take so we needed to express exactly how we felt as we took off the blindfolds, on camera. You could clearly see that there were some things I loved, and some things I didn't. Anyone who knows me could read my face, *"Ohhh, hmmm, ahhhh."*

I had drinks and food arranged already for the whole crew to celebrate after we were done filming. While they were relaxing in the kitchen, I was already taking off the 100 white bows and exposed screws they installed in my headboard. We had a huge bedroom with vaulted ceilings, where the designers had hung hundreds of meters of silk, which did look amazing. I knew there was no way they would have kept to their budget if my mom and her husband hadn't donated all the fabric from their store, Dressew Supply.

Inexpensive Surprise Parties

Once I blindfolded Ralph and drove him around for an hour. I pretended we were at the US border and had a friend act as the border guard. This was pre-9/11, I suspect nowadays that no one could have a blindfold on. We parked a little while later and I took him into BC Place Stadium, still blindfolded, and guided him up the stairs to our seats. Everyone in our section noticed us as I made the *'Please be silent'* universal sign. Then counted down *"-5,4,3,2,1-"* taking off his blindfold as the whole section yelled *"Surprise!".* I had brought him to a soccer game in our own city, an exhibition game with two professional European teams. It took him about thirty minutes to recalibrate that we were still in Vancouver!

Have Marriage Check-ups

Ralph and I have been business partners shortly after first meeting, working together most days. When our fifth-year anniversary was approaching, I sat down with him. I couldn't believe that we were still happily married.

Thinking back on all the things we had been through, I remember saying to him, *"I feel we've learned more about each other in five years than most couples could in ten."* We decided from that moment, at the end of every five years, we would sit and calmly discuss how our relationship was going. How am I doing as your wife, your partner and your lover? And the same for him.

We discuss whatever is on each other's minds. We suggest things that we would like changed or would like more of each other. We discuss if our marriage is still something we both want to continue with, or has it run its course. If we both agree to stay married for the next five years, then we will renew our vows and re-commit to each other. We agree to try our hardest to make the other one feel loved, respected, listened to and fulfilled.

One line he used at the beginning of our relationship when we fought was, *"You might as well forgive me now, because eventually you will."* That drove me nuts! He doesn't say that anymore. One thing I did at the beginning that drove him nuts was calling him my "First Husband." He didn't find that funny and I don't say that now!

Most couples don't do the sit down "check-up". They just go through the motions. They may have kids, experience deaths, moved cities, had the house renovated or changed jobs. All of these life-altering moments can change you. As we go on in years, our needs and desires change. We may not having the sex life like we used to. We may be tempted to look outside our relationship for what we need, instead of doing the relationship check-up with the person we committed to spend our lives with.

I am not suggesting that every couple should renew their vows every five years like we do, but the check-up conversation is a vital tool to keep a relationship moving forward.

And that's how our friends started calling us "The Newlyweds."

Celebrating Anniversaries

Our 5th anniversary ceremony was in Hawaii. We invited Ralph's brother Joe and his wife to join us. We arrived after dark to our hotel. As I usually do when on vacation (a habit from my back-packing days), I washed our traveling clothes in the bathroom and hung them on the balcony to dry. We woke up late the next morning to find them blown over the golf course we now overlooked. We ran after our unmentionables that were blowing across the ninth fairway!

The next day we met our wedding officiant who happened to be another Kiwi. He instantly fell in love with my husband. We did the rehearsal with him and then met him the next day out at the water's edge of the hotel grounds for the ceremony. As he was speaking, he only looked at Ralph. I just kept smiling. All of a sudden, a helicopter flew high overhead and dumped thousands of rose pedals above us as we stood near black volcanic rocks. Apparently, the pilot was a good friend of the officiant and they did this as a surprise for us. It was all very romantic, for all of us. The ceremony finished with all the guys performing the haka. I will just add this officiant to the long list of people around the world that have also fallen in love with my wonderful husband.

For our 10th anniversary, we took a cruise in the Caribbean. One of our ports was the island of St. Thomas which is a former Danish colony. We got all dolled-up on board and took a taxi to our elopement hotel. The officiant met us at the wedding arch on the beach. It was a perfect sunny day once again. Tourists all came to watch. Then we had lunch at a table on the beach, and after, stripped down to our swim suits and went for a swim. We took a cab back to the boat in time for sailing away. Very romantic. The whole thing costs less than $500. So, if you are thinking of eloping or renewing, this is a very inexpensive way to do it.

On a big adventure for our 15th anniversary vow renewal, we took a four-week cruise in the Presidential Suite on an all-inclusive Silversea Cruise ship from Singapore around Sri Lanka and India, finishing in Dubai. Coincidentally, the Head Sommelier on our ship was from Saskatoon, my birth town and we ended up getting all the best wines and champagne.

While we were in Indian waters, we donned traditional Indian wedding clothes and makeup, and arranged for the ship's captain came to our room to perform the ceremony. We had met a few other passengers aboard so we invited them to join us for the ceremony and dinner afterwards. No haka at this one. We danced to Bollywood soundtracks instead. FYI, captains can only marry people if they are a registered Justice of the Peace. Originally, captains were granted the power in case one of the crew members died and were buried at sea but this does not extend to weddings. But they all can, of course, preside over a renewal of vows.

For our 20th anniversary, we were on another big adventure around Asia. While we were in Chang Mai, Thailand, we arranged for a traditional Buddhist ceremony. It was easily 35°C or 95F that day and, as a woman, I was required to be completely covered up. Our guide who arranged the ceremony brought us to one of the most famous temples, Wat Phra That Doi Suthep. We walked up the 309 stairs and met the monks in the temple. The tourists and the locals were all buzzing around because they had heard that a senior Buddhist monk was coming to do the ceremony. Monks do not accept money for the ceremonies, so we presented them with donations of first aid baskets. The ceremony began with the senior monk holding a ball of string. As he chanted, he passed the string inch by inch down to the other three monks, then back again. The ceremony took over an hour and we were on our knees the whole time. The monks didn't seem to be bothered. Meanwhile, my husband and I were melting from the heat and our legs were falling asleep. At the end of the chant, the head monk made bracelets out of the string and we were to wear them until they naturally wore off.

I had a new wedding ring for this event, so we asked the head monk to bless it. Ralph handed him the ring. The monk jumped up and said something like, "Holy cow, big diamond!!" We are still laughing about that. After the ceremony, we were asked to go around the village ringing the bells and putting coins in all the cups while making wishes for our loved ones still with us, and those who had passed. Within minutes, strangers came up to congratulate us, but really, they just wanted to see the ring they heard about.

The Dhara Dhevi Hotel, where we stayed at in Chang Mai was incredible. This property will take your breath away. The deluxe villas with private pools make you forget all about life. There are great bike paths around the

60-acre property. It has a superb spa and a choice of restaurants. It is a little way off the beaten path, so rent a car or driver if you go there.

On latest vow renewal, we toured the South Pacific for our big 25th anniversary. After exploring Fiji and Australia, we boarded a cruise from Sydney to Hawaii. Our first port of call was Paihia, near the northern tip of New Zealand in the Bay of Islands. Here we decided to invite our Kiwi friends and family to join us for a traditional Maori ceremony at the Waitangi Treaty Grounds, near where our ship moored. My husband's best man from our first wedding, Andy, had previously been the manager of these famous grounds and with the support of the local iwi or people, arranged for us to celebrate our 25th anniversary in true New Zealand style.

We were staying in the penthouse suite on the Celebrity Solstice so we got to be the first passengers off the ship that morning. But we had to take the 20-minute tender crossing which had our guests waiting longer than planned. I think they expected us to be helicoptered in from the ship.

Our guests came from all over New Zealand to meet us on the grounds. I was praying for sunshine all week because my custom-made dress was made of silk, and if it rained, I would have been screwed. It turned out to be a perfect fall day. We were confronted by six Maori and their battle cry challenge. They placed a peace offering before us. Ralph was advised to pick it up, while maintaining eye contact, which meant we came in peace. Then our best man introduced us in the Maori language, after which we were all allowed to proceed with the traditional greeting reception, through the touching of forehead-to-forehead and nose-to-nose.

After that, our guests formed a circle where we exchanged our vows. Ralph welcomed everyone and declared his on-going love for me. He reminded me of what he said twenty-five years before, "*That he couldn't wait to have memories with me*", and then promised me many more to come.

To his surprise, music began playing. I started singing. I sang the first verse, and the rest of the guests joined in for the chorus (pre-planned weeks before). He was blown away. There wasn't a dry eye in the crowd.

I planned to do this flash mob for my husband months earlier when we met the band *Chicago* backstage at a concert. They were just inducted into the Rock and Roll Hall of Fame, and their tour stopped in Vancouver. They were all excited about performing that night and we had a great conversation with them backstage. I couldn't help but notice the tables of food and booze they had preassigned. It looked like they were going to have a massive party after the show. Their intimate concert will go down as one of my favorites. They had tons of energy as they played mostly their old songs, including *You're the Inspiration.* That's where I got the idea for our 25th vow renewal.

I had secretly been taking singing lessons from my cousin Kayla, who is a professional singing coach. I always thought I was tone deaf, but it turns out that I am not. I have a very large comfort zone and I rarely get nervous about anything, but singing was the one of them.

Every time I practiced the song, I would tear up. It was so emotional. The words were exactly how I felt about our life together. I knew the lyrics and pitch, but I still never made it through one practice session without crying. (Did I mention I am a sap? I can tear up over a TV commercial, and every heartwarming movie, unlike my cold-hearted friend, Vicki, who laughs at me when this happens).

After the ceremony, we headed up to the restaurant for a traditional hangi. The Maori people of New Zealand have cooked their food in this underground oven for centuries. They dig a hole, put fired hot rocks down at the base, and then cover their food in cheesecloth material (traditionally they used large leaves). They cover it with more hot rocks and then dig it all up eight to ten hours later. They usually cook fish or meat and root vegetables in them. It's a lot of work and takes time, if you ask me – but people love it.

Afterwards, we all had a few glasses of our favorite wine brought in by Ralph's sister, (thanks very much Margaret) and a few thoughtful speeches. Most of our guests already knew each other, so it was a relaxing afternoon full of love and laughter. As with most ports of call, we had to be back by 5pm. We paid the bill for the celebration, and they all walked us back to the dock to catch a tender back to the ship. As we were saying our goodbyes, all hugging and kissing, hundreds of shipmates piled out of tour buses to join us in the long line back on board. We caught the eye of our private concierge and he took us straight to the front of the line, to the pleasure of our cheering guests. Our Kiwi family and friends emailed us pictures late into the night of the dinner they shared together, while we continued on our honeymoon cruise to French Polynesia and Hawaii.

Then there was the epic 25th surprise anniversary party back in Vancouver that just about everyone else in our life had prepared for us on our return.

One couple invited us, as a decoy, to an underground dinner party, while others were secretly planning a big surprise get-together. Apparently, these supper club parties happen all over the world, where you go to strangers home for dinner and bring your own drinks. At the end of the night, you contribute whatever money you consider the meal was worth. I was excited to meet some new people and a have new experience.

Sadly the day we were scheduled for this dinner we had to cancel because Ralph's aunt from Belfast suddenly passed away and he decided that he should go to the funeral to represent the overseas relatives. Meantime and unbeknownst to us, the surprise party was moved on a month. On the morning of that next date, Ralph went for a quick bike ride around Stanley Park. He must have been distracted because he crashed into a parking truck at high speed and was rushed to the hospital. I arrived at emergency a few minutes after the ambulance got there, I was terrified. He had a cracked sternum, broken ribs, a bruised lung and bruised heart. The cardiologist that attended to him said he had only seen these kind of serious injures twice before. Once, the guy was kicked in the chest by a horse, and the other was a guy was kicked in the chest by a bull! (Interesting that they were all men hey?) I called our dinner dates and told them what happened and that we wouldn't be able to make the underground dinner, again. I also called some other friends and when I told them what happened, one of them decided to spill the beans. They were having a huge 25th anniversary surprise party for us that night. I was heartbroken for all the preparation they had done, and even more, surprised that I hadn't caught wind of it.

They decided to proceed with the party as the food was already ordered. We Skyped them later that night and I was thrilled to see all the people in our lives gathered as one. We could see they were having a great time and were all so proud of themselves for keeping it under wraps. They told me that no one wanted to email or call me all week in case they blew the surprise.

The next day when calling all of them to thank them, I told them, *"If I ever want to rob a bank, I know who the sneaky people are that I could get to assist me!"*

Thank you to all of you for pulling this off...it will go down in history as *the best party we never attended!*

How to Keep Connected to Your Partner

Most of our friends accept the fact that we are always kissing. Not a day goes by without telling each other, *"I love you"*. If I could clone Ralph, I would make a fortune. I know all my girlfriends think he is the perfect man, and yes ladies, he is. He has put up with all the times that I got mad at him, yelled at him, gotten jealous, was PMS'ing and overreacted.

I don't know how he has remained so patient with me all these years, but I am grateful for it every single day. Thankfully there is not too much nowadays we argue about. However, when we do, we go to our separate home offices and close the doors for some cooling off time. If the door stays closed, that means the other one should not interrupt. It's amazing what a 30-minute "timeout" can do for a dispute. We make it a point that whenever one of us gets home, the other will get up and greet them. Sometimes we may be busy, but we still try to welcome the other home.

Every chance we get, we turn up a song and have a quick dance at any time of the day. When our puppy was around, he didn't like us dancing. He thought we were hurting each other or something. We often had to get up on the island in the kitchen and dance there. That is not a reflection of our dancing skills. I was actually the Dirty Dancing Champion when I was young! And Ralph and I took many dancing lessons together.

We started "Midnight Margaritas" when I started menopause and had trouble sleeping. We made a pact that if one of us wakes up in the middle of the night and can't get back to sleep, we can call "Midnight Margarita". That person would go make a couple of Margaritas and turn the music up loud. The other person would wake up and get out of bed for a quick dance and a quick drink, then we would go back to bed and get back to sleep.

We love going to comedy clubs and to concerts. We meditate and exercise daily, and we love biking. Our favorite moments are still cuddling while watching a movie at home on our big screen, or cuddling in bed and watching TV on Sunday mornings together.

Take Time Out to Be Grateful

Happy Hour is a daily event for us. Not necessarily to have a drink, but to talk. Even if we've both been at home all day, we still love 5 o'clock happy hour to share whatever we learned that day. In the summer, we salute the cruise ships departing in the Vancouver harbor. In the winter, we watch (and supervise) the progress on the construction sites around us.

When we moved into our penthouse, we had to get used to living with seagulls on the roof. This can be a challenge. In the first year we moved in, while having happy hour on the balcony, we were dive-bombed by protective seagull parents.

They had made their nest on the roof and wanted no one to get near, so the next spring, we placed plastic owls on the roof to keep them away. Nope, that didn't work! Ralph would get out the ladder and regularly checked the roof of the building for a nest. But the following year, he didn't get up there early enough. A nest was discovered with two large eggs, the size you would expect an ostrich to have laid. The parents were not there, so my husband took the eggs and destroyed them. About an hour later, he felt guilty, so he went to the fridge and got two store eggs, then climbed back up to the roof and placed them in the nest. I laughed for days thinking about what the seagull parents must have thought. *"Wow those eggs don't look like the right size!"* And if they ever could have hatched, they'd say, *"Come on little one, just flap your wings. You can fly if you try hard enough."*

We supervise all the tops of buildings below us from our balcony now and know where all the seagulls' nests are being built. One year a building across from us had two chicks. I called them Jack and Jill. They cried day and night for food from their parents. Once they were big enough, they were encouraged by the parents to start to learn to fly. Jill was doing great. It took her only a few days to lift herself up. Her brother (I have no idea what sexes they actually were) was a little slower. He would try to just fly up the two feet to the top of the air-conditioning vents. That took about a week for him to do that. Finally, he flapped his little wings and rose up to the sky We were cheering for him.

Divide the Chores

We are always hosting parties. I do all the prep, shopping, party games, and cooking while Ralph does the cleanup, garbage and recycling. He likes to wear Merino wool which can't be put in the dryer, and I am allergic to wool, so he insists on separating all the laundry.

One day, he asked me what I wanted for dinner and I replied, *"Can't you decide for me for once!"* He got upset as I am such a picky eater. In fairness,

I am always on some sort of weird diet and he needs specific food because he exercises so much. Now, I do all my meals and assist him with his.

I have final say with all the things indoors at our place, and he has final say on all outdoors.

We both love traveling and we travel very well with each other. I do all the bookings because I have a specific standard that pleases me. One time he did the booking and it didn't turn out well, so now I do it all! He does office accounts, finances and real estate paperwork.

Wait Three Weeks

It's not like we have not had our problems. There have been a couple of times I thought for sure we were done. This shocks everyone when I tell them that. We both have said and done things that we shouldn't have. One of my closest friends, Sally, gave me a great piece of advice years before; if things are going sideways, you should wait three weeks. If in three weeks you still feel the same, then do something about it. I've passed that advice on to friends going through rough patches.

Career vs. Relationships

Another theory that I agree with, is that at any one time in your life, you will need to work hard at your career, then other times you will need to be working on a relationship. For most people, it is very hard to work on both at the same time. So, if you go through a rough patch, think about which one you should be focusing on at that particular time.

Think Twice Before Having an Affair

No one said that getting married will instantly stop you from being attracted to other people. It is what you do about your thoughts that count. I have no problem with someone closing their eyes and imagining being with someone else. But the second you take action, you could destroy your relationship forever. Sorry, Sir Richard Branson, you are just my fantasy, it's just not going to happen between us!

In my opinion, if you do make a mistake and take things too far with someone in a moment of time, please, do not think you need to relieve your guilt by confessing to your partner. Talk to a friend who you can trust. I told Ralph from the beginning that if he ever has a one night stand, to never tell me. It would break us if I knew and if it was just a mistake, he would have to deal with why he did it.

When we were married for about seven years and operating two school campuses, a gal came in looking for Ralph at our new campus. I told her he would be over shortly and I asked her how she knew him. *"Oh, I'm his girlfriend."*

Our receptionist heard this and froze. I replied *"Oh, I didn't know he had one!"* and asked her how long they have been seeing each other, to which she replied that they had just met at a seminar. Minutes later my husband came in and in front of her I remarked *"Ralph, I didn't know you had a girlfriend."* He looked at me with a confused expression, and greeted the gal. He introduced her to me and I declared I was his wife. He explained they had in fact met at a seminar, but she had been mistaken about the situation. Our receptionist wanted to hide under the desk and the gal probably wanted too as well. She tried to apologize that she must have misunderstood his feelings.

I was very proud of how I handled that, as I have been guilty of being jealous before. But I believed Ralph. He can be oblivious of his charms most of the time, and I am sure more than one gal has mistaken his kindness for something more. He just does not have it in him to cheat.

During a gridlocked journey heading out of town for the weekend one summer, my friend and I decided to stop at the zoo. It was the middle of the day in middle of a heat wave. The only animals that were out of their hiding spots were bunnies, deer and birds. We were just about to leave when the lady at the exit told us to go over to the lions' den as they're going to be fed. The bleachers in front of the enclosure area was a couple of feet from the fence. The keepers first hosed down the two lionesses and the lion, then they then took a huge piece of meat jammed into a large bone, and held it high on our side of the fence so the lion had to jump up on the other side of the fence to get his lunch. He let off a huge roar, ran up to the fence, grabbed the meat and devoured it. I turned to my friend and said, *"I just got turned on by that lion!"* Later that night at a restaurant, the waiter came over and asked us how our day was. I replied, *"I am thinking about having an affair with someone I met today and I don't know if I should share this with my husband."*

He inquired, *"Where did you meet him?"*

"I met him at the zoo!"

"Ahh, so which animal was it?" he asked, not missing a beat.

"The lion," I replied.

"Oh, so in that case, you probably don't need to tell your husband, as it will be just a one night stand."

Keep Learning New Things

I feel we all need to keep growing to keep our relationships healthy. Both of us have always taken one course or another though the years.

Caesar salad is one of my favorite dishes. (There are different stories about who invented the first one, some say it was an Italian chef who moved to Mexico.) I applied as a food writer for a local paper once, and my concept was to evaluate all restaurants' Caesar salads. I even told them they didn't have to pay me. I never heard back from them. One day, I will start a blog just on Caesar salad.

Then I completed a Private Investigation course. In my earlier life I really wanted to become a police officer, but was too short at the time I applied. (Turns out my mom and my cousin, Peter also wanted to be a cop! Who knew?)

My husband was very supportive by giving me Christmas presents that year, filled with PI gadgets. There were voice-changing devices and super range listening devices, etc. I truly felt this was going to be my new business. In BC at that time, you needed to work for a registered PI company before you could open your own agency. One time, I was working undercover for an agency, getting information from a Russian mob guy at a bar. ***And then it happened!*** I discovered that if they suspected me, they would hurt my family first, before hurting me. I came home and told Ralph that it was not for me and - boom - that dream ended. Trust me, it sounds much more glamorous on TV than the actual work is.

My next adventure was taking my helicopter pilot's license. I was never interested in working as a pilot, but my husband's dream at that time was to own his own island. I am not into boats, so I looked into flying. I went to a seized property auction with a police friend of mine and a Robinson R22 helicopter sold for $50,000 (they are worth a whole lot more new). I asked around and they said that there are very few pilots who want a two-seater.

They can't make money just taking one passenger, or if they want it for private use, most have more than one person in their family.

I love flying the Robinson R22, especially with Geoff, my instructor. We spend half the time laughing. One of my favorite memories with Geoff, was once when we were lifting off. For years, I flew one of three helicopters at the airport, so the aircraft phonetic call signs - like Alpha or Bravo, were ingrained in my head. But this day, we took a new chopper up. I had the blades rolling as I radioed the tower for permission to lift off. I looked down on the panel for the letters, but instead of the correct names, I spat out the first thing that came into my mind over the airwaves. My coach just about split a gut. I still don't know how I kept flying with tears of laughter coming down my face. The call letters were something like N L T F. You will just have to guess what came out of my mouth. Nope, think harder... think of the very worst words that start with those letters and then imagine hearing them on the airwaves. (Did I mention that I do have a potty mouth sometimes?)

Flying taught me a lot about double checking no matter how repetitive the task may be. It also taught me about being totally aware of every single thing around me.

Simple Things You Can Do For Your Partner

Ask your mate what you can do to make them feel truly loved. Then do it.

Boast about their accomplishments in front of others.

Slip little love notes in their luggage if they are going away, or under their pillow if you are going.

Celebrate the little successes and accomplishments as they happen.

Tell them you love them daily.

Don't use these words during an argument: "You always"... "You never"...

If your spouse picks a good movie, a good restaurant, or cooks a tasty meal, praise them.

Listen to them when they have a challenge. You don't have to give them a solution, just listen.

Don't bring your cell phone to bed or to the dinner table.

Ladies, don't talk to your partner if they are watching a game, unless it is about the game.

Drop hints about what you want for a gift, and then act surprised when they get it for you.

Look in each other's eyes for thirty seconds at least once a week.

Dress up for one another and go on a weekly or monthly date.

Have Sex. Countless studies have concurred that when a couple has sex, a hormone is released that is picked up in the partner's brain that reminds them of you. Even if it is quickie, make time for sex.

When going through a hard time, write a letter to each other with the things you love about them and the things that hurt you, with examples of how they could communicate better.

When times get tough, do a relationship check-up for each other:

A. How am I doing as your partner? 1-5
B. How am I doing as a parent (if you have kids or pets)? 1-5
C. How am I doing as your lover? 1-5
D. How am I doing as a provider? 1-5

Then do the same for yourself. Your spouse may rate low in one area, but how are they in another? As long as the points in total are high, then maybe things are going okay. Ralph has proven to me that "forever love" is a real thing and not just in the movies. I thank the universe every single day that we are together. I am so grateful that I get to be the one who gets to be his wife.

Choosing your spouse is the biggest decision you will ever make in your life. Everything that comes after will be different. Make sure you know yourself well. Talk to your friends and family about your partner when things start to get serious. Do not rush into a marriage. Live together first. Do not confuse good sex with good love. If you have any instincts that things are not feeling right, don't marry them.

'A couple was getting married, and it was only three days before the wedding. The bride calls her mother with some bad news.

"Mom," she says, "I just found out that my fiancé's mother has bought the exact same dress as you to wear to the wedding."

The bride's mother thinks for a minute. "Don't worry," she tells her daughter. "I'll just go and buy another dress to wear to the ceremony."

"But mother," says the bride, "that dress cost a fortune. What will you do with it? It's such a waste not to use it."

"Who said I won't use it?" her mother asked. "I'll just wear it to the rehearsal dinner."'

—*Anonymous*

Help Wanted

Starting Out

"I can honestly say that I have never gone into any business purely to make money. If that is the sole motive then I believe you are better off not doing it. A business has to be involving, it has to be fun, and it has to exercise your creative instincts."

—*Richard Branson*

Ralph and I started our first business together, with an MLM (multi-level marketing) product called Dermashield. It was this amazing product that you put on your hands as a foam and when it dried, it kept anything from penetrating through the skin for up to eight hours. Many industries, like painters, mechanics, or anyone working with harsh chemicals or toxic substances found the product useful. Just as we were getting big industrial orders, the company that distributed it in Canada had legal disputes and closed down.

I am not saying that MLM is a good or bad business strategy, but it just wasn't for us. You are encouraged to use every connection you have to join your network to have them sell or use the product. Unfortunately, most people we met seemed more interested in the 'compensation' than the benefit of the product to their customer. We have had acquaintances get involved in MLM and they have tried their darndest to get us to just handover a list of all of our personal and business contacts. I just say no.

Our next adventure was opening a pizza restaurant with all-natural, healthy pizzas and fresh juices. We had a great time, working long hours and at one point, had lineups out the door, even after one of our best customers ended up with a Band-Aid in her pizza. When our competitors offered a "Buy one, get one free" concept, we offered a "Get one free" deal. Almost every one of the 200 customers that came for a free slice on the first day asked, *"Why are you giving free pizza away?"* Our answer: *"If you try our pizza, we know you will become a regular."*

The whole concept for this deal, was to set up the restaurant with good sales and then flip it quickly. We found a buyer after three months. I don't necessarily suggest trying this yourself, as we got very lucky and made good money in a short time. We had two other partners at that time, my brother and his girlfriend, and we all felt ecstatic with our share of the sale.

Researching for Opportunities

We knew the two markets in Vancouver that were exploding were tourism and the baby boomers retiring. We opted for the tourist education market. I had been contracted as a marketing consultant with a local college that was teaching English as a Second Language (ESL) programs.

That college had a waiting list for those classes. The Director of the program was retiring so I took him for lunch. He said to me, *"You know, if I was 20 years younger I would start my own English school!"* I took this back to Ralph and along with my brother and his girlfriend, we agreed to open a school aimed at foreign students.

Checking Out the Competition

The first thing we did when we decided to open a school was to visit all the competition. There were only a few private ESL schools in Vancouver at the time (there were over 80 in Vancouver when we sold 24 years later).

When we visited the competition, we acted like we had a friend looking for ESL lessons. It is amazing what kind of information you can get from a business's reception about the market.

We asked things like:

What countries do your clients come from?

What ages are they?

What qualifications do your teachers have?

Do your students register with you directly or through agencies?

What commission do you pay your agents?

Which big agencies do you work with?

Where do you advertise that you get the most success from?

What kind of classes are the most popular?

I know over the years we have had many other school operators come visit our business, using the same kind of strategy. One new school actually copied our slogan and concept, but because we didn't trademark it, there was nothing we could do, except insist they change it. They stayed in business less than a year. Mimicking a concept doesn't assure success.

Things Got Difficult

Things were very hard for us the first few years. Those were the days when we would get a student registration, with a deposit check through the mail, and would immediately bank it just pay an outstanding bill. ***And then it happened!*** We were almost a quarter million dollars in debt when my brother and his girlfriend walked out on our partnership. They left us with most of the debt, and because I was the only one with good credit at the beginning, most bills were in my name. We didn't talk to them for years after that. And now, I tell everyone that wants to listen to be cautious about getting into business with a family member.

I remember one of my darkest days when I was down to my last $5. I was heading out to get a sandwich on Robson Street, when I came upon an eccentric lady psychic who gave readings as she traveled with two white ducks in a baby carriage. Although she charged $20 a session, I offered her my $5 as I only had one question. *"Will we still be in business in a couple of months?"* I asked her.

She replied, *"Not only for a couple of months, will you have the business 20 years from now."* I have never forgotten her.

Fortunately for us, our commercial landlord went bankrupt before we just about did. When the new owner of the building came to meet us, we were able to renegotiate a lower rent, and it helped save our business. We got to know a very lovely Taiwanese man, Johnny, who along with his family, were students of ours. I can't remember how we had the guts to ask him, but he ended up investing $50,000 for share ownership of the school. We agreed on a time frame that we would pay him back, while we assisted him to achieve his residency in Canada. If it wasn't for his faith in us, we would have gone under.

No matter what our financial situation, our commitment when we hired someone was to make sure they got paid on time for work done. One of the things I am most proud of is that we never missed a payroll date, even if it meant personal sacrifice. We had to pawn our wedding rings one time in year two to have enough funds to pay staff.

Diversifying

After five years, we were finally out of debt, sales were rolling in and we were eager to expand. There was a vacant commercial space a block from our campus, so we took the plunge. The biggest mistake we made was not to have diversified our client base. We were 40% filled with South Korean students. When Korea had an economic meltdown, many Korean parents wanted their children to return home, creating a daily line-up at my desk of students withdrawing from the school, all wanting refunds. Our bank balance was once again getting depleted. We had signed a two-year lease on that second campus and we struggled to keep it full in our second year. We tried to sublease it but there were no takers, so we continued paying the expensive rent and almost went bankrupt once again. In time, we developed markets in nearly 90 countries, so that wouldn't happen again.

Branding

We learned valuable lessons along the way, including how we identified ourselves in the international language market. Our school, CSLI was short for Canadian as a Second Language Institute, a play on the ESL term (English as a Second Language) but our focus was offering English programs with a Canadian flavor: Canadian teachers, Canada based curriculum, introducing Canadian speakers and cultural activities, along with Canadian family homestay experiences. Some joked about our business name but we soon became recognized among the multitude of language schools emerging. Canada, and especially Vancouver in the 1990s was quickly becoming one of the most sought-after cities for foreign students to learn English, along with London, New York, LA, Sydney, Auckland and later Toronto, Dublin, Cape Town and Malta.

Our strategy was simple. While it is possible to learn a language anywhere, most people are motivated by lasting results, which best comes from immersing themselves in a safe encouraging community. All this while experiencing adventure, mixing with the locals and exploring with new found friends. This made British Columbia and Vancouver ideal. But more than the traditional academic approach we focused strongly on expression through activities and sharing, encouraging more interaction and bonding.

Our motto was *"Uniting the World with English"*, as we always believed that if more cultures spent time understanding each other, the world would be a much better place. It gave me so much joy seeing students from different nations mixing at break times and making connections with other cultures. Despite their limited English skills, we really encouraged students to communicate with others and to make new friends. And I never got tired of graduates praising how CSLI changed their lives, helped achieve personal goals, all while creating better world citizens. We remain very close to many of our alumni from over the years, even though I sometimes have challenges with their names. (I took the Dale Carnegie name memorization course three times!)

Later we evolved into CSLI representing *"Care Share Learn Inspire"*, a clearer vision of our business and school, something our staff fully embraced. Social media with the likes of Facebook were becoming popular and we were amongst the first to engage directly with our youth market, effectively allowing them to drive our marketing campaign overseas. While other schools were spending half of their income on promotions like education trade-shows and hustling for agents to represent them, we focused on delivering quality product at home and encouraging our students to tell their friends about us. We stayed in touch by sending birthday greetings after they returned home, along with our digital monthly newsletters. CSLI had excellent "friends and family" referral and student return rates, some who came back many times over the years.

At the same time we were growing, Vancouver was also branding itself as the new *Hollywood North* Most of our more recent staff didn't know I had been teaching in the first few years, as well as running the business. I recall while teaching one class, taking the students (mostly Asian at the time) onto Robson Street for an activity. The second they opened the door to the street, they screamed and ran up to this guy in shorts and a t-shirt. I had no idea who he was, as our students were going nuts. I went up to him, shook his hand and said, *"Hi, my name is Lori-Ann. Who are you?"*

Well, my students were mortified when I asked that. His manager, who was with him, gave me his background and that he was very popular in Asia, but not in North America yet. He was in Canada to do his first English movie, called *Rush Hour*. Jackie Chan signed autographs and patiently waited so each student could take a picture with him. Thanks Jackie for an exciting class!

Leveraging

After ten years in business, we were still working 60-hour weeks, but were also looking to buy a home. We spent a couple of years trying to find the perfect home at a great price. The housing market in Vancouver was depressed at the time, so we knew it could be a good time to buy. At first, we were only looking at condos downtown, close to the office. Although we didn't have the budget, we fell in love with one that had an incredible view of the Stanley Park for $500,000. It was in foreclosure, so we were required to go to court to present our offer. We were surprised when the judge told us there were others who expressed interest, and instructed us all to go outside and write down our best offer. It was a very strange situation, as we all kept looking at each other, trying to figure out the top bid. We returned and the judge congratulated the top bidder. We were in shock when we discovered it wasn't us, losing out by $1000! Our real estate agent could not believe the judge didn't order a rebid with the offers being so close!

We went home drained. We had searched for months to find the perfect place to the max of our budget. I then called up a psychic who told me, we were never meant to have bought that condo. He then said we will buy a house - not a condo - and it would be on a mountain. I chuckled at that because I never considered a house. I called up a new real estate agent and shared our sob story. We agreed to clear a day that week for him to show us properties on the North Shore Mountains, telling him very clearly *"Do not show us anything out of our price range!"*

We toured a dozen houses that day and the last one we came to was empty, as the owners had just moved back overseas. As soon as I walked in,

I fell in love with the open plan, huge master bedroom and a million dollar view of the entire city. When our agent handed me the spec sheet, I saw it was $325,000 over our budget. I started whacking him over the head with it and reminded him once again about our budget and our agreement. The listing agent said they had two deals completely fall apart and he had a ton of showings, but no more offers.

The owners had dramatically dropped the asking price twice by then, but I asked him if he thought the owners would take a low-ball offer. All he said was, *"You never know, put it in writing!"* We left and went home. Ralph left town the next day for a conference, and we agreed that I would try to low-ball, the only subject being an inspection. To my surprise, they accepted my offer of 30% less than the asking price! I was very excited. Our inspector came the next day, and had the report ready the following day. He faxed it over with seventeen pages of problems. My heart sank. Ralph came back home that night and read the report. We agreed the deal was dead, but said he would talk to the inspector to discuss the report. I went to bed exhausted. ***And then it happened!*** The next morning, I suggested we go for a run as my nerves were shot. Ralph agreed, but said we should stop by the realtor's office. When I asked why, he revealed, *"To pick up our house keys. I countered the original offer by dropping our price another 20% and they accepted it."* I screamed and then yelled at him for not telling me sooner. Our real estate agent couldn't believe it. We had bought a house at half price!

New Lease Negotiations

Before we could negotiate our lease renewal on our school location, a competing school, which was also located in the building, muscled in and took our space. We needed to find a new business location at the same time as we were closing the deal on our new home. Many of the buildings we looked at had high rents and overheads. We came across a new building in Yaletown, at that time on the outskirts of the inner city, but it was on the ground floor with lots of windows. One of our biggest challenges in our old location was that we were on popular Robson Street, but at basement level, and not as appealing for our educational agents or our students. We loved the new space as we could build to our own specifications, but there would be serious construction costs involved.

This Yaletown location was 11,000 square feet and was part of Concord Pacific Developments, owned by Sir Li Ka-shing and managed by Terry Hui, his CEO in Vancouver. We approached them about leasing it, but after a while, discovered that Concord clearly did not have the appetite for managing property. They wanted to sell, and we didn't have the money for a large down payment. Ralph pitched their marketing man, Dan Ulinder, on the vision of having an international college within their new community. Dan was a past professor at the University of British Columbia, and loved the idea. Financing remained the issue and Ralph would regularly deliver specialty coffees for Concord staff at their sales center in the hope of keeping the deal warm.

Fortunately, it was still a soft market and because of the close relationship HSBC had with Concord, Dan eventually showed Ralph the 'secret handshake' to get the bank to come to the party. ***And then it happened!*** Against all odds, we got the loan to buy the building. We will be eternally grateful to both Dan (who sadly passed away the year after) and Terry for this incredible opportunity.

With some high risk financial maneuvers and smart negotiating advice, we were able to come up with a deal that worked. We took out a second mortgage on our new home, as the market value of our house was double. We bought the Yaletown property for $2million with support from the seller for the all improvements, but knowing a $1million balloon payment would be hanging over our heads for the next two years. When this payment came due, property values had increased significantly and we were able to refinance the building and cover this looming debt.

The space was an empty shell, but with a city-compliant engineer and a creative designer (thanks Brian), we were able to complete construction to code in 60 days, even though the city inspectors were on strike all this time. Try building anything in 60 days, so how we did it was nothing short of a miracle. Contractors were flexible because the economy was flat, and we were able to push electricians to work over painters and carpet layers to get the job done. We moved out all our furniture from our old location into a semi-truck on the Thursday and we finished moving furniture into the new location in the wee early hours of Monday. That same day the city inspectors, who conveniently for us, returned back to work! They grumbled about us building without normal process, but our paperwork was in order and we received our occupancy permit.

And that's how we managed to buy a house and a school property with very little money down. In today's market that would be near impossible! Or is it?

What we were learning, was the power of leverage. My husband had studied real estate and over our first ten years together had been searching for opportunities like our first home and our new school location.

As our business grew, it produced regular cash flow. Rather than having these funds, along with our profits sit in bank accounts, we would borrow and invest in other real estate opportunities. It was more through smart real estate leveraging that we became wealthy, than through the profits of the school. Imagine investing $100,000 as down payment on a $2million property, using the rental income to pay off the mortgage and expenses, all while the property appreciates in value. Over time, we were generating 100 times our investment. Our school business was never this profitable but our properties were.

Treat All Clients Like Royalty

A few years later, we were partnering with a Canadian company, Bombardier, a manufacturer of airplanes. As all aviation communication is in English, the Kingdom of Saudi Arabia decided to send their engineers and pilots overseas to learn western culture and the language. Along with Bombardier, we competed with New Zealand, Australia, USA, and England. *And then it happened!* We were awarded the largest contract we ever received. The bid preparation took us two years, but out of all the schools from around the world, we received the engineers, while a university in Saskatchewan won the pilot's contract. This was our biggest challenge in our fifteen years of doing business.

With these fifty-four Saudi engineers our challenges included:

Teaching them our alphabet and to read left to right instead of right to left. You try that!

Taking them from Beginner to College level English in less than two years.

Figuring out who has the highest social ranking over and above the military ranking. First born boys, from first born dads from a first wife hold the highest rank. These were usually the social leaders of the group.

Socially immersing them, all while they travelled, married and had families. We had one student who came in one Monday morning joyously saying that his wife had a baby over the weekend. Then the very next Monday the same guy came in and said the same thing. It took my brain an extra few seconds to realize he had more than one wife.

Homestay issues were plentiful. As these men were used to having most things done for them, their leaders wanted them to experience life with typical Canadians. Our homestay families had many challenges dealing with smoking, attitude, halal diets, extracurricular friends, health issues, loneliness and other cultural differences.

Saudi Arabia has over 15,000 members in their royal family. A number of the junior princes studied with us, so we had a great reputation with the royal family, many graduating before we had any idea who they were. In the middle of the engineer contract, one of the senior princes and his entourage came to inspect our school. We literally rolled out the red carpet for them. As women shouldn't make physical contact with Saudi men, I kept reminding my staff to bow instead of shaking hands. Out of respect, I also asked all our female staff to cover up their arms and legs, which in the middle of summer was an unusual request. When the group arrived, Ralph opened up the doors and what did I do? I extended my hand… oops! The prince ignored it, gave our management team a quick bow then immediately asked to meet his subjects. He was either very generous to them if they were doing well, or extremely hard on them if they were at the bottom of the class. This is not something I fondly remember.

Funny story though: Canada almost didn't get the contract. When Bombardier and government officials were first touring the Saudis, they were impressed with our school and we were assured we would meet again. But when their officials were taken to Robson Street for lunch, it was a hot summer day, and on seeing the restaurant servers in scantily dressed shorts and t-shirts, the Saudis became concerned their students would be morally corrupted. They reconsidered the deal, but fortunately they found the same in other Western countries and accepted that this was part of the education.

As more of our Middle Eastern students started to enroll, we learned more about their cultures. What we didn't understand right away was how and why women covered up. I can tell you after talking to Muslim women in the West for over a decade now, it is the women who choose how much to cover up. Some just cover the head, some head to toe, and not because their husbands insist.

Although our policy was to mix students nationalities in classes as much as possible, we had special classrooms for Middle Eastern women (if they preferred), and for student prayer. They had a female teacher and a room without windows, so passersby couldn't see in. They would come to class covered up, but when the door was closed, they would loosen up. Many were dressed head to toe in designer clothes and only wore the best jeans, the flashiest jewellery and a full face of makeup.

Selling Our Business

Selling up was the most stressful experience I have ever been through, but we learned some very valuable lessons in the process. After 24 years in the business we both felt proud of our accomplishments and just wanted a change. We had the best team ever, the business was profitable, our school had a solid reputation and our markets were expanding. A big factor in selling was the ever imposing regulations and red tape by provincial government in British Columbia.

Apart from the success of CSLI we were proud that we had helped establish the international language industry as one of Canada's major export industries. CSLI was instrumental in establishing Languages Canada, the national association of private language schools, promoting and representing English and French school owners in the private sector. Private schools, on the recommendation of the Canadian government, organized themselves into a national body. We established stringent quality standards, developed a student fee protection fund, bilingual (French & English) protocols and sponsored trade missions and education fairs abroad. Many of our students went on to training colleges and universities after acquiring sufficient language skills. By 2015, the private education sector, largely through Languages Canada and colleges, were generating $2billion into the Canadian economy, much of this into Vancouver and BC. But when we saw government was more interested in protecting public sector and union jobs, than supporting small business owners and building trade, we became disillusioned.

We had a great relationship with our management and staff and wanted to handle the process of selling CSLI discreetly, so we kept it private. It was business as usual with our educational agents, our students and staff, so accessing prospective buyers within the industry was not easy. The international language industry was maturing and there was a lot of consolidation, mergers and acquisitions of individually-owned schools, with the intent of creating worldwide education brands. Private equity and investors from outside the industry were also buying schools, colleges, and training operations.

Ralph and I would tour prospective buyers discreetly through the school under the guise that they were potential educational agents. What exhausted me most, was our first group of potential buyers. Their broker would text us every few days, assuring us that a formal offer was on its way, stringing us along. Initially we were looking at selling both the business and the premises, which complicated the deal, but after a tiring twelve months, we gave up on them.

We then used a broker that specialized in selling schools, however we still ended up doing most of the work. My husband spent hundreds of hours answering all their questions and due diligence. Our lawyers did an amazing job and we should have involved them earlier. They put their personal life on hold the last week of negotiations. I don't think I would have made it through the sale without our caring lawyers Michael and Silvana. ***And then it happened!*** After two years of struggling to get the right deal, we finally had one.

We told our General Manager on the Wednesday (although still waiting for the deposit), the rest of the managers individually on Thursday morning, then the rest of the staff at noon. I told them I would be in early Friday if they want to come in early to talk. One by one they showed up distressed. *"I didn't sleep last night!"*, *"I got drunk last night!"*, and *"I got drunk and didn't sleep last night!"* We had our final team meeting at nine that morning. Tears were shed, some frustration, shock on some of their faces was heart breaking for me, but I knew it was time for me to get out of the business. The buyer's non-disclosure was restrictive and it didn't allow easy communication with all those that we had worked with over the years, staff, suppliers and local and overseas agents.

The last question my team asked was, how long I will be staying for the transition with the new owners. I told them I would be leaving in 20 minutes, which was part of the agreement, and we had a plane booked the next day for a Mexican vacation. And that was that. After twenty-four years teaching over 20,000 students from eighty-nine nations, we were done. Because we decided to keep the ownership of our building, Ralph's new job is being a landlord and we remain happy collecting the rent.

Starting my own businesses and building them up over many years was a real joy and challenge. Then reaching the pinnacle of success by selling the school as a world-renowned award-winning operation is something I am very proud of. More than getting the price we wanted, we found a buyer that would continue our legacy, provide a financially sound foundation and growth opportunity for our employees, suppliers and most of all, our clients.

In starting CSLI we discovered more than we expected. We always loved traveling and engaging others, but we learned so much more over the years in uniting nations of people. We felt we created something much bigger than ourselves. It was a huge honor and responsibility to manage tens of thousands of students, thousands of homestay families, hundreds of employees, and a lifetime of lessons. But boy, it was worth it. To all of you who have made our school such a success, I offer a very big thank you. Thanks for the hugs, tears, and lessons we have all shared and learned along the way. I wish you only the best success in the future.

'The sales chief, the HR chief, and the boss of a company are on their way to lunch when they stumble upon a beat up, but valuable looking brass container.

The sales chief picks it up and starts cleaning it with his handkerchief. Suddenly, a genie emerges out of a curtain of purple smoke. The genie is grateful to be set free, and offers them each a wish.

The HR chief is wide-eyed and ecstatic. She says, "I want to be living on a beautiful beach in Jamaica with a sailboat and enough money to make me happy for the rest of my life." Poof! She disappears.

The sales chief says, "I want to be happily married to a wealthy supermodel with penthouses in New York, Paris, and Hong Kong." Presto! He vanishes.

"And how about you?" asks the Genie, looking at the boss. The boss scowls and says, "I want both those idiots back in the office by 2 PM."'

—*Anonymous*

Going Out on
Your Own

STARTING AND RUNNING YOUR OWN BUSINESS

"Starting a business is hard, but if you do it right, the prosperous reward in the end is worth all the hard work, sweat, and tears you will have gone through. If your business fails, don't become discouraged. Many successful businesspeople failed repeatedly before they found their way to success. For example, Gordon Ramsay was forced to shut down many of his restaurants. If he simply gave up after seeing his first restaurant fail, what would have happened to him? He'd just simply become another failed restaurant owner with shattered dreams and an empty bank account. That didn't happen, because Gordon Ramsay decided to keep going. Today, he's one of the most well-known chefs and restaurateurs in the world. He just kept on truckin', and so should you."

—*Chiara Fucarino*

If you are thinking of going out on your own, here are some things to keep in mind:

Don't Work with Family Members

Ralph and I started out as business partners and then became lovers, but I still stand my ground if you are thinking about working with a family member, don't! Most of our arguments over the years were business and money disagreements.

Even though we did well on our first business deal with my brother and his girlfriend, our second deal with them was a disaster. If you do decide to have a partnership or joint venture, a great idea is to establish an arbitrator, an impartial person that all partners respect. So, when you get into a deadlock, you can call on the arbitrator to determine an outcome that must be accepted by all partners. Also decide on a timeframe for goals and agree upon exit strategies.

Talk to Your Bank First

One of the best tips I can give you, if you are thinking of starting your own business, is to get a line of credit and an increased limit on your credit cards while you are still an employee. There is no guarantee the bank will give you credit once you are self-employed. Try to get the ones that give the most points, cash back and the lowest interest rates. If you travel a lot, then get ones with Air Miles. Try to use your cards for most purchases over $20 (check the fine print of your card for exemptions, I didn't know I was not collecting points on purchases under $20).

Nowadays, you can use your credit card points for many other things than just travel. You can buy anything from gift cards to cars. Make sure you pay them off at the end of each month, to avoid ruining your entire credit history. If you have a large credit card balance, talk to your bank about getting a line for credit to pay off your card, because the interest rate can be much less.

Make sure you have clearly budgeted your start-up costs, having funds for at least six months operation. Ideally you should not be borrowing to start a business. And, of course, having a business plan before you quit your job is wise. It is a romantic thought to want to work for yourself, but the reality is it is extremely hard. Set an absolute limit as to what you're willing to spend and lose before reconsidering your dream.

Pay Your Bills on Time

We almost went bankrupt and I know how important cash flow is, but your reputation and your credit record are also at risk. If you just don't have the funds available to pay a bill, call and assure your supplier when the payment will be made. Also pay your staff and temps promptly. When we had substitute teachers come teach at the last minute, they always had their check ready for them by the end of their shift. Other schools would mail out check weeks later and would wonder why it was hard finding staff. I remember what it was like living paycheck to paycheck.

Go to Auctions

My heart breaks when I see new businesses start up and spend a lot of money on renovations and brand new furniture. When we started furnishing our school, we went to every auction in town. Many times, we bought things inexpensively that looked brand new. I am sorry to see businesses go bankrupt and have their property auctioned off, but that doesn't stop me from finding great deals.

If you do go to auctions, especially if you are starting your own business, go there with a firm maximum you are willing to pay for each item. Check out each piece the day before if you can, as some may have scratches or damage where others may look brand new. Each piece has its own number. You can bid online, but you may only see a small photo of the lot you want. When you succeed with top bid on a multi-unit lot, you can usually tell the auctioneer exactly which items you want. If you don't, the other bidders may take the good ones and leave you the marked ones.

Also, remember to factor in the auction company's commission. It can be as high as 19%. And check delivery costs plus taxes. There is usually a delivery company who you can book on the site. You almost always need to pick up the items that day or the end of the following day. After paying all these costs and you are still well below half of wholesale value for an item you need, then it may be worth it. Remember there are no payment terms on purchases.

Listen when the auctioneer says you must take the whole lot when you only need a few items. I ended up having to take all the files inside filing cabinets, which cost me disposal costs and inconvenience.

Make sure you know everything about the electronics you are bidding on. I bought a bunch of computers once and they didn't come with hard drives. Know what you are buying.

Check to see how outdated something is. I've purchased photocopiers over the years at auctions and probably spent more fixing them than leasing new or refurbished ones. So, buyer beware, all things are final sale at auction houses.

Hiring

One of the best questions in a job interview you can ask a potential employee is: *"What is the most important value in your professional life?"* Their answer determines how to best manage them. If they sought recognition, I gave them job titles that would suit them. If they prioritized family, I would help to keep their schedule flexible or provide some days working from home. Some wanted the money, so I managed to give them more projects and rewarded them accordingly. Some had the need to travel, so I would help them by extending their holiday weeks, even working for us as they traveled. The more you know about each staff member's goals and desires, the more you can motivate them.

Employee Contracts

In our first year, a teacher applied for a job on a Friday, we hired her to start the following Monday. She showed up Monday morning with piercings all over her face and was dressed inappropriately. One of her students came up to me at morning break and said she was freaked out by the teacher's appearance and wanted to change class. I asked the teacher to go home and change, and take her piercings out or she will not be able to work at the school. She claimed wrongful dismissal and we ended up in Small Claims Court. We were told she had no case, and that she had actually been in his court before. He also explained he could not make a judgement, and suggested it was better to settle. We ended up paying her to get rid of the case, which upset me for weeks.

I felt so silly for not having written a dress code into our contracts and so angry that she would do that to a small business that couldn't afford this kinds of disruption. Why is it that some people just assume you are wealthy because you own your own small business? We immediately went to a lawyer to create a proper contract. We made it with all the "dos and don'ts" of working for us. Nowadays, you can print one off a generic version from the Internet, but make sure they have regulations that are relevant to the area in which the work is being performed.

Reference Lessons

Another major staff challenge came a few years later. We had hired a manager from outside the company (we usually try to promote from within). She was still working at another school when she applied and asked us not to call her present employer for a reference check, but gave us others to call. Her other references were glowing, so we hired her, but still had suspicions. I would check her work and performance. She appeared to be producing good results, assuring us of the group sales she was closing. Her student applications would be in the database with personal details such as passport numbers and birth dates, but one by one, as her students were due to arrive, they would have their visa denied, postpone or just cancel. My spidey-senses where tingling about her. I came in one morning and went through her emails and the files, and couldn't find communication from these clients. When she came to work I asked her where the emails were. She replied, they were having trouble sending to the school's email address, so they sent it to her personal address. *"Okay,"* I said, *"open your personal email and show me."* She agreed, but had to run out to another meeting. You guessed it, she never returned! It turned out she was a pathological liar. I called her references back and they were either disconnected or didn't return my calls. She worked for a total of six weeks and cost us about $50,000 in bogus work, courier fees and stolen cash.

Our new policy from that day on was that if an applicant doesn't want you to talk to their present employer, make sure their contract has a probationary stipulation. This means that after they are hired, you will have their permission to contact their previous employer before the probation can be lifted. If they disagree - trust me - don't hire them.

Unfortunately, I learned this lesson a second time while I was on the board of a charity. We were interviewing for a new Executive Director to run the office and raise funding. The applicant also asked us not to contact his current employer. We hired him and months later, when he wasn't performing, we discovered he wasn't even honest about his job title in his previous position.

Everyone should be hired with a probationary period.

Conducting a reference check is an important business practice, which surprisingly, is not always done. There is no legal impediment in asking prospective candidates to provide reference names and to give you permission to contact their previous employers. Reference checking is different than employment verification. Verification is just to confirm that they did work there and for how long. Reference checks gather information about the applicant's performance, skills, weaknesses and areas that require growth. Every candidate should have a reference check.

Ask the candidate to supply the CEO or owner's contact information of the companies they worked for. The owner may not know the applicant, but if it was an employee who they had issues with, they will probably know them. When you call a company, call the main reception number and ask them to verify the job title of the reference person you are calling about. Try to avoid a cell phone number for a work reference.

I found out that one of my past teachers made herself a verbal reference for another person, claiming she was the owner of my school. Another employee used our letterhead to make her own reference letter and sign my name. Fortunately, it doesn't take much nowadays to Google or check on LinkedIn for a list of company's officers and photos.

Reference letters often tell more in what is not written than what is, so check for gaps. If the HR department wrote a reference letter rather than their direct supervisor, try to find out why. Never take a photocopied degree as proof, you need to see the original. If they have no local references, you still must call their overseas work references. Get a translator if need be.

If at any time you are having challenges getting or contacting any reference, be on high alert. I am not saying you shouldn't hire them, but I am saying double check their work often. If you get a surprise call requesting a reference for a past employee that you let go, or a current staff member that isn't performing well, be careful what you say. Verify who you are speaking with. A lot of Human Resource departments will have standard questions. If you agree to answer them, feel free not to answer questions you are uncomfortable with, and allow them to read between the lines.

Suggestions for Employees

If you are looking for a job and need references, try to find the most senior person in the company who knows your work, to be your reference. Try not to use references that are no longer working for that company.

Please don't miss an interview, or just **not** show up for a shift. You never know how small your industry community may be. We knew the names of many staff from other schools that had burned their owners. Please give more than just a few days' notice when leaving. It's your our co-workers who will have to cover your load.

Don't just stop doing your work if you are frustrated with your job. Talk to your boss. We are not mind readers. Tell us your concerns. Please don't stop working when your boss is away. This just makes you and your co-workers lose pride in the work done.

Let your supervisors know how to best way to communicate with you. Generally, I found most men need to see something in writing, rather than just hear it. Please don't cry about how or what a co-worker or client said. It is not life and death. Keep things in perspective.

Ask your boss what you should be doing to be more valuable for the company to get promoted or receive a raise. We love proactive people. Bosses love to know that when someone says, *"Consider it done!"* that it will get done without a reminder.

Do not discuss politics or religion at work. This can be done outside of the office. Do not swear or use slurs at work. You never know who is listening and who you may offend. Treat your co-workers and supervisors with respect.

Providing Excellent Customer Service

Our business consistently won best customer service awards and here are some ways for you and your team to give great service to your clients.

Smile and Make Eye Contact

Always greet a new customer with a smile and a hello. My staff and I would always get up off our chairs to acknowledge a new customer as they walked in.

I learned how not to welcome while on my first trip to Vegas. I was so excited, announcing my arrival, *"Hi, can I check-in?"*

The check-in lady behind the front desk was sitting down, chewing gum and talking to another employee. *"Just one minute,"* she replied dryly.

I made sure my staff never treated a customer like that.

Memorize Your Customers' Names and Learn to Pronounce Them Properly

They say that a person's name is the sweetest word they can hear, so use it as much as possible. When you meet a new person, the best way to memorize their name is to use it three times as you meet them. *"Hi, what is your name? Is it Pete or Peter? Nice to meet you Pete. What do you Pete?"* If the name is unusual for you, ask them if you are pronouncing it correctly. I always encouraged my staff to learn and call new students by their names, especially when saying good morning or goodbye. We gave all new students name tags on their first day, so staff and other students recognize them as new, giving us all a chance memorize their names early.

Make Your Clients Feel Cared For

One of the simplest, most popular things we did was have a coffee mug for each student, with their name already on it, when they arrived. They felt they were part of a family when they were here. It was a small thing to do, but it turned out to be one of students' favorite memories of the school. The only place I could find so many unique mugs for 300 students at the school was at the Salvation Army Thrift Shop. I would go to the manager, who knew me as a regular, and asked for a deal on fifty or 100 different mugs at a time. The most I ever paid was fifty cents each.

My mom and her husband's business is also in downtown Vancouver. They often stop to help tourists when they have their maps out, trying to get somewhere. One Saturday, they saw a young Japanese girl looking lost. They asked her what she was looking for and she explained she was trying to find her new English school. Mom smiled when she recognized it was my school, and then offered to drive her to the school to show her where it was. The girl happily agreed. They all got into my mom's Rolls Royce and took her. They then invited her to come to their home for dinner, a 30-minute drive away, and again, the girl happily accepted. They all had a lovely dinner, then they drove her back to her homestay. When my mom told me this story I laughed, but when this girl came to school Monday I warned her never get to into a stranger's car ever again!

She replied, *"But they had a nice car, so they must be nice people!"*

Acting Quickly May Save a Bad Tweet

An example of acting quickly was when one day a student wrote in his school review, *"The owners of the school don't care about their students"*. I was shocked. I went to his class and asked him to come into the hall for a moment. I gently asked him why he felt that way and he said, *"Because the table tennis bats are terrible."* It is always surprising what clients feel is important.

I thanked him, grabbed my purse and took off. Twenty minutes later, the students were having their coffee break and as he came out of class, I presented him with brand new professional grade bats. You would think these kind of things should have no bearing on your business, but I can assure you, everything inside your business walls is how clients judge you. I could have replaced them in a week and he may have been happy, but seeing that he was listened to by the owner of the school gave him pride and made him feel special. Each time I saw me after, he would say, *"I love this school!"*

We also had one agent, that every time she visited our school, she went straight to the microwaves to see if they were clean. It was her way of seeing how much we care about her clients.

Make Up for Mistakes

Things happen that can be beyond your control. When it does, you need to act quickly to rectify it. Offering clients a discount can be one way, but it may not be enough for them to use your company again. You need to say sorry quickly, even if it is not your fault. Have we not learned from those who have publicly fallen? Just say you are sorry! We always had gift certificates in the office for all our administration to access. The staff were trained to listen to clients who had a complaint, even if it wasn't directly our fault, they were empowered to remedy as best as they could by giving a gift with our apologies. We could have waited until the end of the day, but that is never good enough in my books.

One example of this, was when Ralph and I went to a new restaurant that had just been promoted on the news during a cooking segment. The chef on TV made an incredible gnocchi dish and we told the server that is why we came. The gnocchi came and it was tough and overcooked so when the server came to ask how it was, we told her. She could have just taken it off our bill, but we probably would never have returned. Instead the kitchen made us two fresh dishes and brought them out with an extra glass of wine. They were delicious. We have returned there many times since.

Naughty Chef

Harumi Kurihara, a celebrity homemaker and television personality in Japan is often called the "Martha Stewart of Japan." We first met her when she came to study English at our school. For each dinner, she would sample food from different chefs at restaurants around the city. The first time she came, she had a camera crew following her around for her TV show. I won't forget the day that show aired in Japan. We received hundreds of emails from past students and agents that saw us on her show. The second time she came she just focused on learning English and we spent some private time with her.

One night we took her out for a dinner to a popular Vancouver seafood restaurant. For the reservation, I told the management that she would be joining us. Their chef was a huge fan of hers, so he came over to introduce himself as we arrived, requested a photo with her and offered a specially prepared seafood platter for the table. When the bill came at the end of our evening, we were charged $250 for that "special platter"! Not cool! I didn't make a fuss at the time, but I did send an email to the management. I never heard back from the restaurant!

Be Early for the Holidays

I made sure all my business-related Christmas presents were bought and wrapped by August. We had over 400 gifts to give away every holiday season, as I wanted everyone to feel special - the students, our agents, the staff and our suppliers. Planning early gave me more time to hunt for bargains during the year so when December came, it was a little less stressful for all knowing it was all ready to go.

Have Little Gifts Wrapped

Storage was always filled with wrapped gifts for VIPs, agents, special guests and clients, that just dropped by. There were baby gifts when someone came in with their new baby. There were pet gifts for those with animals.

I made sure that the birthday treats were bought in bulk as every student and staff member received them on their birthday. I understand that not all companies or all people can give these kinds of gifts out, but I sure can tell you we signed a lot of clients with the simple things we did. We entertain a lot at home, so I make sure I have gifts ready to give out there too. If the parents come over and mention their kid's birthday coming up, I just pop into my gift room and get one. It's not the gift, it's the thought.

I often look out for different sales throughout the year. I may not know what I will do with 50 heavily discounted items of the same thing, but they always seem to find a purpose. I use them up between birthday gifts, baby gifts, charity donations and next year's Christmas gifts. Businesses or a busy household can always find a need. Keep a log in your closet of who you have already given that item to. I once gave the same gift to someone's child two years in a row. Oops!

The day after Easter, Halloween, Valentines and Christmas are my "Go" days. Usually starting at Walmart at 7am, I shop for car loads of items that are freshly marked 50% off or more. You have to be quick. While staff and other shoppers are examining individual pieces, I will be taking cases of each. Keep an eye on your shopping cart, as other shoppers may take a few of your items right out of your buggy. After I usually hit retail chains like drug stores as these stores have their discounts from opening. Later in the week I will hit up furnishing stores like Home Sense or Michaels as they take a few days to put everything on sale.

Get Greeting Cards in Bulk

I buy Birthday, Get Well, Sympathy, Congratulatory and Seasons Greeting cards in bulk. As soon as I hear news about a loved one, I go directly to the box and write one out. And really, how much effort does it take to show you care? You could leave it till tomorrow, but doing it the second you think about it, is effective. Of course, having the resources to get things done is a plus, but many times things that don't get done until the last minute are just excuses for not being organized.

Get Gift Cards

Around Christmas and sales seasons, many restaurants have good deals on gift cards, where you can receive extra certificates for free, etc. Be careful to read the fine print on these deals. Some may say you can only use the bonus gift cards at that one location. Some must be used in the next two months, while others have limitations on many you can use at one time. FYI: If you buy credit card gift cards like Visa, you will be charged extra taxes.

When I owned the school, I would negotiate with the managers of nearby restaurants that we used regularly for client or staff meetings. I would ask them how many bonus cards I would get if I bought $5000 worth of certificates. Then, I would play them off each other by showing their competitor's offer. That got me at least $500 more every time.

FYI: It is easier to business expense them that way, rather than expensing the individual restaurant bills separately.

Make Your Washrooms Comfortable and Clean

I made sure our washrooms were always decorated nicely and were cleaned throughout the day. Washrooms are always brought up when we discuss different cultures. I will always remember one amusing incident when all the students were gathered in the lounge, and one of my female teachers came out of the bathroom yelling, *"OK, who pissed all over the toilet and floor?"* After I calmed her down, I felt I needed to address this situation to some of our students. I explained that in Canada we don't step on the toilet and squat, but instead place toilet paper or toilet liners around the rim, before sitting. Another challenge was that so much toilet paper was being used, that it constantly plugged the toilets. It took us years of unclogging before we got smart and installed strong flush Gerber toilets. The most common complaint we received from homestay families was that their international students used whole rolls of toilet paper daily.

Men are no better. We had to install the automatic urinals that flushed upon use, and they were constantly 'missing' … very gross. When we went to World Cup in Germany, the men's urinals at a pub had a tiny soccer goal (with an even tinier ball tied to it) in the pee zone. The objective was to help men aim better by "shooting" the ball into the net. We thought this was a novel way to improve their accuracy, so when I came back home I ordered a few online and installed them in the men's washroom at the school.

It took exactly two days before someone thought that these would make a great souvenir. Gross! I put the last one in Friday morning and it was gone by the morning break!

Tips For Management:

Double Check Staff's Work

We have a friend who also had an English school and one of his employees didn't answer company email for weeks. If you are a small business owner, take my advice and make sure you are constantly checking on staff and their work stations. I don't care if some find this invasive. It is your company and you own the computers. Congratulate them when their emails are answered in a timely fashion, if they are filed and not left in the inbox, praise them publicly for their professionalism and for how organized they are. We later switched to cloud email with all correspondence reviewed regularly by supervisors.

Organize Schedules Early

In business, planning ahead is essential. Clients and agents wanted our study calendar and prices, sometimes two years ahead of time. Staff needed to book their holidays with their families, so they sometimes needed to be approved well ahead of time. If my team waited to the last minute, events would be chaos. Advanced calendars and schedules are what we build our working lives around, so be proactive.

Last One

We marked "last one" on supplies, but just to make sure we had time to order more, we wrote reminders on the last five, so we never got caught out.

Be on Time

I cannot emphasize this enough. No matter what is happening, make sure you plan accordingly and be on time for deadlines, meetings and your scheduled work. And that does not mean you're walking in the door of the business at 9am on the dot. You still have to put your coat away and get your coffee.

To me, that is still late. If you are not a morning person, that is no one's problem but your own. Say good morning to your staff, co-workers and your boss. The longer staff worked for me, the more they realized getting things done before the deadline was always greeted with high fives and a pat on the back. (Ralph just about lost me for good after being late for meetings the first few times in our relationship.)

Set Department Goals and Measure Results

I had goals for all my staff and posted them for everyone to see. It is amazing how often we reach clear goals once we can focus on it. Our administrative staff had sales goals every month and if the team reached them, they would get different rewards, such as cash, days off with pay, massages, lunch, etc. Our teachers always had evaluation goals and incentives as our clients expected the best, during slow seasons or peak seasons. Our staff performed like no other and I believe they enjoyed their jobs as they constantly achieved high evaluations month after month and year after year.

Like any good learning center, we depended on regular client feedback. Our international students were asked to regularly complete performance evaluations on their classes, teachers, on the school in general, and even on themselves, to make sure we were consistently on top of our game. Our clients (our students and their families) spent hard earned money to come to our school, and there were plenty of other schools to choose from, if they were not getting results they wanted. We had programs that ranged from one to 50 weeks with starts every Monday and graduations every Friday, so we challenged our students to be the best they could be in the time they were with us.

Your own goals need to be where you can see them every day. Check them off, add to them and visualize them all coming to you.

Answer Clients Quickly

On our website, we guaranteed that all inquiries would be answered within 24 hours during the work week. I can't tell you how many people said they chose our company because we answered them first. Some said that other schools never answered them at all! I remember once as a client, calling a company informing them that, *"No one answered the email I sent you last week."*

Their reply was *"We answer emails in the order we receive them"*. I highly disagree with that approach as it could not have taken more than one minute to have answered mine. I would have my staff skim all their correspondence first thing in the morning, and prioritize, answering the easy ones first, so they have more time to focus on the lengthy ones. We developed templates to simplify replies as staring at so many unanswered emails, can be distracting and overwhelming.

Train your Sales People

Business is tough. Motivating your staff and greeting each customer, as if they were the most important person in your life, is where you can have the greatest success.

We trained our sales team to start with the same question for each client: *"What is the most important thing for you in choosing a **school**?"* You can change the last word to adapt this question to your product or service. Listen carefully to each client's response before trying your standard "pitch", as it can save you time and a sale.

If you are talking to a client or customer and the phone rings, leave the phone. The person who is standing in front of you is more likely to buy your product or service now, and the person on the phone can be called back. I can't tell you how many times I have been at a counter waiting for service and the clerk is talking to another store or staff member on the phone. Establish your sales priority, have back-up, and focus on the sale standing right in front of you.

If you are free and the phone does ring, answer it in a slow, friendly tone. You may be run off your feet, but that is not the concern of your customer who is on the phone. I trained my team to actually smile while answering the phone as it is conveyed in their tone.

If you work in a retail setting as a store sales person, please never redirect a customer to another till without actually helping collect their items off the first counter. I have walked out of stores that have done that to me.

If you work in a restaurant, know that Ralph and I have a system for tipping. We started years ago when we had a horrible server. He was not just rude to us, but to the tables around us. You know the kind, when you have to ask for the same thing several times. I wanted to pay the bill so he would not a get a cent for a tip, and we decided to carry forward the normal tip amount to the next time. For that night's dinner, the tip would have been around $50. Our breakfast server the next day was amazing and she got the whole $50 tip carried forward, and an explanation why.

Drop Clients

There are always the extremely difficult clients that, no matter what you do, they are never ever satisfied. They may not even realize how much you have been trying to please them. My advice is to drop that client ASAP. I know this is a challenging thing to do when you start out, but as long as your quality standards are high, follow the 80/20 Rule and seek better customers.

Diversify

Please listen to me when I say, do not put all your eggs in one basket. Use your marketing budget to gain clients from different markets. I can't tell you how many companies I know that went under when they were just working with one client, or one market.

Thank Your Team Often for Their Results

I think we had some of the most dedicated, loyal staff. Many had been with us for ten to twenty years. I often have to call them at the office after closing time, to tell them to go home.

When I handed out paychecks, I would always try give them to the person directly and say, *"Thanks for your hard work!"* You are not being generous by giving them their paycheck, they have earned it. And if those words can't roll off your tongue easily with an employee, ask yourself why? Maybe they are in need of a performance review?

While we were overseas on business trips, some of our competitors would complain that their staff would drop the ball and slack off while they were not in the office. I would tell them that I felt my team worked harder to reach company goals when I was not in the office! Many employees have become close friends. However as their boss, I always made it clear that my job is to measure work performance, and that criticism is always constructive, and never personal.

Time Out

Try not to bother your staff or co-workers on their day off or on a break. Employees need a time out from work to refresh and regroup. Do not contact them on their vacation or days off. I always had a policy that two people must know every position inside and out. So, when someone was on vacation, they don't need to think about work.

Discuss Mental Health

You won't believe the kind of things we had to deal with involving staff and students' personal lives. There included abortions, birth control, babies, divorces, suicide attempts, fights, arrests, deaths, surgeries, major illnesses, postpartum and winter depression, car accidents, illnesses and drug abuse and much more. They needed help to deal with their emotions (and sometimes we needed help too) when a disaster happened in their home countries and when they could not get in touch with their own families. After 9/11, we brought in counselors for both staff and students.

We had many teenage students who were "shipped off" overseas because the parents just wanted a break. These kids were usually unhappy and usually late for classes, or just didn't show up. A few would wander around the malls or beaches, or just ended up causing trouble and getting dismissed.

Parents, please make sure your kids have their medication when they leave home, as well as a medical notes if they have a condition. We had one 18-year-old boy walk into my school for his first day, stating his name and saying that he wanted to kill himself. His parents had flown him to Canada without his medication. I asked why he didn't bring it, and he told me his mom didn't want anyone to think he was strange. We had a few of these situations.

Mental health is talked about more and more these days in the Western world, but in many countries, it is still taboo. I am not saying these parents were bad as I am sure they needed relief from their stress, but unfortunately, the homestay families, my staff and I were left to handle difficult situations.

So please managers, discuss these issues with your staff and provide resources they need to help.

The Put-Up-Withs

Every year I asked my team what their "Put-up-withs" were, you know, those work interrupters. I then made a list of all the little or big things that irritated them at work and then took immediate action on the ones that I could fix fast.

I was only in the office a couple days a week by this stage, so I wanted to show them that I cared. If I waited for weeks to fix their requests, it wouldn't have been half as effective. One person wanted a bigger computer monitor. I ran out and bought one and it was installed an hour later while she was meeting with a client. Another wanted a new chair so, I gave her mine and I got a new one later that week. A few weeks later at a staff meeting, we would check off the list to make sure they were all done. I know the staff got used to me doing things quickly and well ahead of time. When we sold the business and the new owner took over, staff had a reality check when decisions would take weeks or sometimes months.

Be Transparent

We would close the school at least one day a year for a paid Professional Development Day. I think the staff got a lot out of the team building, training sessions and the social events around them. We lost many great teachers to the public school boards as understandably they received better pay, conditions and security than we ever could offer. However we were thrilled to take them back during their summer public school holidays, as this was our busiest time and they loved the work atmosphere at CSLI.

The biggest pushback we received was usually over teacher salaries. Ralph did an amazing presentation to our staff at one of these sessions outlining the significant costs in running a private school business, using a simple pie-chart to compare operating costs of private schools versus public schools. It was hard competing with the public sector (and their unions) for international English students, given that we were required to pay enormous taxes (income, federal & provincial sales taxes, employer taxes, property taxes and capital gains), and operating costs like international marketing, advertising, agent commissions, mortgage payments, medical plans, strata & operating costs, that the public schools are generally not required to pay.

Showing our staff all the costs to run the business gave them a real insight into how challenging running a business can be. Although not everyone can appreciate the challenging costs of a small business, we did our best to help our people understand the realities and I think they showed incredible loyalty as a result. We also lost a few staff-who thought they could start their own school, none of whom are still in business.

Team Building

Some events we have organized with our team include fire walking, public speaking, zip trekking, river rafting, the gun range, curling, board breaking, rock climbing, repelling and sky diving.

We have had a few parties up at our house on the mountain where we bused everyone up from downtown. We had a murder mystery, and - one of the most challenging - a scavenger hunt involving all of our neighbors.

In solving the puzzle, they discovered we were taking everyone to Las Vegas for the weekend. It was a blast.

One of my favorite end of year events was when we all gathered at the school, walked the entire staff and their spouses to the nearby Miele demonstration kitchen, complete with six self-contained kitchens in one room. We put everyone into teams and we had our very own Iron Chef competition. We brought in hundreds of food items and a full bar (one team was the cocktail making team to serve our chefs). It was so much fun, with great teamwork and lots of dancing afterwards, but no drinking and driving. For such events we usually chartered a bus to pick everyone up or paid for cabs to take everyone home.

Another year we took them to the Dark Table restaurant and then a nightclub. One of the most unique experiences is dark dining. There's different versions in many countries, all meant to provide an appreciation of how much we depend on our sight. Here we had an entire meal in pitch-black, sensing the taste and the texture of the food rather than through its normal visual appeal. When they say "dark" they mean completely dark. We were lead through a busy jammed packed restaurant, to our table by mostly blind staff, where at first, we had no idea how far we were from each other. The noise level got very loud, so at one point when I wanted to give a speech to our group, I clinked my glass. The entire restaurant went quiet, as no one knew who I was addressing.

People came away with very different experiences. Some loved it, some felt claustrophobic, and some thought it was their best meal ever. I had a sensational experience and it certainly gave everyone an insight to what the visually impaired have to go through every day.

We always tried to make these team-building activities a surprise, getting our team out of their comfort zone on pro-D days, and having them to experience something new. They were taught to juggle, fire-walk, salsa, play the drums, box and yoga. They never knew what was planned ahead of time, and I was always so proud of them jumping right in.

When the school was about 10-years old, we treated the entire team by taking them on a Caribbean seven-day cruise. Ralph stayed and we hired past staff members to work for the week, while twenty of us had a fab time. We all flew to Miami and I arranged a bus to pick them up and take them to the cruise ship. I was meeting my best friend and chosen ship roommate

Sally, in Miami and went to her hotel before we boarded the ship. We all had the rooms on the same floor on the ship and when we arrived at ours, I was shocked to see all the other rooms were vacant. The whistle blew, the ship left port with still no sign of my people. An hour later I heard a loud, drunk mob come down the hallway. Apparently, my staff bribed the driver of the tour bus to stop by the beach after picking up some "refreshments." I was relieved to see they all made it aboard, but still yelled at them for almost giving me a heart attack.

We often took staff away for the weekend retreats. At the end of the day, I cannot say specifically why our team remained so loyal, but these trips always gave us great stories to share and laugh about.

Suggestions for Employers on Events

Take a copy of everyone's passport if you are taking them out of the country in case someone disappears (like one staff member of mine did in Vegas when he partied all night at another hotel).

At some yearly events, just take the staff and not their spouses, as spouses can change the chemistry in team bonding. If spouses are invited, encourage mixing with other team members.

Put a designated driver sticker on the drivers to ensure they do not have alcohol. Know diet restrictions and keep them in mind when catering.

Don't do anything that involves playing on ice (one 'elf' ended up in the hospital during our Christmas costume curling tournament. How's the head Mikey?). Or protect appropriately.

Keep things top secret, as we get much more enjoyment out of being surprised.

Celebrate as Often as You Can

After we finish our school years, we rarely get a chance to be given awards. Top sales people or an actor may get awards, but most adults don't usually receive enough recognition for their efforts.

When I was in Toastmasters, we received constant reinforcement with ribbons for "Best Speech" or "Best Table Topics," etc. This shows that someone a long time ago knew most people do like to be acknowledged for their efforts, especially to reinforce growth, learning and improvement.

When I started our school, I implemented a "Student of the Month" award. The staff would nominate a student (out of the 200-300 each month) who had worked the hardest, participated the most and was a role model for others. They also received a return flight ticket back for our tenth anniversary party and a one month scholarship. We had our onsite dormitory at that time, so for the reunion, we flew dozens of students back to Vancouver for that one month of celebration. We worked very hard to ensure our students had a memorable month of events and reunion, many declaring it one of their most enjoyable achievements.

I also introduced the "Ambassador of the Year" award. This annual award was given to the person who had showed the greatest contribution in bridging international relations between their home country and ours. Winners included those who introduced others to the school, those who helped mentor other students or those who helped the school improve with new ideas. This award gave the person and their immediate family, free English lessons for life. It is amazing how so many of the ambassadors are still close friends of ours today, and will be for life.

Students could study from one week to two years, so we had graduation ceremonies regularly. We celebrated our "Student of the Class" awards once a month with each teacher deciding the medal winner. At the time, I wondered if people would keep their medals, but when I later saw photos of students back home with the awards proudly displayed, it showed me people do feel good about themselves when they are recognized. Graduations ceremonies became spectacular events, and were celebrated with international themes, parties & competitions such as Iron Chef, Olympics, Oscar Night, Beach BBQ games and Halloween costume contests.

We gave various kinds of recognition awards to our team. Some accepted them with excitement while others felt humbles by the attention. One award was our "Teacher of the Month." All teachers were evaluated each month, including by their students. The teacher (or teachers) with the highest evaluation were usually called into my office, we would do the drum roll and then present them with the "High Score" bonus. If the teachers earned a perfect score they would get a much bigger one.

We had the "Green Award" for staff who made the greatest environmental contribution at the office. Most people who know me, know I am not a big recycler or environmentalist. Now, don't get mad at me, Ralph does all the recycling for the both of us. But after seeing how much paper we wasted at the office, I implemented a "Green Award" for the employee who would be most creative in saving costs while helping the environment.

We also encouraged our team to publicly recognize their co-workers. A favorite of mine was the "Cappuccino Awards". After every busy season, I bought fifty $5 Starbucks cards and everyone is given one to award to the team member who supported them the most. It is always uplifting to see heartfelt open appreciation expressed between co-workers. It also shows who the team players were.

I felt humbled by my staff, family and friends when I was nominated in 2004 for a "Woman of the Year" business award. We all dressed up to the nines and went to the gala at the Westin Bayshore Hotel. The other four women in my category had doctorate degrees, (apparently a prerequisite). I didn't win that particular award, but later that night, my friends presented me with their very own Woman of the Year Award. (I guess they would have kept the trophy if I had won?) I felt their award was way more valuable than the other, but I now have a joke going around that I have my Doctorate in Celebration Events, so you can just call me Doctor Lori-Ann.

I truly feel I found my purpose in life and that is to celebrate, celebrate people's accomplishments, even those little moments in life, as often as possible.

If You Are Looking at Selling Your Business:

First, ask yourself if you are mentally or emotionally ready to exit from your business. How dependent is the business on you? If so, how can you change that? Ralph and I slowly removed ourselves from the day to day operations, so we knew the business could run without us.

Would your business be severely impacted by the loss of a key client? What is the true value of what you are selling? If you are not a good negotiator find someone who is, as the process can get emotional and drawn out.

Decide if you are willing to stay on as an employee, under contract or a minority shareholder if asked, or do you want out from day one? Remember you are no longer in charge or carry the responsibility or ownership. There is usually a transition period where the new owner may want you around, but this is negotiable. It is not unusual for there to be an indemnity period where you and your selling partners may remain liable for what you have stated in your financials and disclosures which include taxes, contract obligations, employment contracts, debt collection, leases and creditors.

Be prepared to do your homework. Prepare accurate, complete records for due diligence as you will need this for each and every candidate. Have your financials polished for at least the previous three years. If your business is not making a profit, your price might just be the devalued assets you have. Most sellers think their value is higher because of all the blood, sweat and tears that they put in, but that is not usually the case. It's all about the profitability or upside, or the uniqueness and potential of your product or service.

Businesses are usually assessed on its EBITDA (Earnings before Interest, Taxes, Depreciation, and Amortization), effectively its business performance or profitability: how much money your business makes each year after you remove irregular non-operating expenses, including what you take from your business for your personal use. Multiply this amount by the industry multiple (which can be anything from 2-3 times and up) to determine your selling price. This multiple tells you how many years it will take the new owner to recover their investment, if things are run at the current level. This is why your figures need to be carefully scrutinized, yet it does not mean this is all the business is worth. Valuing start-ups and new tech companies are harder, as they may yet show profit and are valued more on their hidden potential. The TV show "Shark Tank" reveals how challenging it is to determine true value.

Never deal with someone you do not trust, no matter what the offer. Non-disclosure agreements are worthless if someone can't keep it private. Don't be drawn into extended negotiations that may prevent you from considering better offers elsewhere as this may weaken your position. Be willing to say no to exclusivities, non-competes and other restrictions.

Always make every effort to be paid out in full at closing in cash as there is no certainty that installments or hold-backs will be delivered to you as promised. There may be tax benefits to be paid out in installments or in shares but there is no guarantee that your buyer will be in business in the future. Ask for more than what you think your business is worth. Remember once you determine the price, you still have closing costs: legal and accounting fees, agent commission (if you used a broker), and final corporate and capital gains taxes so build this on top of your asking price. You are selling the business that may have been providing you an income, so sell when you are ready to move on. Finally, be patient as the process of finding a buyer and selling it to her may take some time.

Preferably your buyer is someone who knows the industry or your product, and ideally knows your business intimately. This means they should have no doubt as to what they are buying into and its value, and in that case, the process should be smoother and shorter. Our goal was to sell to an established but expanding Canadian owned company in the education business and this is what we eventually and successfully found.

> *'A shopkeeper was dismayed when a brand new business much like his own, opened up next door and erected a huge sign which read 'BEST QUALITY'.*
>
> *He was horrified when another competitor opened up next door on his right, and announced its arrival with an even larger sign, reading 'LOWEST PRICES'.*
>
> *The shopkeeper panicked, until he got an idea. He put the biggest sign of all over his own shop. It read 'MAIN ENTRANCE'*
>
> *—Anonymous*

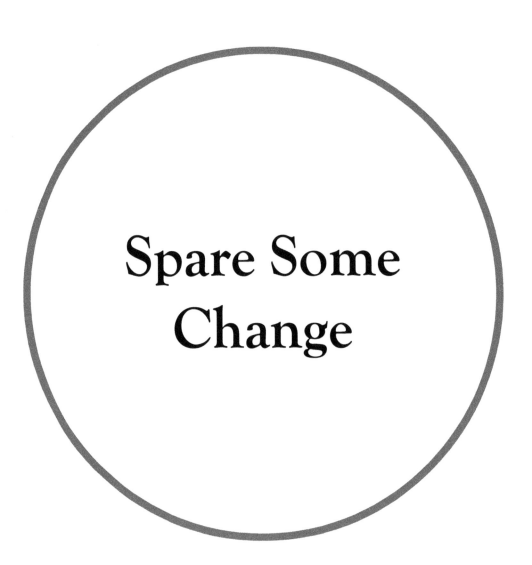

Spare Some Change

GIVE BACK TO THE COMMUNITY

"The smallest act of kindness is worth more than the grandest intention."

—*Oscar Wilde*

One of the most important values in our lives has been the power of gratitude. Appreciating whatever we had, whenever we had it. Every morning, we start the day declaring something we are grateful for. We try to celebrate life and its small victories as they come along. This is the essence of success but there is no better way to feel grateful for what you have, than by sharing or giving.

I am always involved with one charity or another. When I eventually choose Vancouver as my home, I started a program for seniors at the local community center, called Wheelchair Travels. Each week I would have a slide show, video, or a speaker to discuss places and tours that are exciting, but accessible for the elderly. The best part was, that they could ask questions and feel like their needs were being considered. Some of them would come week after week just for the presentation while others signed up for the tours.

Having no children of our own, we try more to take care of others. For twenty-five years we help support children through Children International, a global non-profit that helps children and their family in poverty. Doing this kind of giving back was great when we only had a few dollars a month to spare. Our main reason for going to Chile one year, was to meet one of the children we had sponsored since the age of five. We had to go through many channels, as the organization wished to protect the privacy of the families involved. We first met the liaison near Valparaiso, in a very poor area of town. It was bucketing down rain, so we were soaking wet when we met the family in their humble home. But maybe this helped to make us look more approachable. Maria was sixteen by then and we had a good chat about staying in school and not getting pregnant or marrying young, as many in poor families do.

Our school, CSLI sponsored eight children from around the world through Children International and featured them in our school programs, involving our students as a community project. We recommend this organization if you are seeking a legitimate impacting cause.

We have also been sponsoring the Terry Fox Cancer Foundation for over twenty years. Terry's brother, Fred, and his mom Betty, have been to our school for presentations and fundraising events where we would auction off items and services donated by staff, homestay families and even students. We made it a fun event where I performed as the auctioneer, and students actively participated in bidding, making it a great learning exercise and a favourite annual event. Staff and students also participated in the annual Terry Fox Run. It's always a worthy cause to get people involved as everyone knows someone who has had cancer.

We were very excited when Vancouver got the Winter Olympic Games in 2010. A friend of ours, Jamie Stirling, was chosen to be the guide skier for a partially sighted cross-country skier in the Paralympic Games. This athlete could only see shadows, so he needed a guide to ski ahead to make it around the course. Guides like Jamie are not paid for their training or for all the time off work, so our school arranged fundraising events and we presented a cheque to him in front of everyone. I think Jamie was very touched because after the Paralympics, he presented his signed Olympic jersey to us.

We have done fundraising for other athletes over the years. It takes a lot of money to be the best in your country, and then the best in the world, so we are happy to have contributed in some way. We are now sponsoring a young figure skater who, we hope, will be in the next Olympics. Go get 'em Sophia!

Christmas Giveaway

One year, instead of doing a big expensive staff Christmas party, we gave everyone $250 each to do something nice for someone in need. We set no other parameters and they didn't need to share their story, if they didn't want to. The low-key party we expected turned out to be one of the most memorable and a tear-jerker night for all. One by one, each one of our team made a presentation on how they impacted less fortunate people's lives. They were some of the most loving, touching and creative stories I have ever heard. I was so proud of all of them and will remember those stories for many years to come.

Rose Charities

And then it happened! When the big tsunami hit in Southeast Asia on December 26th 2004, Ralph woke up the next day saying, *"I can't just sit here and do nothing!"* We got busy looking for where we could help the most, identifying Sri Lanka as our focus. When we watched the local news, there was a Sri Lankan man named Anthony living in Vancouver who lost 36 of his family members in the tsunami. We called up the TV station and asked for his contact information. My husband met with Anthony, and local members of the Sri Lankan community who were now coordinating with Rose Charities, a local NGO (Non-Government Organization) with ties to BC Children's Hospital. Ralph offered to pay for the man's flight so they could both go to his village of Kalmunai on the eastern coast to assist in the emergency. Global TV asked to follow them and the Rose medical team with a camera crew back to Sri Lanka.

As I booked his flight and hotel to the capital city of Colombo, I don't remember being as scared as I was that day. Ralph had a calling and I understood that, but he said he had no idea when he was coming home and that was very worrying for me to hear. I raced to the department stores to buy as many supplies that I could think of: fishing nets, first aid kits, cell phones, school supplies, water purification kits, etc.

When checking-in at the airport with a lot of excess luggage, I asked the airline if they could give us a break on the extra luggage fees as Ralph was bringing supplies to survivors. I think because we were one of the first who acted, (it was less than seventy-two hours since the tsunami), they didn't charge us for the extra baggage. He left a week ahead of the main party to help make arrangements for them on the Sri Lankan east coast, to identify projects to prioritize, and then rendezvoused back in Colombo.

Following their 30-hour flight to Sri Lanka, Ralph greeted the incoming party (Anthony and some of his family, the Rose Charities medical volunteers, and the Global news crew) off their flight and shuttled them to their Colombo hotel, where they spread out into two bedrooms for six hours rest. I remember calling him at their hotel at 11pm that night, his time. He answered and quickly whispered he would call me back, as he was busy. I was a bit shocked. It turns out, on arrival, they were meeting with the Sri Lankan Minister of Health in their hotel. In the chaos there was little coordination between international aid groups and government, and given there was a civil war still going on at the time, the government were cautious, even suspicious of help. Many of the poorer, devastated areas in the north and east were isolated and in real need.

It took them a 12-hour journey on mostly unpaved road through Tamil Tiger (LTTE) resistance country to the east coast of Sri Lanka, through checkpoints and debris. They arrived in Anthony's village, Kalmunai, to find over 500 meters of their shoreline missing. Anyone who had a hut or home on the waterfront had disappeared. People were walking out to sea to see in hope of finding missing loved ones, some so hopeless they committed suicide. Ralph did not speak Tamil, but he managed to convey to some these survivors, with Anthony's help, a sense of hope, that they were destined to rebuild the village and its future. In Ralph's book, he wrote about his experience, about going around the communities and the hospital, consoling and encouraging survivors. Telephone reception was weak in the village, so I would watch the 6pm news just to see the reports from the TV crew on location. They were mostly sleeping on concrete floors near the hospital. It was warm there, and as hard working, exhausted volunteers, sleep came easy.

Ralph stayed for a month and shortly after returning, he joined with Rose Charities and fundraised for these various Sri Lankan projects. Anthony, who lost so many family members, remains there fifteen years on to assist with Rose Charities projects he established, and is now one of the most respected people in the region. We are also assisting Anthony's wife and daughters in Vancouver from where they plan to graduate and return to help their father, as doctors and nurses. With the support of Rose Charities and a Swiss foundation, and especially the local Kalmunai community, we have rebuilt the hospital and a local medical clinic, re-established schools, pre-schools, community centers and we have helped set up scholarships for students to go to university in Sri Lanka.

Often after a disaster like this one, people offer to help, but after a while as other disasters occur elsewhere, the money and interest usually flow away. However, our staff and students, and friends continued to support our fundraising efforts for Sri Lankan charities over the years, remaining dedicated as life on the east coast slowly improved.

Anthony and Ralph founded a micro-financing division after emergency relief work became less urgent, supporting mostly mothers in villages to start their own home businesses. It is similar to getting a credit card or a small loan from a bank, except for underprivileged families to help create income. For example, we lend $100 for someone to buy a goat, who was then able to repay the loan slowly as they were able to sell its milk. Other family members made sure the loan was paid back on time, so another person in the community would receive the next one. This growing economy worked hand-in-hand with our social programs as home based jobs like these, allowed parents to send their children to preschool, helping lift families out of poverty. Daycare and education became our priority, and since these programs have begun, thousands of kids have been schooled, with many going onto university, something unheard of ten years ago in this war-torn region.

Charity has led us to micro-finance which in turn led to social enterprise projects, our latest being micro-farms and even an hotel, as tourism and backpackers are attracted here. Our school sponsored a number of staff and friends from Canada to go and support the village, and teach English. We paid for their flights, arranged simple accommodation as they volunteered their time. Big thanks to all who have gone there including Sonia and Jonathan. We were very proud to accept the 2013 Humanitarian Award from Rose Charities International, much of what would have been impossible without their incredible organizational support over the last 15 years. Thank you especially to William, Josie and Yoga. My husband was humbled by the recognition, but I know he deserved it.

Big Brothers

My husband and I had also been involved with Big Brothers for many years. We both had a *"And then it happened!"* moment when Ralph was first paired with his 12- year old boy. I know if this boy didn't have Ralph in his life, he could have gone a very different route. Kris is a man now with children of his own, but we still consider him our own son.

The things this kid had to deal with were just awful, but credit to him, he has stayed away from drugs and doesn't drink, even when he was pressured to. He were proud to see him graduating high school and working very hard at his job. I think kids who grow up in unfortunate situations may have a reason to harbor a grudge, but Ralph's little brother showed remarkable tolerance, patience and love given what he had to put up with, just to survive. I found even greater respect for our First Nations people.

I was involved with the school program at Big Brothers, where I would meet a child once a week and spend a couple of hours one-on-one with them at their school. One of the kids I had was a very sweet, intelligent boy of Asian descent. His mom put him into the Big Brothers program so he could interact with other adults and just to have fun, as his dad was very strict. We ended up being the one of the faces of the Big Brothers Mentoring program. I will always love him.

I will never forget my interview for Big Brothers. I thought running a school of 300 students and close to fifty employees was a challenge. I showed up early for the appointment and was invited into the interviewer's office. She probably asked me a hundred questions, my husband didn't have Anywhere near that many! The woman kept asking me questions about drug use. I replied that I had once smoked some weed and a few "special cookies," but was not a regular user. She asked me again in a roundabout way, and then again. I finally stopped her to ask why she was asking me these sort of questions. She paused and then asked me my date of birth. Once she heard my reply she started laughing. It turned out that my doctor had sent the wrong medical records for my background check to Big Brothers. Apparently, there was someone with a similar name, who went to the same doctor and was into hard drugs. I still chuckle about that day. My interviewer Sue, and I ended up becoming close friends.

Scholarships

Bringing the concept of volunteering to our students was a big part of our school. Many foreign students had never volunteered in their life. Some cultures don't even have a word for "volunteer". Every month we gave deserving students who could not afford to extend, a chance to volunteer part-time at the school, in exchange for continuing half-time studies. They also volunteered at countless numbers of fund-raisers we supported in outside of the school. Each and every student told me they loved the opportunity to help others.

Kids Up Front, Vancouver

One day, a guy named John Dalziel was at a sporting event and was noticing all the empty seats around him. He thought to himself, *"Mmm, I bet some of those seat tickets are sitting on someone's desk at work. There should be a way to give away those tickets to kids who wouldn't normally be able to afford them."* So, he talked to some of his connections and started a charity called Kids Up Front (KUF). The premise was simple: if someone has tickets to any kind of event and can't use them or wants to donate, they give them to KUF and they get them to underprivileged kids. KUF distributes tickets through our partner agencies, and the Vancouver office has over 100 of these agencies, and growing. These partner agencies are other charities like Big Brothers, the Autism Society and sick children charities, like BC Children's Hospital. The partner agency pays a nominal amount yearly to be on the list, and when KUF gets tickets to any sports game, concert, ballet, community events, etc, they send out a notice to each partner, so each can request the number they can use. For example, there is a large construction company that sponsors 300 season tickets to the B.C. Lions football franchise and gives them all to KUF. We send out notices before each event and divide the tickets up as requested. The charity is now Canada-wide and is expanding into other countries. As of 2018, they have given out over two million tickets, worth over $65,000,000.

I went for a psychic reading and asked what I should be doing with my extra time. She said, you need to work more with children. I said, *"Really! I run a school for 300! I would much rather be working with animals!"*

And then it happened! With her advice, I googled local children's charities and came across a friend of a friend. I called her up and asked if she needed any help. She suggested I join the KUF Board of Directors, and set up an interview with them. I recall asking all the questions, and shortly after, I joined the board and was excited to meet some really interesting people. One of the many people I met was the founder, John Dalziel. Along with his wife Vicki, I am now honored to call them both close friends.

As with every small charity, KUF has its ups and downs. Vancouver alone, has over 250 registered charities and we all compete for financial support, so it's tough finding good board members and executive directors, especially as volunteer roles. It is always a challenge raising funds to cover staff and office costs, but we continue to do great work for underprivileged kids. Every event KUF had, our school's staff and students volunteered and did amazing work.

A couple of KUF biggest supporters are Bob Lenarduzzi and Carl Valentine, from the MLS Vancouver Whitecaps soccer organization. As well as running their organization, they are constantly attending countless community events. Every time I have asked them to attend a KUF event, they always show. I know how much time they are away from their families, and it constantly amazes me how much of their free time they give to help others.

Marco Iannuzzi was a Canadian Football League (CFL) wide receiver for the BC Lions who we met through charity circles. We have had the pleasure of meeting and becoming friends with his family. Even though we have met many sports people from all over the world, the one thing that stands out is how dedicated and hardworking Marco is. He earned two degrees at the same time as playing professional football while still helping raise a family of three great young children. Marco also runs his own investment advisory company, and if that isn't enough, you will always find him volunteering at charities all over the country. He retired from football in 2017. I can't imagine how much work professional athletes and their spouses, must have to do when they get traded and have to move cities. You think you don't have the time to commit to charity work, think of how busy someone like Marco is.

Simple Fundraising

We often assist or host charity events with the usual silent and live auction items. I can't tell you how many of my friends I have hit up for donation items over the years. One of my favorite nights was when I rented a small art gallery in Gastown, a trendy area of Vancouver. Everyone was asked to bring two bottles of wine (no homemade), which were then split into two cellars. Each person's name was entered in the draw to win the first cellar. The second, we auctioned off to raise thousands. It was a quick, easy way to raise some good money, even with a small group of participants.

Giving back can be as simple as writing a cheque, entering in a race, holding a fundraiser, spending time playing with a child, or working hours by joining a charity. A word of advice: if you want to join a board, you need to commit to attending regular monthly meetings. The cause of the charity must be close to your heart, so you can remain passionate and dedicated. Most of all, make it fun.

Whatever way you creatively can, get your staff, friends, family and co-workers involved, you can have a huge impact in people's lives. If you only have a couple of hours free every week, this can be life changing. It was for me!

A hurricane blew across the Caribbean. It didn't take long for the expensive yacht to be swamped by high waves, sinking without a trace. There were only two survivors: the boat's owner Dr. Eskin and its steward Benny. Both managed to swim to the closest island. After reaching the deserted strip of land, the steward was crying and very upset that they would never be found. The other man was quite calm, relaxing against a tree.

"Dr. Eskin, how can you be so calm?" cried Benny. "We're going to die on this lonely island. We'll never be discovered here."

"Sit down and listen to what I have to say, Benny," began the confident Dr. Eskin. "Five years ago I gave the United Way $500,000 and another $500,000 to the United Jewish Appeal. I donated the same amounts four years ago. And, three years ago, since I did very well in the stock market, I contributed $750,000 to each. Last year business was good again, so the two charities each got a million dollars."

"So what?" shouted Benny.

"Well!" smiled Dr. Eskin, "It's time for their annual fund drives. They'll find me."

—Anonymous

Wasn't That
a Party?

HOSTING A PARTY

"At every party there are two kinds of people – those who want to go home and those who don't. The trouble is, they are usually married to each other."

—Ann Landers

Ever since I was little, I've loved to cook. The difference between my husband and I is that Ralph is a trained chef, part of his hotel management training, and I am more of a short order cook. He makes every plate look like a masterpiece, making sure each dish looks amazing with final touches. The way I host is to make good comfort food and to not spend the whole time in the kitchen during the party. My motto is *"If God had intended us to follow recipes, he wouldn't have given us grandmothers."*

My parties are not about the perfect dish, they are about the fun, the conversations, the celebrations, the table settings and, of course, the drinks. There are purists, of course, who love making their own cheese (like you Jack) or choose a recipe with ingredients no one has ever heard of (like you Kimmy), but that is not how I roll.

Parents out there, please have your kids in the kitchen as much as you can. I have met so many adults that were raised with their parents or maids doing all the cooking, and they have no idea how to cook anything to take care of themselves.

Ralph says I show love through food. When I go grocery shopping, 80% is for him or someone else that I am thinking of. Anytime someone has a new baby, when there is a death in the family, or someone is moving into a new house, the first thing I do is bring them food.

B.U.R.P. Food and Wine Competition

By far, the ultimate event that we host every year, is our legendary cooking competition named B.U.R.P. (Bacchus's Union of Recipe and Presentation). In honor of Bacchus, the god of wine, the challenge is to discover the perfect food and wine combination using a specific chosen theme.

Every year we invite five couples who are given months of notice to get their creative juices going and plan. On the night of the event, each couple must be prepped and ready to go at their starting time. We pop the champagne and they each draw from a hat the order in which they will be presenting. In turn, each team has exactly thirty minutes to finish cooking, plating and presenting a dish of three bites for twelve people, including themselves. Their wine and food is presented using the theme of the night in whatever manner they choose. Costumes, music, props and such are encouraged as part of their presentation to highlight their story.

As hosts, we don't have time to participate in the cooking event, as it's a full-time job with greetings, introductions, serving drinks, organizing the party games while assisting chefs between courses, and helping clear the kitchen after each presentation. It's our job to keep the evening running seamlessly, ironing over any hiccups by our contestants. As each pair completes and clears their plates, the others score their ballots, (based on a taste, wine pairing and presentation score system). Then the next couple begin their thirty minutes. During the breaks, I have different theme-based games and puzzles, along with great prizes for the winners. Every game, guests choose a different partner.

The contest has become incredibly competitive amongst our "foody" friends. Not just because the grand prizes or the trophy they get to keep, but the bragging rights they have for a year, until they return to defend their title against a new group of frenemies. Some of the themes over the years include: "Grandma's Favorite Recipe", "Aphrodisiacs", "Junk Food", "Fire and Ice", "Food Truck Food", "Brunch for Dinner" and the "Iron Olympics".

The presentations are my favorite part. One winning team (Melanie and Bill) brought a keyboard and sang their engagement song. Another team (Andrea and Boyan) brought in dry ice to create a volcanic culinary landscape. We have had guests prepare music, PowerPoint presentations, food truck props, extravagant video shows, and give-away recipe cards. Many had costumes, even naked service but for an apron, but all were fun and creative. Our guests laugh at Ralph and me because they are doing all the cooking, but they have no idea how much work it takes to plan the event.

Here is what you need, if interested:

A pre-determined theme, and 5 pairs of adventurous guests
Table and chairs for 12
Name tags and table place-cards for all guests (separate partners as this encourages guests to get to know each other)
Five sets of 12 plates and/or bowls
As many as 60 forks, knives and or spoons (teams should let you know what serving dish they will need ahead of time)
12 champagne glasses for the opening toast, and champagne is a must
Two sets of wine glasses per person on the table for red and white wines
Lots of napkins
Music props, Bluetooth, Wi-Fi etc
Bowl, to dispense leftover wine
Jug of water, to rinse out wine glasses
Draw to determine order of service

5 marked envelopes with 10 ballots each (*presenting teams do not vote for themselves*)
1 to 5 points given for food taste, 1 to 5 points for wine pairing, and 1 to 5 points for presentation. A perfect score would be 150 points with 10 people voting. (No half points)
If you are bad at math (or tipsy) use a calculator. Just check to make sure you are counting 10 ballots per envelope, if you are missing one, just average a score)

Four quizzes *(themed) and games such as: wine quizzes or blind tasting, action games such as mini golf, guess the style of wine, Pictionary, charades etc.*
No need for a game while the first team is getting ready (guests are still bonding).

Eight prizes *(small clear wrapped, so guests can choose) for quizzes and games such as: gift cards, baskets of food, boxes of chocolates, candles, toiletries etc.*
When the winners choose a prize, write their name on it, to avoid confusion at the end of the night.

One big grand prize *such as: a weekend away, flight tickets, hotel certificate, concert tickets etc.*

A trophy *with an engraved plate stating the name of the contest, the words "Winners" and the year*
Cash for taxis or limousine to get the guests home safely

From our experience, many teams over think their recipes. My advice for contestants is to simplify your prep and spend time on the presentation aspect. Most of all, be personal, creative, and have fun with it!

The Great 50/50 Event

With all the parties that I arranged over many years, I learned the lessons I needed to throw this "Party of a Lifetime." There is no way it would have turned out as memorable if I hadn't the experience to stay in budget.

Ralph's big 50th birthday was coming up, so I decided to make it a major event. We selected and decided to fly in his closest twenty friends and siblings from all over the world to Vancouver for a huge birthday bash. It wasn't just to celebrate my husband's birthday, but all of his mates' 50ths as well, as many were turning 50 the same year. We lived in West Vancouver at the time, and we had been taking care of the elderly lady next door whose husband died a few years before. She had just moved to a senior home when she heard about our event, and offered us her six-bedroom home during the two weeks our guests would be here.

I planned for months on hundreds of details before they arrived. We had to decide on menus, organize transportation and coordinate events with other local guests. There was a different event arranged each day: golfing, hiking, business seminars, massages, zip trekking, international cooking contest, wine tasting, sailing, comedy shows and psychic readings.

We rented some modern "manly" furniture for the house and put up a huge sign welcoming all to the "The Clubhouse." I set up all bathrooms with dozens of towels and stocked them with fresh toiletries. Each guest had a Canadian welcome basket ready on arrival in their shared bedroom. I obtained everything in the baskets at half-price at a store close-out sale months before. There was new bedding for all the beds, and we restocked the fridge and the bar daily.

It was the hardest I had worked in years, making sure "The Clubhouse" was cleaned every day and, as you can imagine having all of them partying, they made quite a mess. I prepared a buffet breakfast for the twenty plus every morning and a spectacular sit-down dinner most nights. I washed and replaced loads of towels daily. We had snacks, booze, games, prizes, and photo shoots capturing the whole thing. After dinner every night, we had a birthday cake celebrating one of our guests' 50th birthdays. I was shopping at Costco every day and prepared all the meals, so that was a huge budget saver.

The Grand Finale was a dinner and dancing extravaganza for 100 people with a live band at a booked out North Vancouver restaurant. I negotiated to bring in my own alcohol instead of buying the higher-priced restaurant booze, as well as some extra food, so this kept the price way down. Volunteers from my school joined me and we spent the day decorating the restaurant in the theme of Austin Powers. All guests were to dress up as their "Alter Ego" from monks to devils and everything in between.

I was dressed as a police officer, naturally and had a martini in my hand, directing guests who were parking around the restaurant. My husband was Lawrence of Arabia. (Don't ask… as he can barely handle one wife!) I had given a song sheet for all the guys to practice in between their events, and their performance of *My Way* was indeed stellar. I covered the restaurant walls with photos of the all the events of the past two weeks. And what happens? The real police show up…as I always say, it is not a good party unless the cops pop by. (They also showed up for his big 40th birthday surprise party!)

To see the joy on their faces faces every one of those days was worth the many, many hours of planning.

Wedding Tips on a Budget:

These lessons I learned the hard way. One year, I hosted three weddings in eight weeks at my home.

The first wedding couple didn't have a lot of money to spend, so I offered to do the food as well as host. It was way too much work. Don't do both! It is challenging enough getting the house ready. They had around 90 guests and the budget for food was $2000. I did all the shopping, decorating, cooking and was also the witness at the ceremony. The wedding day was cold, so all the guests stayed inside. Our house had an open-plan concept, but most people hung out around the kitchen area. The second I took something out of the fridge or oven, the guests in the kitchen area pounced on the trays. I literally had to rope off a section or I couldn't get the food out to the other guests. Most of the food I served were ready-made appetizers. I garnished them with fresh ingredients before serving and they looked homemade.

*The first lesson about weddings is to **not tell your** suppliers you are having a wedding.*

Just say "event or party." As soon as you use the word "wedding" the price goes up. For example, I had been using the same makeup lady for many years for all my events. The second I said that I was in the wedding party, the price almost doubled.

If You Are Hosting, Let Someone Else Cater

For the next wedding I was hosting, I didn't do the food. The groom for this wedding worked in a restaurant and he had chefs come to my place. They probably came up to me twenty times asking if I had a bowl, or a spice or something else. I ended up staying near the kitchen the whole time again.

What they really hadn't planned on was my stove having a glass top. The restaurant world, of course, uses gas. So, the frying pans they brought where all cast iron. After the last guest left, I was cleaning up in the kitchen and discovered my previously pristine stove was totally scratched. The cost of the new one was $500!

If you are preparing for a large crowd, talk to your local food trucks. You would be amazed how inexpensive they are and how they do all the catering for you.

Always Have a Back-up Plan

Just in case the caterer doesn't show up or there are traffic issues, at least have the number ready for your favorite restaurant that delivers. Make sure you have the cell phone number of the people delivering to your event. Once, we waited for over an hour because the driver got lost and couldn't call.

Do Your Own Table Arrangements

I buy cases of vases for a bargain and order flowers from a wholesaler like Costco, but make sure they have a couple of weeks to have exactly what you want. If you don't have vases, the dollar stores are a good place to start, and they don't always have to match. We have a friend who recently sold the Costco flower business they operated since Costco opened in Canada. When she explained that flowers for weddings were a large part of their market, I offered my cousin floral arrangements for all the tables as her wedding gift. She was getting quotes of $75 and more, per table! Everyone thought my arrangements looked amazing and my total cost for all twenty tables was under $200.

I have also had great deals from the florists when shopping for an event that is the same day. One time I got a car load of flowers for almost nothing from a store on Sunday because Mondays they get their new deliveries and they would have thrown them out. When flowers don't need to last long, florists are usually happy to give a good deal.

Non-traditional Wedding Cake

The most reasonable deal on wedding cakes are on non-tiered ones. But if you must have a tiered one, you can rent a fake cake for your wedding pictures, but have the kitchen serve portions using regular cake. You can also ask your bakery to make the top tiered layer of the cake real and then have fake ones for the other tiers, as it is much cheaper. Or skip the cake cutting part of the ceremony and serve a selection of desserts, a macaron display, a wall of donuts or a lavish candy buffet.

Home Weddings

There's no need for physical wedding invitations. Most are online these days.

Please have your makeup done by someone professional or a friend who is really good at it. Sephora or Mac do a top job. Staff there all do their own makeup, so look at their faces before you make your appointment and request the person whose makeup you like the look of most. Again, don't tell them it is for your wedding, but make sure you request makeup for photographs. It is a different style of application. Use hair pieces instead of spending hours at a salon. For one wedding, I brought the bride breakfast at her hairdresser's salon. She was there for four hours having her hair washed, dried, set and pinned up. A hair piece would look almost exactly the same and it would have taken thirty minutes, tops.

For condos or apartments, have someone positioned at the front door in the lobby to greet guests and buzz them up. Borrow or rent a rolling clothes rack from a retail store and have hangers for guest coats at the entrance of your suite. Ask your neighbors if you can use their parking spots and let them know about the event. If you have someone reliable, have them be a valet, so more cars can be squeezed in. If you want a limousine, you can book them for pick-up and drop off times, instead of paying for them to sit and wait all day. It's much cheaper.

Try and get your friends to do something for the wedding instead of a gift. You could also put some suggestions on your registry. Please don't put anything ridiculously expensive on your registry list, even as a joke. It may come across that you actually expect someone to get that for you.

Arrange someone to put the wedding gifts and envelopes away somewhere safe. Put them in the trunk of a car, in an out-of-the-way cupboard, or in a locked room. I was at a wedding where a stranger joined the party and stole some cash envelopes. Attach cards or names to gifts in case they get separated.

Professional photographers are dependable, but expensive. So, to save costs, ask them to do just an hour shoot at the ceremony instead of the entire reception. Get a reliable friend or friends to shoot the rest.

If children will be attending, have a room with activities or games where they can go play. Hire a babysitter to entertain them. Make sure you have snacks in their room.

The music can be done with your Bluetooth now, so you don't really need to have a DJ or band. Just make sure you have checked the playlist and have a backup list with a friend ready to go. If you want to hire a band, contact them directly. They are usually listed on many other "agent" sites, but you can negotiate a better rate if you contact them directly. Talent usually requires a "Green Room" or somewhere they can go to get ready and take their breaks. They expect food and drinks as well as a tip in cash. All this needs to be negotiated before you hire them. Make sure you have clearly discussed the set-up needs and timing, the tempo and the kind of songs you expect, how much electric power they will need, and the finish time.

One time I had a pizza and a dozen bottles of beer ready for the four-piece band, but they asked for more. I was in the middle of a big party so of course I gave them more but got angry later when I saw how much they had consumed. And the worst part was, the female singer wore high heels that had no padding so I had over 100 heel indents in my hardwood floor. I asked to see the bottom on the singer's high heels with the next band I hired.

If you are having a garden wedding, provide bug spray and umbrellas. If you are using the lawn, tell the ladies beforehand so they don't wear high heels.

And finally, I know you think you are so busy before the wedding, but have your addressed envelopes ready for the thank-you cards for when you get back from your honeymoon. At the latest, it should happen a month after the wedding. Whoever said that in this day and age you can send thank you cards up to six months later is very mistaken!

If you are asked to host an event at your place, make sure you discuss all these details with them as well as costs before you agree to it.

Checklist:
> How many, who's paying and who is coordinating it?
> Are all the guests known to them or will there be strangers attending?
> Parking details (neighbors)?
> Do you need a coat rack and hangers?
> Where do people put their bags and purses?
> Check to make sure the caterer is someone responsible if they are using your kitchen.
> Are extension cords or other catering equipment needed?

If they are renting equipment, who is delivering, setting up and collecting?

When are deliveries expected? You can be spending a lot of time waiting for deliveries and pickups.

Do you need a liquor license or servers for this event?

What things should you move out of the way, or remove to avoid damage?

Discuss what happens if there is damage or something goes missing?

What is the backup plan if the weather is bad?

Are children or pets attending and who will watch them?

Who is cleaning up during and after the event?

Will there be live music? What equipment is needed? What volume is acceptable?

What will be the agreed-upon finishing time?

Tips for Parties of 12 to 300:

These tips for throwing a party are simple and easy. They come from over thirty years of trial and error. Many of these you may know, but I am often surprised that some people don't know the basics. Guests have complimented me how they love my big parties, because I make everyone feel comfortable and think of everything. Remember, it's all about the celebration, entertaining and having fun, and not how much time you spend in the kitchen, or away from the party.

Sit-Down Meals

Table Settings

My priority for parties is the table setting. My tables always have a different look, I think it is my artistic side that gives me pleasure to do that. Often, I will start setting the table a week ahead of time just to help inspire a new table masterpiece. Of course, you don't have to set your table that far ahead, but please set it before your guests arrive. I can't tell you how often we would go to friends for dinner and they haven't started setting the table yet. Did they think we weren't going to show up?

My tablecloths are almost always just a unique piece of fabric. Look in the clearance section at any fabric store, about 4 ½ yards for a 12-person table. I don't usually use place cards, but if I am inviting a group of people who don't know each other, I may. Place a charger (bigger than the dinner plate) first. If you are serving on a table without a tablecloth, then use a placemat, then the charger, then the dinner plate. The forks go on the left and the knives – sharp-end facing inwards - go on the right of the setting. If your first course is a soup then add your large spoon on the right of the knife. If your starter needs a fork and knife, then place them about an inch higher outside the first fork and knife.

Napkins

I use a napkin ring around a wrinkle-free cloth napkin but you can just lay the napkin neatly folded on the plate. Only use a paper napkin if it is a causal lunch or brunch, but not for a sit-down dinner. Sourcing crisp white napkins will never be a challenge for me because I bought a car load from a guy who was closing down his shop. I have thousands. So, every party I use new ones, then wash and give away to charity. So, if you see a deal somewhere, buy them in bulk; it saves a lot of time on ironing.

Wine Glasses

If you are changing the type of wine for each course, then place two wine glasses on the top right side of the settings. A smaller water glass is placed on the top left of the wine glasses. Get these ready ahead of time, so you can check for spots on glasses.

Flowers & Candles

These should be low enough to see across the table. Candles are great, but use new ones or electric ones. Do not use scented candles on the dining table, as they could compete with the flavors of the food. Save the scented candles and light them in the guest washroom. Make sure the guest washroom has a full roll of toilet paper and fresh, clean towels. I also have vases close by in case my guests bring flowers as a hostess gift.

Name Tags

One of the things my friends tell me they like about my parties is that I have name tags for all my guests, if guests don't know each other. Some people might find this weird, but a lot of people suck at remembering people's names. This way, no one has to ask your name a second time. I will often write a tag line under the name that might say their spouse's name, job title, what country they are from, etc, as conversation starters.

Signs

Because most guests don't want to ask where the washroom is, I always put an obvious sign pointing to them. We have the fancy toilets that open, close and flush automatically but I show clear instructions as some guests aren't familiar with them. I also put signs in my kitchen for the garbage and recycling bins, for those offering to help.

Have Glasses & Drinks Ready

I like to have glasses, cocktails, beer, wine and soft drinks ready on the counter as soon as my guests come in. I find people are less hesitant to meet and mingle with the other guests when they have a drink in their hand. If you're using matching wine glasses and have more than six people, you may want to use wineglass rings so guests know which one is theirs if they put it down. You can also get special pens to write guests names on the glasses that wash off in the dishwasher.

You don't have to be a wine expert to have the wines ready. My suggestions that would please the majority of a guests, would be a white wine such as Pinot Gris or Chardonnay. For reds, I suggest Pinot Noir or a Cabernet Sauvignon. Chill the white wines very well, the reds should be room temperature. If the red wine has a cork, you should open it earlier to decant it, or to let it breathe. I find screw tops are more convenient at parties and not a reflection of quality.

A nice summer cocktail to offer, could be an aperitif served with a cherry or lemon twist over lots of ice. In the winter, I like to serve a Caesar. Most countries around the world know that a Bloody Mary is made from tomato juice and vodka, but may be unfamiliar with a Caesar drink mix which is made with clam juice. Don't worry, it doesn't taste fishy at all.

Mott's Clamato juice had a country wide contest to come up with a new recipe for their Caesar cocktails. A very good friend of ours, Boyan, entered and won a year's supply of Mott's Caesar mix for his winning combination. His recipe uses a unique tequila instead of the traditional vodka and is served with Ukrainian garlic pickle. When Ralph had his big 50th birthday party, Boyan made it for all the guys from around the world and most loved it.

For a brunch, I would suggest freshly blended fruit smoothies, or mimosas composed of one part moderately priced champagne (or a 'brut' sparkling wine, so the drink isn't too sweet) and one part chilled orange juice. Pour the champagne in the glass first and wait for the bubbles to subside, then add the juice. Mango or papaya works great too. If you have non-drinkers, it is nice to have sparkling water or flavored water to serve in their wine glasses.

Appetizers

Always ask your guests ahead of time for any food allergies or restrictions. If you are planning to serve the meal much later than the start of your party, then you may need to serve appetizers when the guests start to arrive. Finger food that can be eaten using just a paper napkin or a small plate.

Preheat your Oven or Barbeque

You should have the oven at the correct preheated temperature before the first course is served. If you are serving a fish for the main, you could put the fish in the oven or on the barbeque as everyone is sitting down for their first course. The carbs (potatoes, rice, or pasta) and the veggies should be already cooked and may only need a couple of minutes to finish them off or reheat.

Soup

If you are starting with soup, you can use store-bought soup, and just add fresh herbs or chives and a dollop of sour cream on top. Make sure the bowls have been warmed in the oven to keep the soup hot. If serving chilled summer soups, have the bowls in the fridge.

Salad

If you are serving meat as the main, then a light salad is best. If you are serving seafood as the main, you can make the salad richer by adding cooked and cooled beets, shrimp, feta and olives, etc.

Bread

I usually serve bread in a basket on the table so guests can help themselves. If you have room on your table to place a small plate for the bread, then place on the left side by the forks. Garlic bread is always a hit. If you use other breads that do not already have butter or oil, then you need to have butter or oil and balsamic in small dishes around the table. Make sure the butter is at room temperature by putting it on the table an hour before.

Serving

Serve the first course on top of the pre-set dinner plate before you call your guests to the table. It is easier than serving over everyone. Hot starters like soup, may get cold before everyone sits, so prepare guests in advance.

Toasting

Guests will sometimes be bringing a glass to the table. If they are switching from red to white or vice versa, always serve it in a new glass. A toast should be made before anyone starts to eat to welcome your guests. If you have a large table, you don't need to clink all your guests, just raise your glass towards them with warm eye contact. Recognize any special occasion or simply express gratitude.

Clearing Courses

Only stand up to clear the plates when everyone is completely finished their dish. (Right Sally?) Then remove by lifting from the larger dinner plate underneath the appetizer. This more likely prevents dropping cutlery or getting your fingers in bowls. Set aside the dinner plates, but consider putting used dishes and cutlery straight into the dishwasher to save on kitchen clean up later.

Timing: The main course should be served about 30 minutes after you sit down for the first course.

Plating

Again, you should heat up the plates first if serving hot food. Make sure you have enough counter space to set all the plates out. Generally, the carb should be plated first, then the protein, then the veggies. Tidy up any drippings, while adding fresh herbs, sauce or garnish. If you have an optional sauce, then put the sauce on the table and guests can either help themselves, or you can go around and pour sauce for them.

I like to ask about the hunger level of my friends, so I can give more to those who prefer more. I don't do this with people I don't know as well, as they may feel uncomfortable. Serve women and senior guests first, from their left, so you are not interfering with their wine glasses.

Of course you always have the option of bringing food to the table for everyone to serve themselves.

If you are planning on serving a hot dessert like a pie or cake, make it ahead of time, or place it in the oven after you take the main dishes out. Shut the oven off and let it slowly reheat.

After everyone is completely finished their main course, then clear all the plates and utensils. Depending on the number of your guests and the space of your home, you can decide where to serve dessert. Timing: The dessert should be served about an hour after the main course was served.

Desserts

I like to serve dessert, liqueurs or port and coffee (usually decaf) on the patio or in the living room so people can get up and stretch. I could easily make dessert, but my friends have so many dietary restrictions, I find having platters of small assorted sweets work great. Have your dessert platter arranged (chilled or heated) so you can just pull it out and serve. If you decide to serve a cake or pie, add your special touch to the plate, like a swirl of fruit purée under a piece of cheesecake, or drizzle chocolate over it. Add fresh mint or fresh fruit to the plate. Find out who is having their birthday next and put a sparkler in their dessert (even if it is weeks away) and sing happy birthday to them.

Buffets

The Menu

Write down your menu ahead of time. Don't do things from scratch if others have perfected it, ie. pastry, bread, sauces, and desserts. Have everything on your list bought by the day before the event.

When catering for those with different food restrictions, always have some dishes without gluten (even salad dressing can contain some gluten so put it on the side), dairy, eggs, meat or shellfish, and best to avoid peanuts so check ingredients. My calculation is one dish for every two people attending. With ten people I would make five dishes, twenty people, ten dishes, etc. That includes sweets.

Preparation

Set up your buffet-table days before, if you can. I like to put different levels on a buffet. You can put a box or bowl under the tablecloth or use a three-tier plate if you have them. Put the bowls and dishes out with a note to remind you what food goes where, and include the serving utensils. Remember to include the small bowls and dishes used for dips and sauces.

Add decorative touches to the table such as flower petals, fall leaves, rocks, small flower arrangements in short vases to ensure they won't tip over when someone is reaching across the buffet.

Plates and napkins should be set out on two sides of the table, if you are able to walk around it. I have separate plates that are very light weight for buffets. If you are using paper plates, get the strong ones and make sure the food can be eaten with one hand, then you can use paper napkins. If something requires a knife, then you should be using a real plate and silverware. I find it easier to have meat that is cut up, pulled or shredded. Skewers or shish kebabs are also good choices.

Prep the night before by having all your pots, pans and bowls on the counter ready to go. You can cut up veggies that you are going to roast the day before. I often do pans of fried onions the day before (and anything time consuming), wrapped and sealed well.

If you are serving wine, prepare for at least two glasses for everyone on a separate table. Check to make sure the glasses are clean and ready the day before. A large container for ice is the easiest way to cool all beverages. Wine, beer, soda and juices, as well and a chilled pitcher of water should be available, with slices of lemon, oranges or cucumber in it, and ideally a sparkling water option.

Day of the Event

As soon as you are ready to start your prep, preheat the oven or barbeque. The dishes that take the longest to prepare should be started first. Get the pots of water heated up. One item that has changed my life is an electric three-pot warmer, as it can be used to finish cooking dishes. Have your coffee cups and coffee/tea maker filled and ready to go for those who want that option.

Time Saving Creative Hints

An easy way to make you look like the perfect host is to buy pre-made items and add your touch to it. An example is lasagne. It is much cheaper (and easier) to buy one than to get all the ingredients in one. Just add your touches on top, like fresh spinach, herbs, mushrooms, sliced tomatoes and more cheese (no one will know you didn't do it from scratch).

Pre-made, packaged salads are a game changer. All I do is add a few extra items and the salad is made in minutes.

Whole Foods can be very expensive, but the one thing that is a steal is the cooked bacon on their breakfast buffet. As they charge by weight, I get the bacon that is crisp. The most I ever paid was about $12 for the equivalent of four packets of bacon. Pretty much every staff breakfast or brunch party I host, I include their bacon. We are vegetarians, so cooking meat is not my favorite thing to do. Cooked bacon freezes and defrosts really well.

A Brunch Buffet to Please Everyone

I always have a freshly made fruit salad with berries and also like a colorful green salad on the buffet. Include at least one bakery basket item for person, preferably freshly baked croissants, with some nice jam on a side dish, or pancakes or waffles. Put all condiments in small dishes with a small spoon. There is nothing tackier that a bottle of ketchup on a buffet table.

One meat dish, a carbohydrate dish of rice or hash browns (with mushrooms and onions).

Seafood: either sushi (ordered in fresh), shrimp or cooked fish and finally a roasted or barbequed veggies platter.

Quiche is an easy way to make you look like a great cook and avoid the whole egg thing. I only use the pre-made pie crusts, and I usually don't prebake (blind bake) the crusts as I find they are better straight from the freezer. Preheat the oven to 375°F. (Why make your own when someone else had perfected it?) For your ingredients, there's no need to use a recipe. Just look in your fridge and freezer and see what you have.

If you are using frozen ingredients like spinach, defrost it in the microwave, make sure it is drained well, and then pat dry with a paper towel so crusts remain crisp. Start a frying pan with onion and butter or oil. Add to the pan all chopped items, like mushrooms, asparagus, pre-cooked potatoes or sweet potatoes, broccoli, fresh spinach, cooked meats, etc.

Then whip six eggs, salt and pepper. Sometimes I use a heaping tablespoon of canned cream soup (mushroom or broccoli also works well). Season lightly, as the cheese you will be adding will make it salty enough. Put the veggies and ham or bacon in first, then add any kind of cheese, then the egg mixture on top.

I like to put the pie pan on a bigger spill tray in case of overflow. Cook for 20 minutes, then turn the temperature down to 350°F for another 20 minutes. Check by tapping the top of the quiche. If the top of the quiche still moves, return to the oven for ten minutes. Take the quiche out to rest at least 15 minutes before serving. You seriously cannot go wrong with this. If you want a gluten free quiche, use cauliflower snow (pulverized into tiny pieces), add butter and Parmesan cheese to make the crust. Cook at 375°F till crispy. Then add veggies and meat, top it with cheese and the egg mixture. Cook for 20 minutes and then reduce to 350°F for another ten minutes, or until done.

Prepare a packet Hollandaise or Béarnaise sauce with the quiche, and put condiments in small dishes with a spoon.

Always Confirm Portions When Catering

I spoil my guests with the amount of food and drinks I serve at my parties. So when I hired a caterer one time, I gave them a big budget. When I offered to help them unload, I was curious when they said the two of them could easily manage. They brought in a six small trays of delicate, tiny morsels. I thought *"Hmmm, this can't be all the food they were serving for 50 people"*. Luckily, I always stock extra frozen appetizers. I ran through both freezers and all my cupboards for anything I could serve as my guests were starting to arrive. The funny thing was that a lot of my catered food was still left over at the end of the night, while my store-bought appetizers were all gone.

Catering for Hundreds of Hotdogs & Hamburgers

Before you decide to do this yourself, consider getting someone else to, as this can be messy, time-consuming and in the end, it may not save you money. Ideally, if you can strike a great deal with McDonalds or a local food truck, then have someone else cook, even serve, so you can focus on the kids, fundraising or having fun with your friends at the event. Compare costs.

Shopping for Hundreds:

For those big family BBQs or fundraiser events: Your big box grocery stores stock the least expensive hamburgers and hotdogs. Just make sure the hotdogs are precooked and don't have casings on them that need to be removed. (I spent an hour doing that one time!) Chicken dogs are usually cheaper and a good idea if you have guests who may not eat pork. Chicken burgers can be cheaper or more expensive than beef, so watch for deals. Also, buy veggie versions of both (Beyond Meat is our fav), but please don't cook them in the same pans as the meat ones.

If I am buying a large amount, I ask for a good price directly to the store's section manager, I usually get it, especially if I mention it's for a fundraiser or charity. Supermarkets have budgets for these types of community drives. If you know the exact number of guests, buy 10% more burgers and hotdogs, but if you are having a family and friends gathering, you should plan on 1.5 hot dogs and burgers per person.

For hamburgers, you can buy fewer buns than the amount of patties, as people double-up. I like to have sliced tomatoes and sliced cheese ready (one per burger), but don't buy the processed cheese with the plastic casings around each slice. (That also took me an hour to remove one time!)

You can make fried onions the day before if you want, or just serve them raw. They should be diced for hotdogs and sliced for burgers. Hint: add a little sugar to fried onions to make them a little sweeter.

If you are serving coleslaw or potato salad, get it from a big box store and make sure it stays refrigerated before you serve. Remember that you would need forks for this scenario. If you are not serving a salad, then I would serve them with a bag of potato chips. I stock up after Halloween for the best prices on the small bags. Remember napkins, plates, drinks and forks for serving cheese, onions and tomatoes. You'll also need many large garbage bags.

Condiments: You can usually purchase mustard and ketchup in bulk, but relish is harder to find. I have seen them at the dollar store, but it's a pain because they are small packages, so buy extra when you see them in big containers to store some for next time. Quantity is not an exact science. If you have mostly kids at your event, they will use more ketchup and less of everything else. Try to always buy squeeze or pump bottles, or you will need to be using a spoon which is a mess.

Ketchup, large bottle should serve 30
Mustard, medium squeeze mustard: 20
Relish, medium squeeze: 20
Mayonnaise, medium squeeze: 20
Sliced Onions: 1 large: 10
Cheese slices: 1/1

Cooking Hundreds of Hotdogs

Preheat the oven to 300°F. Fill large pots 4/5 water on top of the stove and turn to high. As soon as the water is bubbling, add the hotdogs to the top of the water. Cook for about 15 minutes, then transfer to a disposable tinfoil tray that has a couple inches of water at the bottom, cover with tinfoil and put in the oven on.

Take them out when you are ready to serve or if you are transporting, layering the trays in a big box and covering with a towel. Leave the water in the trays to stop them from getting dried out. If you are barbequing, you need to start pre-cooking at least an hour before guests are coming. Keep them warm with foil dishes with some water. You can always put them back for a quick warm up.

Cooking Hundreds of Burgers

Preheat your oven to 400°F. Spray your frying pans with non-stick spray and have them on high heat ready on top of the stove. Place the burgers side by side in the pans. Do not overlap. Then start cooking other hamburgers lying flat in trays in the oven. They will cook faster in the frying pans, but precooking them in the oven this way helps. If they are frozen, I put plates in the microwave to unthaw them. Cook them to medium well and then transfer to big tinfoil dishes. I like to put some of the grease on top so they don't dry out. If you work hard, you can do 150 in an hour, (right Suzy!).

Final Checking and Preparation

Open the sealed part of the condiment containers before your event. Make sure your buns are already sliced when purchased. If you are having your event in a park, get a large roll of fabric from a clearance fabric store and roll it out on the picnic tables or on the ground (but watch for bugs). One five-meter or six yards line for every 50 people should be enough.

Speed things along by having the plates ready with a bun on it, then have people serving condiments, and others putting the meat on at the end of the line. Another person could be handing out drinks. I like the juice boxes, because if you drop them, they don't spill.

Funny Costco Story

President Bill Clinton was in Vancouver to give a speech to a small group of people who paid a lot of money for the opportunity to have dinner with him. I had bought two tickets and I asked around to my friends and family to see who wanted to meet him as much as I did. My brother was the most excited, so I took him. We were all warned ahead of time that we must bring picture ID before we would be allowed in. At the last minute, I changed evening purses, and left my driver's license in the other one. I only remembered that as I was parking at the event. Luckily, I remembered that I had my Costco card in the car. I confidently approached the registration table and explained. And, yes… I got a meeting with a President by showing only my Costco card as ID. I told the manager of Costco my episode and he ended up putting that story in their newsletter.

`A trucker stopped at a local Denny's restaurant and placed his order. He said, "I want three flat tires, a pair of headlights and a pair of running boards."

The waitress didn't want to appear clueless, so she went to the kitchen and asked the cook, "This guy out there just ordered three flat tires, a pair of headlights and a pair of running boards. What does he think this place is... an auto parts store?"

"No," the cook said. "Three flat tires means three pancakes, a pair of headlights is for two eggs sunnyside up, and running boards are two slices of crisp bacon. It's a special trucker version of our `Grand Slam Breakfast.'"

"Oh, Okay." replied the waitress. She thought about it for a moment and then spooned up a bowl of beans and gave it to the customer.

The trucker asked, "What are the beans for?"

She replied, "I thought while you were waiting for the flat tires, headlights and running boards, you might as well gas up!!"'

—*Anonymous*

Lifestyles of the Rich and Famous

NEVER GIVE UPS

'Probably the worst thing you can hear when you're wearing a bikini is "Good for you!"'

—*E. Bayne*

I truly believe that no matter how much (or little) money or time you have, I bet you wouldn't give up the one thing that makes you feel the happiest. I asked some of my friends, and their "Never Give Up" list included coffee, their car, ice-cream, bread, purses, shoes, plastic surgeries, beer, wine, skiing, designer clothes, iPhones and such. Therefore, you may be like me, and are thrifty about many of your purchases, but when it comes to some things, price is no object.

The thing that I would hate to give up is traveling first-class. I will probably shop at Walmart until the end of my time, because paying more than $50 for a pair of jeans would make me crazy. (They all look the same to me anyway.) But I need my first-class travel. I never squirm about the price because this kind of travel gives me a feeling of security. I have stayed at some really horrible hotels and taken some awful flights that made me think I was a prisoner and not a customer. When I stay in the big suites, or fly in first or business-class, I feel special and more protected. I prefer nonstop flights to where I want to go, and I always book row one, sometimes buying the seat that is in the middle of us, if I can't get business class. (It is surprisingly inexpensive for the spare seat.)

After we started making good money in our business, I spoiled us by traveling in the most comfortable way possible. Ralph is happy with basic comforts, (his "never give up" things are his bicycles), but I find great pleasure in booking some of the very best resorts, biggest rooms, and unique locations. Many of our friends say each of our trips is like a trip of a lifetime, but shouldn't all trips be?

Here are some of our travel adventures and a few places you may want to put on your bucket list.

North America

I had booked the biggest room of any cruise ship, the Garden Villa, a 6000 square feet (557 meters) three-bedroom suite on the NCL Pearl to the Caribbean for the two of us. We both love cruising which we do at least once a year. I had heard about this suite and was thrilled to find out it was available on the dates I wanted. The big rooms always sell out first, but they had a last-minute cancellation.

A few days before we left, we received a phone call from CNBC in the US requesting to follow us around the ship all week. I, of course, said sure! The one hour documentary, *Cruise Inc: Big Money on the High Seas* was to be about how cruise ships make their money. They also followed a young honeymooning couple who booked the smallest, cheapest room, and a family of four in the mid-priced room.

From the moment our limo arrived at the port, the cameras were on us. We were swiftly checked-in the VIP line. The rest of the guests in the regular line-up were baffled.

"Who are they?"

"I don't recognize them!"

"No, idea, but take their picture!"

One of the first shoots they did was of us entering our big suite. The host asked, *"How many people are traveling with you in this room?"*

Our replied, *"Only us and our imaginary friends."*

The camera crew followed us to the restaurants, the shows, the nightclub and just hanging out on one of our many private decks. We had an enjoyable time meeting lots of people on board who wanted to know who we were, and why the cameras were on us. We hosted some shipmates for private dinners in our suite, served by our butler. But by the second day, Ralph had had enough of all the cameras.

Months later when we were yet again, out of the country, the show aired on TV. We were on it for a total of two minutes! Not quite the amount I was hoping for, but it still was fun. They are still screening that show around the world on CNBC, CNN, and on the NCL cruise TV channel. The best part of this story was, a few years later, we were flying home out of Istanbul at the end of a big holiday on a very early flight. We woke at 3:00 am to shower and pack. I clicked on the TV's only English channel, and screamed for my husband! Our episode of that show was playing yet again.

We have booked this room twice since because we loved it so much. It sleeps up to eight, so the second time we invited friends. Like most big rooms on ships, it had a grand piano and a large dining room. You are provided a few complementary bottles of alcohol for your bar. They still may charge you extra for specialty restaurant dining, (which I think is tacky) so try to negotiate that in with your rate.

Canada

Quebec

Ralph and I bundled up and went to the Quebec Winter Carnival festival in Quebec City. We had a great time with all the outdoor events and drove up to the north to the ice hotel, Hôtel de Glace, for a very unique experience. We arrived there before the other guests, so reception suggested we check out all the rooms and choose the style we liked. Each was carved out of ice with unique themes and incredible designs. It was so amusing watching the housekeepers walking around with ice picks and fresh snow instead of the usual vacuums and towels. The beds were designed from blocks of ice but insulated with a foam layer and decorative animal pelts, and topped with quality winter sleeping bags.

After we chose our room we went out of the village for a snowmobile adventure. Ralph had never been on one so we had a blast playing in the fields, and later headed onto the dog sled tours. If you are a dog lover, you really need to check it out. There must have been seventy or eighty Huskies there, and because our puppy was a Husky, we had special feelings for these ones. I had a blast giving them treats and cuddles, and they got so excited when their harnesses were on, knowing it was time for a run.

We returned to the hotel exhausted. The other guests had checked in and were enjoying ice glasses of vodka, poured through an ice dragon that ran the length of the bar. The dance floor was carpeted with fresh snow and we danced for hours at the nightclub. Wear warm boots if you go, as we retreated occasionally to the sauna to recoup.

And then we went for the "How to Sleep on Ice" lesson where we were advised to change from our day clothes since body moisture in the fabric would chill and freeze overnight. They also suggested before sleeping to take off our shoes and put them in the bottom of our sleeping bag along with our toiletries. We rezipped our two single sleeping bags to form a double bed. I had stuck a bottle of champagne in the snow beside our bed when we first checked in, so by the time we got back to our room later that night, it had frozen. Our bartender suggested that we put it in the bar fridge to defrost it, and to keep it "warm" enough to drink.

I don't think we got a lot of sleep that night, but we couldn't have cared less. It was such a unique experience living in luxury sub-zero temperatures. Some guests couldn't handle the cold, and moved early to a room in the regular hotel nearby to sleep. Breakfast was also served at the warm hotel and I think everyone was happy to have a hot cup of coffee in the morning.

This ice hotel is on my best resort list, but there are now a few ice hotels around the world, so pick one near you. It will be a night you will always remember. They all have little wedding chapels, intricately carved to stunning effect, so a small wedding would be so incredible. I recommend this as a "must-do" for your bucket list.

FYI, most Canadians have never been to all of the ten provinces or even to the other side of the country. I traveled to over 100 countries before we went to see the east coast provinces. I am sure you know that the people of the province of Quebec speak French, but did you know that New Brunswick also has French as their official language? Our language school had many French speaking Canadians come study English in Vancouver which may surprise you, considering it was on the other side of the continent. Although most Francophones were taught English at school, few were able to practice conversing in English in their communities. We even had one young gal from Quebec who had no idea that the rest of the country barely used

French. When I was growing up in Saskatchewan, my selection of language courses were German, Ukrainian, and Russian. Not many took French.

Today many Canadian parents outside of Quebec will put their kids through intensive French programs, while Mandarin Chinese, Spanish and Japanese classes are also popular, as they have career and business applications.

Toronto

As a birthday surprise, my husband booked Sally and I in the best suite at the Ritz-Carlton during a visit in Toronto. We took the train from Montreal to Toronto, which I highly recommend over driving or flying.

When we arrived at the train station, two gentlemen were there waiting to take us to the hotel. One of them was the General Manger, and at the time I thought, wow, that must be a lot of work to greet every guest this personally. When we arrived, it seemed that all the staff knew my name. We were given a glass of champagne and checked in, and it wasn't until then that I realized we were staying in the Ritz-Carlton Suite. We were escorted up to our room, and when we opened the door we walked into a truly luxurious 11-room suite. The only thing out of place was a rolling cot that they had set up in the main living room. Ralph knows that when I travel with friends, we like to have separate bedrooms. Even though the suite was huge, oddly, it only had one bedroom. I laughed when I saw the cot and asked for it be removed. After a few drinks, we took pictures of Sally posing in all the places she could possibly sleep. Some were of her pretending to sleep on the top of the fridge, on the treadmill in our personal gym, in the huge bathtub, on top of the desk in our office, and on top of the ten-person dining table.

The suite was blanketed with lilies, which I love, with many arrangements courtesy of the hotel, although Ralph also sent bouquets. It wasn't until the second day that Sally confided in me that she was allergic to them, so I gathered them up and put them all in our office. They filled the whole room.

The entire staff must have been told it was my birthday (presumably at a staff meeting) as they all recognized and congratulated me. The first day or so, it was fun. I loved it when the staff would run down the hallway to stop the elevator or just to greet us. They must have Googled me because they knew about my business and charity work and where I was from. (We do the same thing at my business when a VIP visits with my team). The concierge in the Club Lounge almost jumped over her desk the minute we walked in to welcome us. Anything I wanted was quickly brought at no extra charge. But after a couple of days it became overwhelming and I started avoiding the attention. I guess that is how someone famous must feel at times.

We had excellent service and it was a great room, but it's not one I need to go back to. The main reason is that it was the middle of summer and it didn't have a balcony, and I need to get fresh air. Another thing to remember if you stay at expensive places like this, is to make sure you have a sizeable credit card credit limit. If you are not a regular or if you have not reserved, a pre-charge may be taken on arrival.

We were brought back to reality lining up for the CN Tower in Toronto. That was a big mistake. After we bought tickets, we discovered it was an hour's wait to get up the elevator. It wasn't until we came down that we found that for a few dollars more we could have bought a VIP ticket that bypasses the line. So, if you ever go up one of those lookout towers in any city, ask the waiting time or if they have an express line. Ask also what the minimum cover charge is for the viewing restaurant.

Ottawa

This adventure came about because I was out of the country when Oprah came to Vancouver. Instead I found scalper tickets for her Ottawa show and invited my mom. I bought front row seats for my mom and I and another couple of tickets for her friend and her daughter to join us. I go to many of these kind of events, so I knew not to get there too early. The stadium is located about forty-five minutes outside the city but my gals insisted we get there before the doors opened. I tried to tell them we didn't need to as there would be in a long lineup to get in, and we already had assigned seating. But they were too excited and went early anyway. When we arrived, we couldn't even see the entrance doors because of all the thousands of women (and maybe eight men) in line.

I gave my group their tickets in case we got separated, and to meet at our seats. And then, there goes my mom, making a bee-line through the crowd insisting, *"Excuse me… excuse me… excuse me!"* until she pushed herself right to the front. We were laughing hysterically from the middle of the crowd as others glared at her. The only person who didn't let her pass was a lady about the same age, who defiantly stood her ground at the door. She looked at my mom and demanded she wait behind. I guess my mom figured that because she had front row seats, she should be first in line.

Please listen to me, unless you don't have reserved seats or love standing in line for hours, always go after the doors open, not at opening. And ladies, be willing to use the men's washrooms at mostly woman events, as I always do.

Meeting Oprah is on many people's bucket list, including mine. It turned out that she was staying at the same hotel we were in, so I sent her a note wishing her a good show and told her our seats were in the front row. At the show, Oprah waved at us and we were thrilled. Her talk was a solid two hours long. Her main message was to listen to your instincts more, and listen less to the others who are negative around you. I could see the teleprompter from my seat and saw that she went off script many times as she chatted with the audience. Technically, we didn't officially meet her, but I felt I could check her off my bucket list anyway.

While we were in Ottawa, a friend of ours, who is an RCMP officer, gave us a city tour. We visited Parliament House and the Governor General's vacation home on a lake where security was so tight no one was allowed to boat there. The best time we had was a private tour of the Governor General's residence. When the Queen or her family come visit, they usually stay there. Our friend told us a story when he once was on guard all night outside Her Majesty's bedroom. Get this: as the house was built in 1838, her private bathroom is across the hall from her bedroom. Therefore, there were times in the middle of the night, she had to go past a guard to do her business. You would think our government could have renovated to have a bathroom inside the suite. Upon hearing this story, my mom chose this perfect opportunity "to go," and use the "Queen's" toilet. I guess we now have a new meaning for "The Throne."

Whistler

In 2001, a girlfriend and I were sitting at the lounge fireplace in the Chateau Whistler having a warm drink after a day of skiing, when a couple sat down in a sofa beside us. I greeted them and then saw it was Pierce Brosnan. He was dating his new girlfriend at the time, and he had just finished his TV show "Remington Steel," that made him so popular. He was even more handsome in person. I asked how they were enjoying Whistler and he responded by saying it was one of his favorite places. His girlfriend was not the friendliest person, she probably thought we were hitting on him. Their drinks came and I offered to treat them, but he declined. We had a nice chat, trying our best to get his girlfriend involved with the conversation, before giving them some privacy.

I won't return to the Whistler Chateau Penthouse Suite until it is renovated. When I first visited Whistler many years before, I would look up at that hotel and visualize staying in that room. So when the opportunity did come, the experience was not very memorable. There were stains on furniture and drapes, and garbage under the sofa. I sure hope Fairmont have renovated it since.

In many cities, there are companies that now do tasting tours, including Whistler. We have been on a few and they a blast, where a guide takes a small group into selected restaurants around the town with sampler items in each. Staff are ready to serve an appetizer and a paired glass of wine or a cocktail where you stay no more than twenty minutes, before moving on to the next place. It's a great way to see the private rooms in these restaurants, their wine cellars, or even sub-zero vodka tasting rooms. I highly recommend you try one in your city or next time you are traveling, as it's an easy way connect with others and discover new places.

Vernon, BC

The Sparkling Hill Resort & Spa is one of our recommendations for anyone visiting British Columbia and is on my Top Resorts list.

It was built by the Swarovski family and has an incredible 3.5 million crystals around the hotel and spa. We went there the first week they opened and have been back many times since. It has a 40,000 square feet spa with just about every service you can imagine. Ralph likes to do the Cryo Cold Chamber, the -110 C room where his nervous and circulatory systems are given a boost. The food is fresh and local, but the view is what I come for. All three penthouse suites are lovely, and the standard rooms are nice also. Always book the lake view when you go.

One year we booked a helicopter that picked us up right at the hotel to go wine tasting. The hotel is in the wine country and we have been collecting wine from the Okanagan every summer. But when you arrive at the vineyard in a helicopter, they really roll out the red carpet for you. We invited a couple friends with us, Kathy and Frank, as they know their wines very well. The only drawback was we didn't have enough room on the helicopter for all our cases of wine we all bought.

Victoria

As part of Mom's big surprise birthday, I flew with her and a friend to Vancouver Island. I had rented two side-by-side penthouses at the Victoria Regent Hotel right on the water.

It was a lovely spring weekend and we were all relaxed and happy to just hang out. Her friend Josie, had never been whale watching before so we offered to treat her to a three-hour tour. We walked over to the dock and I paid for one person. She yelled in her loud Italian voice, *"What? I thought you were coming with me... I am not going without you!"* I then turned to some others that were going and introduced them to her. By the time they were suited up and in their Zodiac, they were best of friends. She didn't even wave goodbye to me.

I went back to the hotel, where Mom and I chatted. We could see the dock from our suites, so we kept an eye out for her boat to return three hours later. But four hours later there was no sign of the Zodiac, so I called their office. The gal there said they had spotted a pod of whales further down the island, and the guests aboard voted to head there. Eight hours later they came back cold, tired and hungry, and there was no bathroom on the boat. I knew Josie was going to blame everything on me. So, before she got back to the hotel, I poured her a very hot bath, a large glass of wine and made her a snack. Later that night she proclaimed she had a fabulous day that she will always remember. If she hadn't gone she would have missed out on an amazing adventure. Sometimes people just need to be nudged out of their comfort zone.

Ralph's Epic Bike Ride Across Canada

I can't understand how someone wakes up at the age of fifty-five and states, *"I am going to bike across Canada!"* As a good wife, I support whatever crazy thing my husband pursues, just as he supports mine. Marathons or bike races. He has run the Knee Knacker 30-mile mountain foot race many times, along with the Grand Fondo Vancouver to Whistler bike race. He ran

26 miles each way, on his "Rim-to-Rim-to-Rim" Grand Canyon adventure as well. So, when he started his ride across Canada, I wanted to be there for him. He first started only biking the trails as I felt the highways were too dangerous, and I still believe many parts are.

It took two days to do Vancouver Island starting at Mile One on the Trans Canada Trail in Victoria. It was a good lesson starting close to home, testing equipment and gear, including a run of punctured tires, with weekend practice runs into the Fraser Valley. Then he resumed riding across the British Columbia mainland, North Vancouver to Hope, up the Coquihalla Highway all the way to the Okanagan on trails, which took two weeks. I joined him in Kelowna when he decided the roads were a better option than the bumpy dirt trails. I followed him for five days driving on the side of the highway with my flasher lights on. I would make sure he had food and water and then would go ahead and check into a hotel. I would have his bath ready, with a cold beer and a big meal. He would arrive and I would wash his clothes, feed and massage him, then put him to bed and do the same thing the next day. Some days he would miss out on all the action. I would be driving my car behind him and a big bear would come running out after Ralph cycled by. I saw many deer while he saw only a few of them.

At the BC border with Alberta, I left him on his own. He had a tracking device on him at all times, sometimes I would follow it to see if he was near a town where he could spend the night. My mom took over as the minder as she checked her iPad throughout the day and sent me updates, like *"He's in Calgary, having lunch at Subway."* He ate a lot of meals at Subways as they are located on main streets and where he was able keep an eye on his gear. Since he was traveling light and unassisted, we named it "the credit card tour". If he needed something he would just buy it. There were some fabulous trails on Cape Breton Island and Prince Edward Island, where I was able to join him. The day he finished in Halifax, Nova Scotia was a great day for me. I couldn't wait to have him home, knowing he was safe and healthy.

USA

Las Vegas

We have been many times, mainly to see the shows. Once we stayed in suite that high rollers usually get for free, but not being heavy gamblers, we paid for ours. That particular night we gambled a little, made $300 and left the chips on our bedside table before going out for dinner. When we came back, the chips were gone. We called the manager who came up with security and we explained what happened. Their casual reaction was a shock to us. They suggested $300 would not be an uncommon maid service tip in a room like ours, so the maids likely took it, and that we didn't have any recourse. I complained to the hotel when I got home and never even received a reply. So, when you go to Vegas, put your chips away before you leave your room.

One show we particularly enjoyed in Vegas was the David Copperfield magic show. We were sitting in row one, and he chose us to come up and help him with a trick, one that would make my husband disappear. But while he was giving the instructions to my husband, I went up behind David and smelled him. (What? He is a good-looking guy!) The women in the audience roared with laughter. We can't remember what happened in the act, but I can still remember how wonderfully David smelled!

If you are planning to go to shows while in Vegas, buy the tickets well ahead of time because they sell out way in advance. If you want to take your chances on the day of a show, go early to the half-price ticket booths or beg your hotel concierge.

One evening we were in the Las Vegas airport waiting for our departure home when a Canadian from our flight, won over $1,000,000 at the slot machine next to us. It was very exciting for everyone. She had to miss her flight (not that she probably cared) because officials had to come to the machine to verify it was a win. They deducted 40% for taxes and prepared a check for the rest.

Atlanta

Before the Olympics in 1996, there was a story that went viral about the state of New Mexico calling the headquarters of the US Olympics for their allocation of tickets. Headquarters, not recognizing that New Mexico was actually a US state, responded by suggesting they talk to their own country's government. Apparently, that person did not know all 50 state names.

A radio station in Vancouver heard about this and was discussing it on air. I called in to say that we were going to Atlanta, and suggested that we see how far we get, posing as athletes? So, we applied to the Olympics from the country of *New Columbia* ("New" from New Zealand and "Columbia" from British Columbia). It sounds like a country, right? We flew down to Atlanta and made it through the first line of entrances for athletes, but we chickened out at the next phase as the security guards were all carrying guns.

The only hotel we could find in Atlanta was an hour by train out of the center. Some people were even renting sleeping bag space on the conference room floors. After a hot day at the events, we stopped for a drink at a bar at a downtown hotel, where we spotted OJ Simpson out partying after his big trial. There were signs welcoming sponsors everywhere. I went up to the front desk and said I was with Sara Lee Corporation, one of the Olympic sponsors at the hotel, and asked if by chance they had rooms left. She said they had plenty for special guests like us and so for $100US we spent the night in a five-star hotel with a welcome gift waiting for us in the room. Sometimes you just have to ask.

While in Atlanta, we went to a popular southern-themed restaurant, where their elaborate buffet was the draw for many tourists. Servers, dressed as Southern Belles, paraded around asking how we were doing. Since we don't eat meat, but like seafood, we had tried some tuna salad. We both thought it was the best we have ever had and went up to the buffet for more. When one of the Southern Belles asked how we were doing, I complimented her on the tuna salad. *"Why Honey"*, she replied, *"that's chicken!"* We had a good laugh as it had been years since tasting some. We attended the amazing Opening Ceremony, where Muhammad Ali made one of his last and greatest public appearances.

Our favorite story at the Olympics occurred when we exchanged tickets with a guy who looked like he had never traded tickets before. We had already been to see the US basketball Dream Team, so we swapped tickets for the gymnastics finals. Remember the one where the American athlete, Kerri Strug injured her leg, but still competed to win gold? As we entered the arena, we were surprised to be shown up to the VIP suites, where a suite host welcomed us to the Lanier Copier corporate suite. Not knowing what to say, I declared we were from the Vancouver office, to which she warmly replied, *"Oh, I heard you might be coming!"* They had a full service buffet and open bar, and were having a blast with the other guests. Hours later Ralph had to spill the beans that we just traded the tickets with some guy (likely from Lanier) and we weren't part of the company. And another couple spoke up that they also bought them the same way and we all had a good laugh. I guess this happens all the time.

Hawaii

I can't count the number of times I have been to Hawaii, but the best hotel penthouse suite I found in Honolulu was at the Ala Moana Hotel. You are probably gathering by now that I love penthouses. If you are traveling with a group, this place is conveniently located right next to the mall and a block from the beach. Sally and I spent two weeks there and loved it.

The hop-on buses in Honolulu are very busy and you might find it easier to take a cab to the starting point. We spent what seemed like an hour, watching bus after bus pass us by and it was frustrating. Then we spotted what looked like a taxi, and I literally jumped in front of it, he stopped and we jumped in. I asked him to take us downtown, he smiled and complied. A couple minutes later he confessed that he was not a regular taxi and only picked up disabled clients. (I did admire how spacious the cab was at the time!) And, he was off duty! We had a good chuckle about this, but when he dropped us downtown and refused payment, I insisted he pick up dinner for his family with the money.

Mom and I went to Hawaii a few times as we always have fun together. On one trip, I booked a nice penthouse right across the street from Waikiki Beach. We were having an excellent time. One morning we went into the ocean for a dip. Mom is not a confident swimmer, so she hung out in the shallow water. She must have tripped because I saw her go underwater. She got up and laughed. We went back to the hotel and she took a nap. She woke up later saying she wasn't feeling great, so I suggested that I go get dinner and bring it back. She didn't eat much and went to bed early. ***And then it happened!*** By the time morning came she was worse, very dizzy and throwing up. I called an ambulance and we took her to a hospital across town. By the time we got there, Mom was out of it. They ran every kind of test they could think of, and kept her overnight, using words like "stroke" and "heart attack".

I ended up sleeping on a bench outside the hospital overnight. I could have gone back to the hotel, but the doctors seemed to want to talk to me regularly about what they were doing for her. The consensus was she had a bad case of vertigo. Our flight back was the next day, so I asked if they thought she would be good enough to fly. They gave me some very strong pills to give her once we boarded the plane, as well as a note declaring her okay to fly.

I got our things packed up and headed for the airport. She was in a wheelchair, so it was not so bad checking in and then we headed for the business class lounge. I poured a large glass of gin and tonic to calm my nerves. We finally boarded the plane and sat in row one, when flight the attendant came over with our menus for the meal. She asked if we would like the chicken or the fish. Mom all of sudden became alert and she proclaimed in a loud voice, *"Chicken, I… want… chicken, I… love… chicken, I… need… chicken."* I can imagine how hungry she probably was, after not eating for the past day and a half. I gave her the pills, suggested she take a nap and said I would wake her for dinner. She slept the rest of the way. When we arrived back to Vancouver and cleared customs, we headed out to Arrivals.

I saw Mom's husband waiting for us and I shoved the wheelchair, with Mom in it, towards him and said, *"She's all yours!"* I was exhausted and headed home.

Before we left Canada, I asked her if she had overseas medical insurance. She didn't, so I immediately bought a ten-day plan from my insurance agent. The plan cost twenty dollars. Her medical bill from the hospital cost thousands and thousands, so don't ever think about going across any border without travel insurance. The older people get, the more expensive insurance can be for traveling out-of-country, but it is an absolute must.

Private Jet Adventures

I have had some great adventures on private jets. I warn you, once you start, it is hard to go back to commercial airlines. For me the issue is customs and immigration. I have never trusted them since the time, when I was twenty years old and travelling on my own, when they must have suspected I was carrying drugs or something illegal. They snapped the heels off my shoes, and smashed all my makeup, all in front of a big line of waiting passengers…and found nothing. Since then, I get tense any time going through immigration. Ralph knows not to chat with me while in the line-up and he does all the talking to the officials. When you fly in a private jet, you are treated very differently. No pat downs, no metal detectors, and usually not having to open luggage for inspection.

Portland

One private jet flight was with the Owner's Circle of the Vancouver MLS Whitecaps soccer team. We flew with the owners out of the MillionAir Terminal in Vancouver, (I know, what a fabulous name hey?), heading down for a game in Portland, Oregon. Just as we were boarding, a luxury SUV pulled up to the jet next to ours and Oprah and her people got out to board their jet. Very cool! We ended up losing the game but we all had a fantastic time.

Scottsdale

On another adventure, I was the top bidder of a luxury jet trip at a charity gala and auction. There were 800 people at this event, organized by the Grizzly Bear Foundation in the Vancouver Convention Centre. The large room was designed as a forest setting, unusually dim, so as soon as this item came up for auction, I stood, determined, and made the first bid. To my delight, there was only one other person bidding on it and he backed down quickly, so I got the trip for a bargain, relatively speaking. Thank you the McLaughlin family, for your donation.

The trip included a private jet for seven people to a majestic villa in the Scottsdale foothills. I carefully selected my friends who I thought would best get along. The night before the departure, a major snow storm hit Vancouver, which is a very unusual occurrence. I was a bit apprehensive if our limo would be able to get through the snow, but the driver picked us all up on time and we left the snow for some much appreciated sunshine. This jet was smaller than the other ones I have taken, as we had to bend over to get to our seats. But the funniest part of the whole trip was the captain explaining the onboard washrooms. We all thought he was joking! Nope! To use the facilities, we had to move luggage into the very tight aisle, duck down through the washroom door, unzipping while bent over. Then flush and try to zipper up while attempting to remain dignified. Not as easy as one would think. We all had drank a lot of champagne by the time we boarded, so everyone accepted the challenge to use the bathroom during our four hour flight We were crying, laughing so hard at everyone's effort to use the toilet, but we all had totally bonded by the time we landed in Scottsdale. A very polite US immigration official met us at the jet door, checked our passports quickly and wished us a good stay. When we returned to Vancouver, there was no immigration official to greet us at all, as it was raining and we were late. We just disembarked, I ran and jumped into the waiting limo, yelling to the others, in my best Ikea ad impersonation *"Start the car! Start the car!"*

There are many jet companies that are all campaigning for your travel dollars. You might be surprised how reasonably priced they can be, especially if you have a group sharing the cost.

Mexico

We have travelled extensively though Mexico, mostly on business but here are our highlights:

Cancun

My favorite part of staying at an all-inclusive resort is all the extra service and freebies, especially staying in the big suites. At one such all-inclusive resort in Cancun, they stocked our full-sized fridge in our Presidential Suite with mini spirit bottles. They are just too cute, I couldn't resist popping a few, along with their expensive toiletries into my suitcase. By the time our last day came, my suitcase was brimming so full of goodies, I had to sacrifice some clothes for the maids.

On another trip to Mexico, my mom and Sally joined me for a week on the beach. Mom loved to fish, so she arranged a deep-sea fishing trip for herself. She came back to the resort with the biggest smile and gloating about how she had caught a massive sailfish. She had it stuffed and it now sits on the wall in her office, I think, just to prove to the fishermen in her life that she reeled it in all by herself. (She claims this fish was the smaller of the two she caught). If you are thinking of bringing a trophy like that back home, you should be aware of the costs. Another suggestion is that most resort chefs will prepare it for dinner while some resorts will even can fish and ship it home.

Our latest discovery in Cancun is at a newly opened (2019) resort that you must try: The Haven Riviera, all-inclusive, adult-only and euro chic. By far our best resort experience to date; superb service, quiet beach, fabulous foodie restaurants, sophisticated chill music. Serenity club suites are a must and the Presidential Suite is the ultimate for luxury and privacy. As always, check for potential interruption from nearby construction.

Puerto Vallarta

One year, we decided we didn't want the usual all-inclusive resorts that we have been to many times, so we rented a private penthouse right on the beach. Now, just to be clear, the accommodation itself is the most important part of a holiday for me, except for flying in row one.

We have stayed, over the years at some fantastic presidential suites, penthouses, master suites, etc. But when I opened the door to this private high-rise named Vallarta Penthouse, I was blown away. The 30-foot-high glass walls opened-up to the beach below. It was heaven. It had four bedrooms, each with a view. It was very private and quiet because we went in October, which is low season. Very few guests were in the building or by the pool. There was no loud music blaring, just peace and decadence. Horseback riding was there on the beach just outside the building early every morning for me.

One morning my husband came running into our suite saying, *"Come quick, there are turtles on the beach!"* I ran down to see them, but I couldn't spot any. He came down a few minutes later and I asked where they were, expecting to see large turtles. He pointed down at my feet. And there they were, dozens of tiny turtles that had just hatched and were making their way to the shoreline.

This penthouse is one of our top places to stay in the world. If you are thinking of a destination wedding or reunion, this place would be great. The open-air lobby below is filled with over-sized furniture and would be perfect for a ceremony. You don't have to rent the penthouse, but if you traveling with a group, the cost divided up is reasonable. Just one bit of advice: when you rent a private villa, read all the fine print. It may state that some things are extra, like we found out the air-conditioning will be billed to us at the end of our stay. I had not read this on the fine print, so I was leaving all the doors open to hear the ocean while having the air-conditioning on. Our air-conditioning bill at the end of the week was USD $1500. Lesson learned.

Europe

Greece

My husband and I have both been to Greece before and after we met, and love it. He came on a holiday to Santorini when he was young, and would end most days with a drink at Franco's, one of those great Fira sunset bars overlooking the Aegean Sea and the boats dotted below. Back then, he got chatting with a guy who worked at a bank in Vancouver. They had a few drinks, and Ralph got up, they said their goodbyes, and he headed back to his hotel. It then dawned on him that he forgot to pay for his drinks. He ran back to Franco's to find that the banker had left, but found a very angry waiter wanting to get paid. Many years later when Ralph moved to Vancouver, he tried contacting banks, to try find this guy to apologize. He wanted him to know he didn't mean to run out on his bill. Ahhh... got to love that Catholic guilt!

When we returned together to Santorini years later, we found the most amazing small hotel in all of Fira. It had an infinity pool and a view that was breathtaking. We stayed there for a few weeks, doing our 5am exercise walking down, and up, the 100plus steps that led down to the main dock, avoiding the droves of donkeys that populated it later in the day. "You, donkey?", their handlers would ask confused tourists. We picked up fresh food daily from the local market, from which we made the best Greek salad. We spent the afternoons reading by the pool, and our nights at the local bars and watching the millions of stars. Pure heaven. When you go there, have sunset drinks at Franco's Bar… it's the best place to watch it.

Spain

We had been to Spain a few times and every visit I fall increasingly more and more in love with Barcelona. Sally and I were going on a seven-day Mediterranean cruise. We met up in Barcelona the night their soccer team was playing in the Euro final. Every time Barcelona scored a goal, fireworks went off all over the city. It was very exciting. I just love the food, sights and the people. You must go there one day and just hang out on Las Ramblas, the main strip.

I am big on getting a spray tan before going on vacation so I don't look a tourist. Sally was pasty white, so I suggested (okay, insisted) that she let me spray tan her that night. When we woke up the next morning, we saw that her bed sheets were completely orange. I guess the product didn't stick, to her.

We boarded our ship later that day that would tour us around the Mediterranean. I had booked the big room, which had two bedrooms. It was a very strange set up. My master bedroom was lovely, but the other bedroom was little and unattractive, almost like servant quarters, so we joked throughout the cruise that Sally was the maid.

The only issue was that most of the ports we stopped at, were hours from the main points of interests, so we just hung out in the ports. We had a great cruise and didn't do much more than walk, dance, eat and drink. I am a seasoned cruiser so I had suggested Sally not to order wine by the glass, but by the bottle and keep it for another meal. Since we both liked different kinds of wine, we both ended up sending bottles back to our room. When we woke up on day six, a day at sea, we had a collection of ten half-empty bottles. So, we looked at each other over breakfast, and agreed, *"Let's get at 'em."*

Later that night we checked our account on the TV for our onboard charges. This cruise was not an all-inclusive and we hadn't hit the casino, spas or excursions, but the bill total looked like we did. I decided it was best I didn't tell my liver what the alcohol total was.

The next morning, we disembarked back in Barcelona with huge hangovers. When we arrived at our hotel, our room wasn't ready, so we walked to Las Ramblas and ordered breakfast. Sally was badly in need of a coffee. The waiter took our order but insisted that when in Spain, we had to have Sangria. We tried to explain we couldn't handle anymore, but lo and behold, he returned with two huge Sangrias. We looked at each other again, *"Let's get at 'em!"*

France

One of the times Ralph and I were in Paris, we took a small tour excursion for wine tasting out of the city. There were eight of us in the van. I noticed that our driver was drinking the samples as much as the guests, but it never dawned on me to tell her that she shouldn't be drinking. An hour into our drive back to the city, most of the guests fell asleep. I was sitting right behind the driver when she inexplicably veered across two lanes of highway traffic. I screamed and the whole van woke up... including the driver! How we didn't get into an accident is beyond me. Needless to say, if you are ever on a wine tour, make sure the driver is not drinking or on the phone, as it's your life you are protecting. Even at home, when drivers are holding their cell phones while driving, I ask them to put it away. And please, whatever you do, wear your seat belt. I have heard too many stories of tourists being seriously hurt because they trusted the drivers. Sometimes I was complacent if I was in the back seat of a taxi or limo, but now I make sure we always wear seat belts.

In 1998, we went to France for World Cup soccer tournament. We had pre-bought tickets to many of the earlier games, but as France was winning their way to the final, the scalper prices were going crazy. (A scalper is someone who buys and sells tickets, usually on the street.) We have bought dozens of tickets from scalpers all over the world for major events. France ended up playing favorites Brazil in the final. We went to the stadium a couple of hours before the game but we could only find single seats for $1000USD each, way above our budget. So, we headed back to the Champs-Élysées to watch the rest of the game at a bar. The game was so exciting and France ended up winning. The bar owner opened a case of champagne and poured all his customers endless glasses. The parties spilled out on to the street and thousands ended up celebrating for days. Not being in the actual stadium was fine with us this time as this occasion was the largest since the liberation of France after the war.

In 2006, Ralph and I were at the World Cup soccer tournament in Germany, so I decide to sneak away for a few days and meet my mom in Paris for a shopping trip. The French Open was on and we asked our hotel concierge, if he could find us tickets to the final. He said there was no chance as they are all sold out. I have been to many events like this, so I was sure we could get scalper tickets, and we headed down to the stadium. There was a short line up at the box office as they had just released last minute tickets, and boom, we were in. Federer was playing Nadal. Great match! We didn't even need to buy tickets from a scalper. This happens more than you know with "sold out" events. Many times, the stadium will release last minute tickets the day of the event. It was 110F that day, but that didn't stop us from cheering.

Germany

A very good friend of ours, Reinhold, a past student at our school, who later became one of our Ambassador of the Year recipients, invited us to his small village in Germany. It is called Oberwesel and is on the Rhine River. Every 2-3 years the village hosts a medieval festival, the *Mediaeval*

Spectaculum, which attracts thousands of visitors from all over Germany and around the world. We arrived in the middle of summer and it was baking hot. Everyone was in costume and our friends decided to make our dress extravagant, so they were heavy and very warm. At this festival, the village transforms into how it was hundreds of years before. No electricity, only lanterns, where modern inventions are off limits. Food was prepared the way they had in the Middle Ages and even the entertainment was authentic.

It was getting towards lunch time when Ralph and I began looking for something to eat. As you can imagine, there were not a lot of willing vegetarian Germans back in those days. We finally spotted something we thought we would be able to eat. It looked like rye bread with mashed potatoes on top. So, we bought two. On our first bite, we looked at each other… hmm, this is different. After the second bite, we knew what it might be, lard! I went somewhere quieter to dispose of it and we drank beer for the rest of the day.

At the festival, our friend's nephew was performing on stage as a fire juggler, like they would have had back in the good old days. We sat in the top row on the bleachers and cheered him on. Unfortunately, he dropped one of his flaming sticks and the surrounding hay bales instantly caught fire. Little children right by the stage were instantly rescued by quick reacting parents, who scooped them up and ran. Others grabbed water buckets and put the fames out in an orderly fashion, avoiding a near disaster, but adding to a memorable day's entertainment!

An especially authentic feature was staying at the local famous Schönburg Castle, a nice hike uphill from the village. We had a top suite facing the river, with breakfast served outside, overlooking fabulous views of the Rhine. It was very romantic. Make sure to book a river view room when you go, and try to be there during Oberwesel's medieval festival as it's quite the adventure. Pack your costume and book the castle early. One night a couple of friendly ghosts popped by to check us out, and the complimentary bottle of sherry came in handy.

A popular way to travel Germany is by river cruise, the scenery is picturesque with magical villages and vineyards. I highly suggest this type of cruise for first-timers as the waters are calm and these ships are smaller and more intimate.

We discovered when sailing down the Rhine in medieval times, the preferred transport route at the time, cargo ships were required to pay substantial portions of their fare for safe passage through each toll. There were so many rulers, gatekeepers and tolls at one point, that a ship could lose most of its load by the time it reached its destination. We plan on going back there one day to bike along the Rhine where the bike lanes are flat and the modern day gatekeepers along the way are now tourist stops, like scenic hotels, tempting wine bars and restaurants.

Central America and the Caribbean

Costa Rica

I love this country. One of my reasons is that the people are so content, Ticos call it *"Pura Vida!"* Rarely did we meet one who wanted to leave their country. They feel they live in the best country in the world. Costa Rica is the kind of place that tourists don't usually just stay in once place. Everyone we met had already come from, or were heading out in the next few days, to another part.

One place on my 'best resorts' from around the world list, is on a surfing beach on the Pacific Coast, near Santa Teresa. It takes forever to get there, but it's so worth it. The Latitude 10 property was developed by two brothers with two master villas and three smaller villas. They decided to rent them out as they were not there often enough. The reason it gets on my top places list, has a lot to do with the locals. Not the human ones, but the ones that live in the trees above. There is a species of spider monkey who rarely touch the ground, they are born and raised and live their entire life in the trees. If a baby fell to the ground, it probably wouldn't survive.

We arrived at sunset and were taken directly to our villa where they had lit dozens of candles all around it. I stepped one foot inside and I was in love with this suite. The large, private bathroom is located outside, and when I say private, I mean we share it with the biggest iguanas and an entire tribe of monkeys up in the trees, who love to play all night.

One night I got up to go to the bathroom and a huge iguana had decided he liked the toilet seat for his bed. He had no intention of leaving so I had to go elsewhere! The monkeys especially loved to come over when we were taking a shower. On the last day, one of them pooped right above me as I was showering. I looked up and I swear he was slapping his knee he found it so funny. They have a private chef who will prepare whatever you feel like eating. If you are a couple, reserve Villa #1. It is the quietest, or bring a group and book the whole resort.

One of my favorite days in Costa Rica, was a journey between towns. Those who travel to the town of Nuevo Arenal, are in for a treat since the original town of Arenal is under water. After a short road trip, we traveled by boat that crossed this man-made flooded valley. At times during the dry season, the level of the lake drops and the remnants of a cemetery, homes and even a church can be seen. This place would have been a blast to scuba dive in. Finally, we were met by horses at the other side of the lake. We rode into town a few hours later through lush countryside. The guide had our luggage waiting at our new hotel, a refreshing shower and dinner, all very cool.

Costa Rica is also a place that offers adventurous activities. When you meet another tourist, regardless of age, the first thing to share is what adventures we all did that day. On our next day, we repelled down a waterfall, and went white-water rafting in a Category 4, which means it was a very fast, raging river. We were having a blast until I tore my shorts wide open. It was a long way back to the bus, so there was nothing much I could do about it. We followed this up with a gondola ride, one of the longest zip treks in the world and hike through a tropical rainforest full of exotic animals and birds.

We moved around to a few different areas of Costa Rica, the last place we stayed, Buena Vista Villas was also lovely. Each guest had their own villa with a view of the sea. They miss my 'best resort" list only because it is a bit of hike down to the beach. One day, I was sunning down at the beach and a staff member told me Ralph wanted to show me something. We headed up to see a sloth climbing down to eye level. He was majestic. We stayed for an hour just watching him. Staff then shared a story about a neighbor who had a huge Rottweiler who was barking incessantly at a sloth. The sloth slowly made his way down the tree and had gripped the dog's temples with his claws. The dog yelped for his life as the slow-moving sloth stared him down. That would have been amusing to see! Now every time we get irritated with each other we pretend to claw the others temples.

On the last day in Coast Rica, Ralph went out for a quick run as I was packing up. I had taken our passports out of the safe early (I had once forgotten to do this in London, only to arrive at the airport without them) and had opened the balcony doors, even though the villa had a sign reminding guests to keep all doors closed at all times. I popped into the shower for just a couple of minutes. When I came into the living room, there were at least fifteen monkeys inside, stealing our left-over lunch and anything else they could get their hands on. I panicked, remembering our passports, and grabbed them in time before scaring the monkeys out.

So, lesson learned. If there is a sign that says to make sure your doors and windows are always closed, it is probably to protect you against some sort of burglar.

Cuba

We were there years before the American tourists returned, and it really felt like we had stepped back in time. The architecture, cars, music and art were amazing. The weirdest thing we found was there were few shops in Havana at the time, a couple for the tourists, while locals were still being issued weekly quotas of bread, dairy and meat. I wouldn't say the locals were particularly friendly to us as we walked around Havana, detached perhaps. Ralph was constantly being asked if he wanted to buy drugs, but never when we were together.

The server at our hotel's restaurant was a local. He was a lawyer, but he found working for US dollar tips made him way more money than practicing law. Dogs were treated well in Cuba, as tourists like me, took food from the hotel buffets to feed them on the beach. Check the forecast before you leave for Cuba as it's not always warm. We ended up shivering in our room for a couple of days, when a cold front came in.

South America

Cusco, Machu Picchu, Peru

Ralph had this on his bucket list for years. I hadn't really heard much about it before, sorry Peru! Machu Picchu is a lost village hidden in the clouds, safe from European invaders until it was rediscovered only 100 years ago by foreigners, completely concealed by vegetation.

One of the first things you are told about this trip is that many people get altitude sickness, so be prepared. Our hotel in Cusco was a very old building that used to be a monastery. Upon check-in at the Belmond Hotel Monasterio, you are offered a special hot tea to drink. It was a very hot day, so a hot drink did not appeal to us, but believe me, when you travel to a high altitude, drink the tea. Another altitude sickness remedy, for an extra cost, is to have oxygen pumped into your room at night, which we opted for.

Ralph and I headed into town for dinner, and discovered it was a national holiday, with locals were lighting fireworks in the main square. We chose a cute little restaurant overlooking the square for dinner. After dinner we joined the locals for the fireworks display, not the kind of display I had ever encountered, as half of the fireworks seemed to be shooting into the crowd. The locals loved it, jumping out of the way, and patting their clothes and hair down from the sparks… yikes!

We returned to our hotel room after and as soon as we entered, a few ghosts showed up. They were friendly ones, just hanging out, and we took a couple of good photos that revealed their cloudy orbs.

We drifted off to sleep with our oxygen pumping in and about two hours later it hit me. I raced to the bathroom and spent the rest of the night losing a couple dress sizes. I will never know if it was the food or the altitude, but it was a bad night!

The next day we boarded the zig zag train to Machu Picchu. It winds slowly up the mountain and ends at the local village, Aguas Calientes. You can hike up or take the long bus ride up at this point. We opted for the bus, although it is a nail biter. Don't look down from the very narrow, unpaved, steep road as there are no barriers to shield you from the valley below.

We were staying the night at the lovely intimate Belmond Sanctuary Lodge, at the entrance to the Machu Picchu ruins. Most other visitors made day trips from Aguas Calientes below and stayed there. I highly suggest staying at this lodge instead. It is pricy, but so worth it. We planned it well, so we could be there on a full moon and at that time the guests at the lodge could explore the ruins at night. Our first trek was just after sunset, only an hour or so before dark as the clouds were rolling in. But at the crack of dawn, we hiked up and had the entire ancient village to ourselves, except for the lamas and stray dogs. Ralph later hired a guide to do a three-hour hike right up to the top of Huayna Picchu, overlooking Machu Picchu. As we departed, I told him my adventures with all the spirits I had seen, while he shared his feelings that he had been here before somehow. It's that sort of mystical place.

Ecuador

From the moment we arrived at the airport, I was in love with this country. I know without a doubt that I had lived another lifetime in Ecuador. There were thousands of roses throughout the airport. I loved the people, the food and the flowers everywhere. We checked into our hotel and at least 100 roses had been placed in our suite. Did you know most roses that we get in Canada come from South America?

On our first night in Quito we went down to the hotel pools where we had them all to ourselves. A major electrical storm quickly blew in as we sheltered under a bridge that crossed the pool. I have never seen so many lightning strikes in so short a time, very romantic.

After touring Quito and the Ciudad Mitad del Mundo, where it's Equatorial line is in the wrong location incidentally, we flew onto the Galapagos Islands. Yes, you must go here one day! You can choose just about any size of touring ship that makes you comfortable. The smaller boats go to places the bigger ones can't, but you may not have the same comforts. Reserve well in advance as there are restrictions on how many people and how many vessels can go at any one time. Make sure you pack your water shoes and ensure your package includes park fees, as they are expensive.

We landed in Baltra a day ahead of the departure of the cruise, with a quick boat ride to Isla Santa Cruz. The Royal Palms Hotel was where we stayed that night, and it was amazing. The Queen of The Netherlands had just checked out of our villa the week before, along with all her entourage. Meals were delivered tastefully to our room, so we ate by the fireplace and then ventured out to meet some of the giant tortoises nearby.

FYI: there are very heavy fines if you ever touch any of the wildlife in the Galapagos, as we were told again and again. But what if it is just not your fault? I was sitting a good distance away from a 100-year-old tortoise, what a beautiful creature he was. He decided that he would like to get a better look at us and started heading our way. (I guess there are no eyeglasses for these old guys.) We got up and moved back but he kept coming, so I just stayed there. He got to about a foot away. It was close enough to look into his eyes and give him a cosmic hug. That's when I figured I would get into trouble if someone saw me and I backed away one last time.

We boarded our ship the next day that held about 90 guests. We were all so excited for our upcoming adventures. Day one, we went to a few islands that remained totally undeveloped except walkways, some revealed the distinct volcanic features that formed them five million years ago. We looked closer at some darker lava rock to discover the ground was actually teaming with hundreds of iguanas.

It was one of our monthly anniversaries the next night, and Ralph had asked the captain if we could have a romantic dinner somewhere private on the ship. The captain arranged for us to have dinner on his private deck. We got to know the captain and his wife well, and to repay his kindness we offered his daughter a one month scholarship to our school in Vancouver including flight and accommodation. They were all blown out of the water! (Get it?)

The next day, we sailed around many of the islands. One of the untouched islands was the home of the infamous Blue-footed Booby bird. The whole crew searched all morning for a sighting. Nada! My husband and I were the first to return to the ship, and I was sitting by the small swimming pool catching some rays, when a bird flew down beside me. I just assumed it was a seagull and then did a double take. Sitting right there was a Blue-footed Booby. Ralph came up to the pool deck and spotted it beside me. He grabbed his camera and started taking photos. The other guests started arriving back and all froze in their tracks when they saw it. The boat pulled anchor, but this bird stayed with me as more and more people came up to the pool area. He shimmied up to me, to where he was no more than a foot away and we locked eyes. He was asking me, *"What's with all those people?"*

I told him, *"You are so beautiful, that they need to remember you by taking a photo."* He stayed for a good hour by my side, then bid adieu! The moral of this story is sometimes you search and search for something, when it actually right in front of you.

Uruguay

My favorite memory here was dining at a lovely restaurant on the water one night in Montevideo. During dinner, we saw this young romantic couple on what looked like their first date. We called the manager over and gave him

$50, saying we wanted to secretly buy them dinner. You have never seen such surprised people. We get a lot of joy travelling to countries that have so much to offer in culture and natural beauty, but where its people may not experience the same comforts and security that we have. We are so spoiled living in such a great country as Canada, but going out for dinner for some people in the world may be a once or twice a year event. So, if you have the opportunity to treat a local, you will be surprised how much happiness you can bring.

Brazil

Not only have we made some amazing Brazilian friends through our business, but we have traveled all over Brazil and adore the country.

One evening we went to the open-air nightclub in São Paulo. I have never seen anything like it before. There were thousands of people and many different styles of music in different large rooms, open until the wee hours of the morning. One thing to watch at a nightclub are your drinks... no, not what you are thinking. Whenever we got up to dance, our drinks were scooped away. We figured it was the staff. It was so hot, we would need a drink to keep cool, and so we would head back up to the bar for another. You see, when you enter this bar, they take your credit card information. They would then hand you a pass card to be scanned for drinks. My bill at the end of the night was over USD $500.

But on the other hand, the best deal in Brazil was when one of our friends took us to a traditional Brazilian barbeque restaurant, one that continuously serves an incredible range of roasted meats to your table. Showing the green light or card on your table, meant *"More please"*, while a red one, *"Enough"*.

Apparently, they have never had customers who didn't eat meat before. Our hosts felt so bad when we told them we didn't, but we insisted on staying as the salad and seafood buffet, which came with the meal, looked fabulous. We couldn't believe our eyes, it was an amazing selection of exotic seafood and fresh salads. When it was time for the bill, our server and the manager had a conference to decide how much they should charge us. The server came over sheepishly and suggested, *"We will have to charge you five dollars each, is that okay?"* It was the best and cheapest buffet ever! If you have any young men who eat you out of house and home, you should really send them to an all-you-can-eat Brazilian barbeque.

Rio de Janeiro

I wanted to honeymoon in Rio, but at that time it was considered too dangerous for tourists. Finally, years later, we went there on a business trip and I fell in love with the city. Their national drink, the caipirinha, is not to be missed. You have to go to the beach and try one…or five! The other memory we have is of everyone in the family wearing the same style of swimwear. This means the granddaughter, mom and grandma wore identical G-strings.

And visit the bar where the song *The Girl from Ipanema* was written. The composers were often spotted there in the 1960s watching the girls come and go from school. One of those girls was a tall, tanned, leggy, long-haired beauty. The guys scribbled a song down on the bar napkins and the rest in history. Not sure what we would call these men today?

Iguazu Falls

This is the largest waterfall system in the world. It borders Paraguay, Brazil and Argentina. So, depending on what side of the falls you are on, you are in a different country. It is an amazing sight to see, especially by helicopter.

We went there when disposable cameras were popular. Having an expensive camera drew the wrong kind of attention in South America at that time. It was there where we met up with a few local coatis, the cheekiest raccoons in the world. My husband was holding the disposable camera after we had taken some shots of the falls. All of a sudden, a large coati grabbed the camera and took off into the bush, joined by a mob of them. Ralph kept shouting at the thing to drop the camera (because they would know English right!!). The animal was tearing the packaging off the camera when Ralph confronted them and grabbed the camera out of their paws. This is not a wise thing to do, but I guess sometimes you just have to stand up for yourself. The camera still worked and produced some great shots.

Chile

This is the land of some of the best value-for-money wine in the world, many never tasted by locals as most are exported. We had to prepare our livers for going as we never met a Chilean bottle we didn't like.

In Santiago, we ended up at the same hotel that the G8 summit was being held, security was very tight. I was dressed to go out for dinner, so I told my husband I would meet him at the lobby lounge. It was quite a big bar, and I thought the service was just slow. I waved the server over twice and he still never came over. Ralph finally arrived and the server came over quickly. I asked the guy why he didn't serve me and his sheepish response was basically that he thought I was a prostitute trying to hook up with someone from the G8. (Should I have been flattered or appalled?)

My advice if you would like to see most of South America at one time, is to go by cruise ship. We spent half our time going to and from airports, to hotels and back, and after a few weeks, it got tiring. Most cities are port cities, so you can access most the main attractions by ship.

South East Asia

Singapore

We took an all-inclusive Silversea cruise from Singapore through India and onto Dubai. We have cruised a lot, but this was the first time on a long, 30-day cruise. We were celebrating our fifteenth-year wedding anniversary, and this was our first really big splurge. When I first saw the price for that trip advertised, I told a neighbor friend how insanely expensive it was. And we agreed only idiots would pay that much. Hours later, I had booked it!

We sailed from Singapore after having a drink at the famous Raffles Hotel, home of the Singapore Sling. Apparently, it is mandatory for every tourist to go and try one.

Sri Lanka

We were on our way to Sri Lanka, an island country with a difficult past. It is also home to the village my husband helped rebuild after the big 2004 tsunami. We didn't go to our village this time. Ralph had a meeting in Colombo and I ventured off on a tour to feed orphan baby elephants.

After a long bumpy ride, our bus arrived at a dried-up river bed. We bought bananas to feed the elephants and they came a runnin'! It was a blast playing with the wee baby ones, but about an hour later, the guides starting screaming for everyone to quickly get back on the bus. We were shocked at the sight of a massive bull elephant pounding down the river bed, at full speed toward us. I guess he didn't like the fact that the kids were getting all the food. We made it safely back to the bus with adrenaline a-pumping.

Sri Lanka is still developing as a tourist destination, where you will find locals most friendly, travel very cheap and food incredibly tasty. Now is the time to visit before the masses discover it.

India

A few days earlier we had reached India at Chennai, then sailed around to Kochi, leaving the cruise ship behind for a tour inland to New Delhi and Agra before reaching the Taj Mahal.

We expected to see massive amounts of needy people, but what we saw intrigued us. After leaving the big cities and traveling to the outskirts, we saw smiling faces, children playing, and very little begging. The children were running beside our bus to wave to us, or to sell us something. Of course there is poverty but there is development transforming this country.

I met one Indian man that had a herd of cattle and he would take his cows to different paddocks. The cows would eat the weeds and then do their business on the fields. The manure helped to feed the ground. The guy would sleep right there with the animals, the farmers would pay him, then head off to another farmer's field to do the same for them.

Mumbai

We witnessed an impressive business in Mumbai, a hot lunch delivery service network using dabbawalas. You may have seen this story on the news, or in the movie *The Lunchbox*. Traditionally, when husbands head off to work, their wives would prepare special meals for them to enjoy for lunch. She would then put the lunch container outside her door in the morning for a dabbawalas to pick up, put on a train, bus, rickshaw or bicycle transferring it up to five or six times, then have it delivered to the husband's office right before noon.

When the husband finishes his lunch, he places the container outside his office door and it would be cleaned and brought back to the wife in the late afternoon. They are also used by commercial meal suppliers in Mumbai, who pay dabbawalas to ferry lunchboxes with ready-cooked meals from central kitchens to customers and back. The remarkable thing about this service is that it is provided for millions every day, and it's mostly performed by illiterate and sometimes disabled people. And the cost is only about eight dollars per month for deliveries six days a week. President Clinton went there to see how the system works and the director of the company explained he could only meet the President after 5 pm, ensuring first that all the deliveries were completed for the day.

Agra

When we finally reached our destination at Agra, our group checked-in to the five-star hotel, Oberoi, with a great view of the Taj Mahal from our room. Our group gathered after lunch at Agra Fort and made our way, along with hundreds and hundreds of people, through the gates and to the Taj. It's a fascinating place. The locals get in free and the tourists are hounded by guides wanting to give you a special tour. The sunset was remarkable. The jewels that used to cover the walls of the buildings have long been stolen by past invaders. I am not convinced that Mumtaz Mahal, the favorite wife of Shah Janan (who built the tomb), is still in the tomb. The guides have different answers if indeed she was ever there or not.

We were offered an opportunity to see the Taj again the following morning and we jumped at the chance. At 6:00 am sharp, we headed through the gate and took off running because it is still a hike before reaching the Taj. We arrived and had the entire grounds to ourselves. The energy was completely different than the busy day before – even magical. I just stood and watched, as the sun was rising and was looking for the perfect photo spot. An Indian man rushed over and gestured for us to follow him. I don't know why we did, but I guess we felt he was a trustworthy soul. He took us up three sets of stairs in an adjacent building and pointed to get our cameras ready. I wondered at that point if he was going to steal our cameras or if we were in for a treat. The sun rose through the windows of the Taj Mahal right towards were we were standing, illuminating the entire tomb as though the gods were smiling on it. It was truly spectacular. If you ever get a chance to go, you really need to try to get there first thing in the morning, free from the masses.

Bali, Indonesia

In 2002, a year after the first devastating bombings, the Indonesian government decided to try and get back tourists by offering very cheap package deals.

We paid $999 per person for ten days in three different five-star resorts, including flight from Vancouver. We jumped at it. As we were checking in at the airport, the lady said, *"OK, I can give you the boarding passes for the first two legs, you will get the others later."* What? Others? Yep, you guessed it, it was a multi stop flight, four airports and 36 hours later we landed in Bali. When we had cleared customs, I ripped up our return tickets and threw them in the garbage. I purchased a more direct flight back later that week. Sometimes when it sounds too good to be true, it can be. So, check the fine print when purchasing a deal of the century. Apart from that experience, the trip was spectacular.

Bali is a very peaceful place. One thing I observed is that few locals drank alcohol, or sold alcohol except at hotels. Indonesia is largely a Muslim country and drinking is frowned upon. We loved the three different hotels and, while walking around the hotel grounds, we noticed all these very tiny temples where locals would come to pray. We were told that although the hotel owner may own the land, they have to respect and build around established family temples, including when developing property, golf courses and beachfronts.

When you go to Bali, the monkey forest is a must for all animal lovers. I can't say that my husband would have gone if I hadn't insisted he go with me. You are greeted a block away from the forested area and given instructions on how to feed the monkeys. They suggested I only have a few peanuts in my hand, but not in my pockets. My husband hid the bag and we headed into the trees. This is not a zoo with fences or gates. As soon as I arrived I saw dozens of monkeys and I headed over to some tiny baby ones. They were the size of my hand. So cute! I held out my offering of peanuts and they didn't get within a foot of me before a group of adult monkeys pounced and took all the goodies. I chuckled and asked Ralph if he got any pictures. I reached into his buttoned-up shirt to get some more nuts, then bam! The adult monkeys saw where the stash of peanuts were and they mobbed poor Ralph. (Oh, was I supposed to be helping him, not laughing my head off? Oops, my bad!)

Thailand

Bangkok is a modern city with pockets of great history. We had an unforgettable dinner at the Sirocco Restaurant and Sky Bar on top of a huge skyscraper, with fantastic views of the whole city and a band that played dance music till the wee hours.

This is a popular destination because the movie, *Hangover 2*, was filmed there, and that is the entire premise of their marketing campaign. You have to make reservations way ahead of time. Our concierge at our hotel was able to get us a table, when normally they are full.

Cambodia

We spent a week exploring all the newly discovered temples that had been covered over by nature. Centuries before, kings would build temples to expand their power and wealth. Over time these kingdoms crumbled from years of neglect but were just recently rediscovered by some of best archaeologists in the world, unearthing these treasures and rehabilitating them for historical and commercial benefits. I highly recommend young archaeologists come visit or volunteer here.

We also almost got caught in a major sand storm one afternoon. I glanced up while in one of the temples. I pointed and asked our private guide what was that in the distance. He said something in his language and then turned to us and shouted to run. We bolted to the parking lot, jumped into the van and boom! A loud noise surrounded the area and a sand storm hit the van hard. We were excited and a little scared at the same time, Indiana Jones style (in fact it was filmed there). All we could see were other tourists scrambling with their umbrellas to shield themselves from the blasting sand. I am sure they were exfoliated by the time they found cover.

Being a white woman, I was stared at when walking around town alone, but I never felt threatened or uneasy. It is a relatively inexpensive place to tour. The tuk-tuks are readily available to ride to any temple or shop. Hostels and beer are very cheap according to loads of backpackers we met. Of all the other countries in the region, I would say Cambodia was my favorite. It is a very young country, in that many of its elderly were killed in the war. Our guide explained to us that the only reason he survived the genocide was that he would go home to his family farm during university break. Working on the land gave him darker skin which gave the ruling Khmer Rouge the impression he was a farm worker and not an academic. If you were pale, wore glasses or read books you likely wouldn't have survived fifty years ago in Cambodia.

Vietnam

Hanoi was surprisingly one of my favorite cities in the region. We got up at five in morning to get some exercise, as it is so humid and hot later in the day. We left our hotel, turned the corner, and bam! I was astonished with the hundreds of older people who were also out at this early hour, all exercising. They were doing Tai Chi, playing badminton, ballroom dancing, jogging and doing yoga, but my favorite was a large group of mature woman "dirty dancing". I had a smile on my face every morning and couldn't wait to wake up early to join them.

From Hanoi, we drove a four-hour trek to board a small but very comfortable cruise ship from Ha Long Bay. The drive was long and uninteresting, so I highly recommend taking a flight from Hanoi instead. The three day cruise around the bay islands was magical, very relaxing. My husband scored me some great pearl jewelry from the small vendors who would row alongside the small cruise ships in their tiny junks brimming with goods, and bargains.

The Philippines

We were invited to a birthday bash in Manila for our neighbor who lives there part-time and works with politicians in the Philippines. The party was at our friend's restaurant in Manila, and we all got dolled-up and enjoyed mingling with the friends and family we knew. I had no idea who most of the others were, but I chatted with them just as easily. Our table included a group of interesting people, including former President Ramos and a lady who was about to throw her hat into the ring to run for presidency. Ramos was a charming man who laughed easily and we chatted like old friends. The other lady only had one thing on her mind and that was trying to get the President's attention and support.

A few days later, we boarded a small plane and headed for a group of small islands called El Nido Resorts to the south. It's one of those resorts you can imagine like in Fiji or Bora Bora. Our cabana hung out over the water with fish that swam up to take bread from our hand. There were fabulous hiking trails and kayaking around the island, snorkeling, diving and remote beaches nearby.

Dinner was at 8 pm for all guests and one night was Earth Hour around the world. Candles by the dozens were lit and great acoustic musicians played during dinner. In pure darkness, we headed back to our villa and decided to go skinny-dipping while everyone was still at dinner. We stripped down and dove in. And then boom! Flashlights lit up the lagoon, and security men came running out from everywhere to tell us to get out of the water quickly. We got our naked butts out and scampered off to our hut. We had been all over this small island for two days and not seen more than a couple of security people. They must have been very discrete, as now we realised everything was being monitored, the reason being that pirates and kidnappers were active in the region. It all seemed so peaceful until we realized the potential danger around us. A few months later there was a kidnapping on another island resort where two Canadians were eventually killed. So, remember you may feel very safe in tranquil parts of the world, but you have to always take precautions.

Japan

Japanese have always played a large part in our business success, something we will always be grateful for. Vancouver is a popular destination for many to study, work or to holiday and we have met so many amazing Japanese people who will always be in our hearts.

One business trip took us to Osaka, and I got lost (nothing surprising about that). I was holding out my map and a man approached me. He didn't speak English, so I just showed him the hotel address and he signaled me to follow him. We walked six blocks to the front of my hotel, we bowed and he left. I watched him walk away from the hotel in the direction where we came from and figured he went way out of his way, just to help me out.

Another time after landing in Tokyo, we were greeted by a dozen student alumni at the airport. They guided us on the train and accompanied us to our hotel. We thanked them and agreed to meet them later for drinks. We napped, and headed out for dinner and while we were walking through the lobby, we recognized all of them, some sleeping on chairs. They spent the whole day there in case we needed something. That pretty much explains the dedication of Japanese people.

A client treated us to dinner at a lovely restaurant one night, the kind where you choose your live lobster from the tank. The chef delivered the platter to us, and it was very beautifully presented. I reached out for a piece with my chopsticks and suddenly, the partially detached lobster's claw grabbed it. I screamed… this was not my kind of fresh sushi.

On another visit to Japan for the soccer World Cup 2002, we were on a train heading to a game, when my husband got very excited and whispered to me: "That's Bobby Charlton sitting there." He is a soccer legend from England's 1966 World Cup win. I, of course, had no idea who that was. He and his wife were in the seats on the other side of the aisle, so I got up and introduced myself and told him that my husband was a huge fan. Ralph had bought some World Cup programs for his brothers and we asked him to sign them, all while having a pleasant conversation. Others on the train soon realized who we were talking to and Bobby got flooded with fans asking for photos or autographs. We chuckled when the others were asked to sit down by the conductor.

In Japan, the stadiums were built miles outside of the big cities. We were told that all the small hotels around those stadiums for World Cup would be full and not to even attempt to find a room. But we packed an overnight bag and decided to take a chance. We took the two-hour train ride from Osaka and went searching for a place to stay. I went into the first small hotel we came to, while my husband waited outside. I used my limited Japanese and pointed to the exotic pictures of the rooms on the wall. Some had a cross over them. I used gestures to communicate to the lady behind the counter that I would like a room, but she shook her head to say no! This same thing happened at the next two hotels. My husband went into the next and he came out a minute later saying we had a room. The woman indicated to us that we could leave our bags with her, and that the room would be ready after the game was over. We headed over to the stadium and saw the longest line from the entrance that I have ever seen. It was at least a kilometer long. So, we went back to the village bar for a drink and lunch to wait for the line to shorten.

The game was great but we were hot and exhausted after it. We headed back to our local hotel, while everyone else waited for the two-hour, standing room only train back to Osaka. We entered our room at the little hotel and went into a fit of laughter. It was a bright red room, lots of plastic, no windows, and a big round bed with a package of condoms on each pillow. It had a mirrored ceiling and a large Jacuzzi. Yep, this was a love hotel! No wonder it wasn't available until late. I don't know how much sleep we got, but we had a good laugh and we slept with our clothes on.

Out of all countries in Asia, I feel Japan is the safest. When you go, you must try the bullet trains between cities. They are fast, comfortable and reliable. And try the box lunches. You have never seen such attention to detail in making these boxes so perfect. I still crave them.

As in most Asian countries, get into the habit of bowing to people you meet; it's a simple way of showing respect. When you hand them a business card, hold out your card facing them using both hands, and when you receive one, take it with both hands and read it out loud staying their full name and their job title. For example "Mr. Natamashi, General Manager." Never put their business card in your back pocket directly, this can be seen as disrespectful. You should always greet the most important person of the group first. When traveling there, try to pack a few gifts from back home for the special people that you may meet and make sure they are wrapped nicely. The same rule applies to giving and receiving gifts, use two hands. Usually you would not open the gift right then. Japanese take great pride in the wrapping of gifts, so admiring the package is a nice thing to do. We were at a Starbucks in Tokyo enjoying a leisurely morning coffee where I watched a sales lady wrap a coffee gift box for what seemed like an hour. It was painful for me to watch. I would have wrapped 50 boxes in the time she took for one, just not as neatly.

South Korea

While in Seoul on business, one of our new agents, took us out for a traditional Korean dinner. We sat on our knees on the floor for the entire dinner. He never explained it was going to be twenty-one long courses, so I politely ate the first few dishes and then I was full. My husband plugged through all the courses. A meal we would never forget.

Being vegetarians can be challenging in Korea. One night we were walking around looking for a place for dinner and there was an English sign that said "Pizza." We sat down and ordered a vegetarian one. When she brought it over, we saw it was covered in bacon. We tried to explain no animals. She tried to convince us this was bacon, and not meat!

But the story I love to tell Koreans is about another time in Seoul. We were walking aimlessly around looking for a place to eat amongst alleys of shops and homes on both sides. We walked past a window and saw two tables of people eating bibimbap, a traditional Korean dish, and there was one table open. This dish is a must try in any Korean restaurant. We entered and asked the little old lady, through body language and basic Korean, if we could sit and have the same as the other guests were eating. She giggled and pointed to the table. We addressed the other guests with a smile. And they often looked our way and smiled back. After dinner, we did the *"pay the bill"* sign language and she shook her head to say no. One of the other guests who spoke a little English explained that this was their home, not a restaurant. We all laughed ourselves to tears. We had just walked into a family's home and ate their dinner.

Shopping for clothes in Korea for a 5' 7" woman was impossible. In Itaewon, Seoul, they have this amazing market that made the most beautiful suits for women, and men. I was a size ten back then and every time I pointed to a suit, the clerk would say: *"No, you too big!"* I started getting a complex about being a size ten, and left empty handed. Even as I walked near another store I could hear, *"Too big!"*

Now it is our standard joke…*"No, you too big!"* But if you are a petite woman, Korea is a great place to shop or have custom clothes made.

Koreans are amongst the most loyal, honest people we know and we are lucky to have many friends there.

Hong Kong

I was attending a trade show in Hong Kong for the education industry, and asked my mom to join me. Those were the days before China took it back in 1997. We had so much fun shopping at the night markets where we bought so many things at such cheap prices. While I was working all day, Mom would be out taking over the town. I have this memorable photo of our hotel room covered with everything we bought, and we had to buy several suitcases to take it all home. Those were also the days when airlines didn't charge you much for extra bags. Hong Kong is not the bargain capital of Asia anymore, so be prepared to spend a lot of money while shopping there.

One evening while in Hong Kong my mom and I headed out in search of an authentic Chinese dinner. We strolled around and came across a very short person (man or woman, I couldn't tell) who indicated there was a fine restaurant upstairs. We accompanied him/her up a small, dark elevator, where I figured we were in for a good adventure, or they would find our bodies one day. We got out of the elevator, entering a huge, very brightly-lit restaurant with at least 200 locals eating. We were shown to our table, but without an English menu and my Cantonese was basic. So, my mom got up and went around to other people's tables looking at what they were eating. Our waiter came over laughing and accompanied her around the tables while she pointed and ordered. The waiter brought her over to the lobster tank so she could choose the one she wanted, then she sat down with me. People were all smiling at us and probably saying something in Cantonese about the "crazy lady". Our waiter came up behind Mom with the live lobster in his hand to check it was the one she wanted, which is common in good restaurants. I saw him approaching but when she turned her head, seeing the live lobster at her eye level, she screamed! The waiter dropped the lobster and it ran for its life under tables. Well, now the whole restaurant was laughing. When all the food came, we could have fed a small village… and the lobster was amazing. Sorry little lobster, you gave it your best to escape!

In Hong Kong, they have a chain of Banana Leaf restaurants. They are a version of fast food places, but we loved the food. While making the naan (bread) as big as basketballs, they would slam it down loudly on the counter to pop it and cook them. The cooks loved scaring patrons with the sound. The prawn curry was amazing. My mouth is still watering talking about it. We ate there at least five times in the few days we were in Hong Kong.

The Middle East

Jerusalem, Israel

Many of us know that this is one of the most religious and embattled places on Earth, but to me it is the most fascinating. Nothing could have prepared me for all the energy there.

Traditionally there are four quarters in the Old City, the Christian Quarter. The Jewish Quarter. The Muslim Quarter. The Armenian Quarter. There are more and more Jewish living in the Muslim quarter, which is causing conflict, especially if a Muslim sells their property outside their faith.

Ladies, when you go the Middle Eastern countries, I suggest making sure your arms and legs are covered with the coolest of fabrics. Wear socks, because you need to take off your shoes before you enter temples, I suggest bringing a scarf for your head. Some female tourists don't do this, but I feel it is more respectful to do so.

The Western Wall, or the Wailing Wall as it is better known, was especially interesting. I could not give do justice in describing the auras and energies there. Guides suggested we have our prayers written out on very small pieces of paper before we went to the wall, as men went to one side and women to the other. We wrote many prayers for our family and friends and put them into to the wall. (I hope they all will come true for all of you.) As I was sticking the notes into cracks of the bricks in the wall, an elderly Jewish lady next to me started crying. Well, actually she was more than crying, wailing would be a better word. I turned to her and held out my arms and she collapsed into them. I held her and told her everything would be okay. I know she didn't speak English, but it was one of those situations where a woman just needed a friend to hold her. If the rest of the world would just hug a stranger for a few minutes, I am sure it would resolve a lot more issues than what our leaders do.

I found the "Steps of Jesus" on the Via Dolorosa to be intriguing. A couple of thousands of years ago, Jesus walked this path carrying his massively heavy cross, to which he would later be nailed. He leaned against a wall, which supposedly to this day, has left an impression of his hand, falling a number of times on this march to his death. I met some religious pilgrims from all over the world, who had saved up for their entire life to come to Jerusalem to touch the marble slab on which Jesus was laid to rest at the Church of the Holy Sepulchre. His exact path in this city is still intact, with no obstructions after all these years. I asked our guides if these sites are the actual places and both guides sided that they probably aren't exact.

We watched a group of very young soldiers doing their mandatory military training in the Old City. And get this, after day one they are issued their gun. This is one of those places where you must pay attention all times, as tensions can run high. Really try to visit Jerusalem, ideally in peaceful times as you won't regret it.

As a treat, Ralph booked us into the King David Hotel overlooking the walls of Old Jerusalem. To my surprise, when we were checking in at the front desk, the receptionist made a call and the manager appeared to take us up to our room. My husband had told the hotel when making the reservation, that it was our anniversary, and requested an upgrade. (All we can do is ask right?) He took us to the top floor and presented us with the Royal Suite. It was a very large penthouse suite overlooking the entire city of Jerusalem. Spectacular vista! US President Obama stayed in this suite the week before, during his Middle-East peace talks. As we were checking out, I made sure to remind the staff that next time Obama comes, tell him that he is staying in the suite that Lori-Ann and Ralph stayed in!

The Dead Sea

A very unique place, but get there soon as it's evaporating and draining quickly. And no splashing, or you could spend a week in the hospital if you get the highly concentrated salt water in your eyes. It's recommended to first cover your body in healing sea mud that is in buckets on the shoreline, let that dry, then shower off. Then slowly enter the water up to your waist and gently lean back. You will be floating magically on of the buoyant water. But getting back up proved impossible, so Ralph had to push my legs down before I could stand up.

Masada

It is a fortress on a plateau that overlooks the Dead Sea, so plan your journey to see both places on the same day. The siege of Masada by the Roman Empire was the first significant Jewish–Roman battle. The Sicarii rebels and their families, living on the plateau in the remains of an old palace, could see the Romans coming, using Jewish slaves to build scaffolding to scale the fortress. As the Roman soldiers were getting closer and closer to the top, the rebels made a decision to kill each other and burn down the remnants of the palace, instead of surrendering to the Romans. Because of their religious beliefs, they couldn't commit suicide, so it is told that ten men killed all 960 of them but one, and he had to kill himself. It is an UNESCO heritage site now and a popular place for tourists.

River Jordan

Amongst other places, we took a private tour to the River Jordan, where Jesus was said to have been baptized. Even the guides admit they have suspicions that this is the actual place. My husband headed to the restroom while a group of people were heading down to the river, so I followed them. It turned out there was minister who performed baptisms there, so I waited my turn. The minister dipped my head into the River Jordan, and I was baptized just as my husband came over in search of me. I think he thought I had lost my mind or was instantly converted. I just felt it was a unique experience to claim I was baptized in the River Jordan.

We had two different drivers from very different backgrounds on our tours through the countryside and the towns, and it was interesting hearing their perspectives. Communities were very clearly demarked along religious lines, so when I told them that I have no idea what religion most of my friends or neighbors were, they just couldn't believe it. Bomb shelters or safety rooms are a must in all newly constructed developments, homes and apartments, just a fact of life here.

Turkey

I have incredible memories of Turkey and a couple ones I wish I could forget. The main reason Ralph wanted to go to Turkey, was that most Kiwis and Aussies, once in their lifetime, go on a patriotic pilgrimage to Gallipoli. It's a small town where the Allies fought a great battle with the Turks in the First World War. There is a beautiful plaque at the memorial in Gallipoli, likely written by their modern founder and war hero, Ataturk.

"Those heroes that shed their blood and lost their lives...You are now lying in the soil of a friendly country. Therefore rest in peace. There is no difference between the Johnnies and the Mehmets to us where they lie side by side here in this country of ours...You, the mothers who sent their sons from faraway countries, wipe away your tears; your sons are now lying in our bosom and are in peace. After having lost their lives on this land they have become our sons as well."

I think it gives sweet comfort to the families of all those that's served in wars and lost their lives fighting, many times so unnecessarily. Who would have thought that this solemn piece of land would come to represent so much to many people at the time? To Turkey, it was a defining moment in the country's history, from the crumbling Ottoman Empire to their war of independence. For Australia and New Zealand, it was the forming of their national identity, with the anniversary of their landings here being known as Anzac Day (April 25th), their Remembrance Day. On the 100th anniversary, so many Kiwis and Aussies wanted to go there, the government had to have a lottery to choose. They allowed 5000 people from Australia and 2000 from New Zealand.

Istanbul

We arrived in Istanbul by cruise ship, our final stop of our cruise. When we slipped into the harbor, we could see history unfolding before us. The incredible temples and buildings were awe inspiring. Our cruise allowed for another night aboard before our final disembarkment.

The one thing I wish I could forget was when we decided to walk to the market as it wasn't far from the ship. It was one of their national holidays and there were literally thousands of people out, mostly men. Getting a taxi was impossible, so we decided to walk. I instantly felt claustrophobic. We never even got close to the market, making our way through the people was an impossible and harrowing experience. We hustled back to the security and calm of our room on the ship.

Then, the next morning we were disembarking and we tried to get a taxi, but it was pandemonium. We finally got a taxi, put our luggage in the trunk and gave a driver our hotel address, he quoted a price, we got in and then he instantly doubled it. Ralph was livid, but I begged him to stay in the taxi and get us out of there. Our hotel was in the old city, and we expected the cabbie to know where it was. He had to stop ten times to ask people who all gave him different directions. We finally got to our hotel and I seriously never wanted to leave my room again. The lesson here is that we should have booked a driver from the cruise ship company or the hotel. Do not just arrive in a foreign land that has a language you don't speak and expect taxi drivers to understand you. I won't make that mistake ever again. Thank God for Uber.

That night, we met up with a good friend, Michelle who came from Hungary to meet up with us. Michelle and my husband promised to keep me safe, when they hired a walking guide to show us around. The tour was fine, except when he asked if we wanted to see some rugs to buy. I said *"No, I want to head back to the hotel"*. And then another guy comes out of a rug shop saying, *"Hey Vancouverites, I used to live there! Come in for a minute!"* Ralph decided to go in. As I am allergic to wool, I stayed out of the shop. A full twenty minutes later he was still in there, getting the hard push to buy something. (My husband is not good at haggling. One time in Mexico he spent ten minutes getting the price of a necklace down a few dollars and then gave him full price because the guy told him he had three kids to feed!)

I went to rescue him. A foolproof way to get out of a situation like that, was to say, *"Sorry, my wife is allergic to wool."*

The next day we got up early and headed out to see the major sites in the old city. The mosques are all active mosques, and all the tourists must vacate them a few times a day, so the locals can pray. The Blue Mosque is one of the most popular, so some of the crafty shopkeepers would lie to passing tourists that the mosque was closed, in an attempt to lure them into their store. They tried unsuccessfully with us.

That afternoon, Ralph took a private driver to Gallipoli, about a six hour drive each way from Istanbul. Michelle and I went to the Ayasofya Hamami Turkish bath and spa near the Blue Mosque.

Built in the 16th century it was one for the books. You really have to try this when you go there. It is like nothing I have ever experienced anywhere in the world. The inside is a large, open area, where women who work there are in full makeup while they are washing their client's hair, lathering up and scrubbing their naked bodies. After a short while you forget you are standing there naked with someone scrubbing your private parts. It was a three-hour event and we floated back to the hotel.

Cappadocia

Leaving Istanbul, we flew to Cappadocia, before driving to these amazing rock formations and the ancient underground village. Now, this place, is very cool. It is one of the "must-dos" if you go to Turkey. All the modern day hotels are built into the caved hillsides and carved out of rock. Historically, they were built this way to repel invading armies, when entire villages would retreat underground structures and blockade themselves.

I wouldn't recommend any specific cave hotel in Cappadocia, as there are so many incredible ones.

Our villa had an underground pool on the bottom level that Ralph almost dove head first into, but I stopped him in time, as it turned out to be two feet deep! The morning sunrise brought us the most remarkable sights of hot air balloons coming up over the hills. We would spot one, then another and another and then instantly a hundred of them. We were so amazed, we took a ride early the next morning, by far the most magical balloon experience ever.

Dubai, UAE

The Middle East was always a bit unnerving for me. We were there when The World Islands were being built on reclaimed land with an unbelievable number of five-star hotels and residences planned, designed on islands shaped like the world map. Massive amounts of sand were being pumped into the ocean, and workers working around the clock. I constantly had so much dust in my eyes from the construction.

Although I was told the shopping is great there, I never found any deals on anything, perhaps in the old markets. Every single sales person in every shop in the nearby mall was male. It was very weird to see them selling women's clothes and undergarments. I always try to be respectful of local customs by covering up my legs and arms as much as possible, but I still felt like I stood out like a sore thumb. When my husband was with me, there were no issues, but when I went shopping by myself, men would make a beeline for me, and casually bump into me. Ralph first thought it was my imagination. So, at the airport, as we were leaving, he sat at a coffee shop as I walked by, and sure enough I was bumped into twice in a minute! If you go there, women, be prepared for this. Get your elbows out.

An interesting thing about the women of the Middle East is dress protocol. Apparently when their child gets married, the mother gets first dibs at the choice of dress to wear at the wedding (and she may need at least 10 dresses for all the pre-wedding events). During fashion week in Paris, they flock there to make their choices. Some fashion houses have developed computer systems for these women, to ensure no one is wearing the same dress to the same event. And from what I was told, many would never wear the same dress twice. Ladies, I am a size 12, and take hand me downs!

Overall Dubai was an incredibly expensive city. A basic room in 2006 at the Four Seasons was over USD $1000 a night. We had lunch at the famous Burj Al-Arab hotel, where the bill was over $500 for the two of us for a couple seafood salads and two glasses of wine. But still worth the experience. Try to book a club level suites in hotels where the private lounges are the best in the world. Their complimentary buffets are of the finest foods and wines, so no need for you to dine anywhere else. Local businessmen would often come to the hotel club floors to drink and entertain their clients.

According to our client, if you are a foreigner living in Dubai over the age of 21, you can buy alcohol in Dubai's restaurants and licensed bars, and some sports clubs, for consumption on the premises. If you wish to drink at home you will need a liquor license; how much you are permitted to buy is dependent on your monthly salary and locals are not allowed to apply. A local can only drink alcohol at licensed locations, if their boss gives them a card giving them permission to do so.

South Pacific

Savusavu, Fiji

My husband had been to Fiji before, but I hadn't. It took us 38 hours door-to-door from Vancouver, but at least we had sleeping pods in business class on Air New Zealand. FYI, pay the extra amount if you can for an upgrade for these long hauls. This was the first airline I had been on where the staff make your seat into a flat bed with a soft mattress and sheets.

The intimate, luxury resort we stayed at, Emaho Sekawa, it is on my best resort list. Perched high on a hill on Fiji's second largest island, Vanua Levu, the resort is surrounded by hundreds of acres of pristine tropical rainforest, with breath-taking panoramic views of the ocean. We had a private villa with a pool, full staff, including a chef who prepared anything we wanted, as well as our own golf cart to take to the beach. We ate fantastic food that was all locally grown or caught.

This was the first time that our view was completely private. There was not one boat in sight and no one on the soft sandy beach, and not a plane in the sky, just peace and quiet. It was just the place to get away from everyone, write a book or just completely go off the grid.

I had forgotten a prescription back in Vancouver, so I asked our host to arrange for a doctor's appointment in town. A taxi took me to the medical clinic. The Fijian doctor was with three locals in his office. As I walked in, he jumped up quickly and told the other three to sit in the lounge. He waved me in with a big smile, asking me how he can help. I told him what I wanted, he handed me the prescription, and I thanked him, and left. Then he called the other three back in his office. I chuckled to myself. The pharmacy was next door, I walked in and there were five locals in front of me. I was in no rush, but the pharmacist told the locals to step aside and he served me first. I felt a little silly and apologized to the others. He filled my prescription, I paid and then he served the others.

The locals were all very friendly and genuine. The day before we were due to depart, the staff were crying to see us leaving. I was touched by their tears, as I know that they genuinely meant it.

There are more than 200 islands in Fiji, so check travel guides for the best place for your needs. This place was perfect for us because we wanted to just veg-out. But if you are more active, the activities were few and expensive. Also, alcohol is expensive on the small islands, so bring your wine from the main cities. Another lovely resort we popped by to see was Namale, Tony Robbins' Resort. I would definitely recommend this resort for honeymooners.

But try not to stay in Nadi, it is just a big touristy city with not a lot of appeal.

French Polynesia

Mo'orea and Bora Bora are both magical islands. Most people want to book the luxury huts over the water, which is what they have seen on TV, so most hotels have that. The Four Seasons on Bora Bora appears to be the most expensive and a favorite for the rich and famous.

But the exact same types of resorts on the Moorea Island, were much cheaper and less touristy. We did the underwater walk where they put a large heavy diving helmet on you, which is attached by an oxygen cord up to the boat. You walk around on the bottom of the ocean to feed the fish and play with manta rays. The other activity was the underwater bike, it's like your personal submarine. Both are real fun, but book early, and if you are not from a cruise ship, you may have to do it on another day, as their guests get first chance.

There is a restaurant called Bloody Mary's that is legendary on Bora Bora. They have lists of all the famous people that have been there. Go for a cold drink and be patient, the service is island slow.

New Zealand

We have been back to New Zealand many times, so one year we decided to send my mother, aunt and uncle as it was their anniversary. They landed safely in Auckland and then rented a car. We had made arrangements for them to stay the night at a friend of Ralph's, who ran a boutique vineyard hotel just south of Auckland. But when we called, our friend said they never arrived. We were a little worried, as my family had never driven on the other side of the road, had just gotten off a very long flight and were not seasoned international travelers. I decided to try the hotel in Wellington we had booked for them for their second night. I called the direct number of the hotel and my uncle answered the phone saying, *"Bucket Tree Lodge, can I help you?"* I burst out laughing recognizing my favorite Uncle Pete's telephone voice. I couldn't believe it. I asked him what the heck was he doing answering the main hotel line. Pete told me they had decided to drive all the way to Wellington that night, and as the hotel manager needed to go out, the manager asked if Pete could answer incoming hotel calls. They acted like it was just another day for them. Lesson learned: just because people are older than you, they can be just as spontaneous and adventurous as ever.

My favorite city in New Zealand is Queenstown. Such a pretty city and lots of things to do. If you are adventurous, try the Shotover Jet boat ride down the Shotover River Canyon. If I ever was to buy a place in New Zealand it would be here.

Australia

I went to Australia many years ago, and Ralph used to work in Australia, but coming back with money gave us a much different experience. The first adventure was trying to figure out how the rental car worked. At the Sydney airport, they upgraded us to a new Mercedes with the controls all on the steering wheel. It took us twenty minutes to get out of the parking stall. The other adventure was remembering to drive on the other side of the road. We left the airport and drove through Sydney on a very busy day. We were thirty minutes away from the airport and I was already frazzled. At one stage, traffic was so bad, I had thoughts of just getting out of the car and leaving it there. This is a lesson for all: if the nice car rental people want to upgrade you to a new, fancy car, then make them accompany you to the car and to show you how to use it.

Blue Mountains, NSW

My husband finally got us out of the city safe and sound, and we drove four hours up to the One and Only Resort in the Wolgan Valley, a 7000 acre reserve and resort. It is an old cattle ranch that has been transformed into a research center where the kangaroos and wombats can roam free, (as well as a few local spirits!). There were more than 5400 kangaroos on the property. The first morning we got up at sunrise to do a bike ride and you just can't imagine how many kangaroos we saw. It was like whack-a-mole. They just kept popping up from the long grass and then they popped down to eat some more.

An interesting thing about kangaroos is that the father teaches the boys to box, not the girls. When the son is good enough to beat the father, he is sent away to start his own family. If not, he stays with his parents. So, when you see a couple of them fighting, they could just be practicing. The other thing we were told, was that female kangaroos can halt a pregnancy up to two times if she is threatened or bad weather is ahead. She can also terminate the pregnancy at will. Ladies, who wouldn't want that?

Wombats have eyes on the sides of their heads, which means they can't see what's directly in front of them. Staff would pad tree trunks around the property because wombats are known to run head first into trees at high speed, if they are startled. Fortunately too, their skulls are very hard, and they are one of the very few marsupials that never stop growing. Perhaps their names comes from the sound it makes hitting an unpadded tree at high speed.

This is a remarkable place for animal enthusiasts or photographers, or to just get away for some quiet reflection, so it makes my top places list. Excursions are included and the chef's creations are some of the best we have ever tasted. Some drinks are complimentary. All the villas have their own private pool and bikes. Villa One is the quietest. They have larger two and three bedroom villas for families. Go with your kids as there is plenty for them to do, or just go by yourselves as it is very romantic.

Kangaroo Island, South Australia

It's funny that they call it that because I only saw one kangaroo, but a lot of wallabies. A friend later pointed out that it wasn't called "Kangaroos Island". Our flight arrived at dusk, and we were greeted by the General Manager before being driven an hour to the Southern Ocean Lodge. He had a night vision screen behind the steering wheel to watch out for nightlife on the road. We dodged dozens of animals on our journey that night.

The tours were included in the package at the Lodge, and we were brought to some amazing sites. One was at the Koala Reserve, and no, we shouldn't say "koala bears" because they are not a bear, and Aussies are sensitive if tourists call them that. They were called bears by the English explorers who thought they looked like a bear. Koalas are very picky about the kind of Eucalyptus leaves they eat, so special types are grown just for them. There are only six species of trees that they eat, but koalas are killing off these trees by eating all the leaves, so conservationists use nets to protect trees to allow them to grow back. Koalas sleep twenty hours a day, eat up to three hours a day and can mate up to an hour a day. The female will mate with a different male every year. But the sad part is that 90% of koalas have chlamydia, a sexually transmitted disease. This is making the females and males infertile and can cause blindness in the offspring. There is a new group on Kangaroo Island that have a less harmful strain than the mainland koalas, and are being bred to help the population survive.

If you are a history buff, Kangaroo Island is the place for you. There have been countless shipwrecks around the island. Each room at the lodge was named after a specific shipwreck. Normally this would not interest me, but a history book that was in our room was dog-eared to our room's namesake. Turns out the captain of the ship that crashed there, has a great-grandson living in Vancouver, and the great-grandson was invited to the island for the recent anniversary of the shipwreck. Small world once again. Shipwreck and treasure hunters head there as well. It's a popular place for long hikes or bike rides.

The self-serve open bar at the Southern Ocean Lodge gets my award for best bar in the world. There was every kind of alcohol you could want. The wine cellar has a magnificent collection of Australian wines and is open to guests to make their own selection. It's perfect for couples, but there's not a lot to do for younger kids at the hotel, apart from the excursions. The Osprey Pavilion room is the best.

Where to Next?

So for all of you, figure out what is the one thing you do not want to compromise on, and what are the things that are not that important. Value for my money… I will stick with Walmart shoes, while sipping on champagne in first-class. What's yours? If you don't travel first class, your children likely will!

'Two priests going on vacation to Hawaii were determined to make this a real vacation by not wearing anything that would identify them as clergy. As soon as the plane landed they headed for a store and bought some really outrageous shorts, shirts, sandals, sunglasses, etc.

The next morning they went to the beach dressed in their "tourist" garb They were sitting on beach chairs, enjoying a drink, the sunshine and the scenery when a "drop dead gorgeous" blonde in a bikini came walking straight towards them. They couldn't help but stare.

As the blonde passed them she smiled and said "Good Morning, Father ~ Good Morning, Father," nodding and addressing each of them individually, then she passed on by. They were both stunned.

How in the world did she know they were priests? So the next day, they went back to the store and bought even more outrageous outfits. These were so loud you could hear them before you even saw them! Once again, in their new attire, they settled down in their chairs to enjoy the sunshine. After a little while, the same gorgeous blonde, wearing a different colored bikini, taking her sweet time, came walking toward them. Again she nodded at each of them, saying "Good morning, Father ~ Good morning, Father," and started to walk away.

One of the priests couldn't stand it any longer and said, "Just a minute, young lady." "Yes, Father?"

"We are priests and proud of it, but I have to know, how in the world do you know we are priests, dressed as we are?" She replied, "Father, it's me, Sister Margaret."'

—Anonymous

Attention
Wanderlusts

VACATIONING

If you are trying to decide what kind of vacation is right for you and your family, here are some tips.

All Inclusive Vacations:

Choose a Five-Star Resort

There is a huge difference between a three, four or five-star all-inclusive resorts, especially with the food and service. There are also a few six-star resorts, but we couldn't tell the difference. Always take the five-star property if you can afford it, even if you book the cheapest room. When you arrive, politely as possible ask for a free upgraded room, or the difference in cost of a better room, as you may be pleasantly surprised. Share with reception what special occasion you are celebrating, and that you wish to surprise your spouse. Upgrades work better in the low season, and in prime weeks, you may not have an option to upgrade without paying.

We have never gone back to the same resort as we like change. Besides hotels change names and ownership so often, it's challenging knowing if the experience will be the same.

Call the Hotel Directly Before You Book

I have adopted the habit of calling the hotel directly, not the 1-800 number, to see if they or other properties around them have construction during my dates. I can't tell you how many times a holiday has been tarnished because of loud construction noise going on nearby.

Kid's Club or Nightclub

Check before you book to see if they have a kid's club, should you have wee ones, so you can have a break too. Or book an adult-only property if you don't want children around. Check to see if they have performances at night or if they have a nightclub. If they don't, the village may be a ghost town after 9 pm.

Don't Take the Free Airport Shuttle

All-inclusive packages usually include a shuttle bus pickup and drop off at the airport. The driver will have to wait to make sure they have all their guests before the bus leaves the airport. That can mean you could be waiting a while, possibly for other flights to land before you depart. And then there may be other hotels where they need to drop guests off, before they get to yours. My suggestion is to pre-order a driver directly from the hotel. It will cost you, but you get there fast and will be showered and on the beach before the people on the bus arrive. This also gives you an opportunity to get a pick of a better room in a less stressful situation.

The same goes for when you leave. The bus will be picking up guests as early as four hours ahead of the flight time. They again, may pick up at other hotels and then arrive at the airport three hours ahead of flights. The check-in counters are crazy three hours before a flight in resort towns. But two hours before the flight there is usually a much shorter line up. We get a driver or a taxi from the hotel to get there two hours ahead of departure time. Resort planes rarely leave right on time, so check before you leave your hotel if there are any delays.

Book a Half-Day Rate

Resorts are also happy for you to pay for a half-day rate if your flight is arriving in the early morning, or leaving late at night, should you prefer a room on arrival or a stay later for a last-minute shower. Nice hotels will sometimes do this for free so always ask.

Take the Excursions, but Stay Overnight

Even though we may be part of an all-inclusive package, we sometimes search for excursion packages that include a luxury hotel close to an attraction. I know you may think that paying for two hotel rooms for the same night is silly, but when you get a chance to enjoy something so magical, after the crowds have gone, it is so worth it. We like to check with TripAdvisor before booking any tour.

One excursion I will always remember was a tour from Cancun, Mexico to Chichén Itza, a pre-Columbian city built by the Maya people. We wanted a night away from the masses of tourists, so booked the hotel right outside the walls of the ruins, where we could experience the grounds with fewer people around. Like everyone else, we arrived hot and sweaty from a long, bumpy bus ride, but we were able relax at our four-star hotel which had a great pool.

We entered the Chichén Itza grounds and I immediately felt at home. When they were handing out maps of the grounds I felt I had been there before and told my husband I would be his guide. I even found a secret passageway that only a few people were in at the time.

While the day tour gathered for their long hot bus ride back to Cancun, we showered and relaxed by our pool until nightfall. The hotel offered a fabulous dinner after which we returned to the ruins for a spectacular evening light show and an intimate story of its history. There were only about twenty of us on a relaxing night with soft music and a star-lit sky. We arranged with the tour company to collect us on the next day's return bus.

Timeshares

Another ploy that all-inclusive resorts do is try to get your hard-earned money by selling you a timeshare. They will usually get your attention by saying that you will get a free dinner cruise, or an excursion if you come to a presentation. My husband and I did this at the first all-inclusive we stayed at. They said it would take an hour, but 90 minutes later, they were not even close to finishing. When I said we were leaving, they got very aggressive, so we just left. We didn't even get our free dinner cruise. Watch out for these timeshares, while the sign-ups may be cheap, your monthly maintenance fees can add up very quickly to a costly investment. Also, trying to get out of the deal you just signed can be costly.

One year we took a group of our students to Mexico for a week. One of the students, Minako, would go to a timeshare meeting every morning. After the presentation, she would just say *"Sorry, no English!"* She would get her bonus voucher and be on her way. She did a different free activity every day, just by going to a different timeshare company each time.

Renting a Fully Staffed Private House:

I have also booked private, fully staffed houses around the world. Here are some things to keep in mind when looking for one.

Check for Nearby Walks

One place we stayed turned out to be on a rock cliff, so we had to take a taxi to go for a morning walk. We had been to Mexico and the Caribbean many times and always had a nice beach to walk or run on, so we assumed private houses that stated water view would be the same. Hotels and villas can sometimes be a little deceptive about their access or location, and some are known to inject overly glowing reviews on travel sites.

Make Sure the Kitchen Is Separate

Another house we rented had the kitchen in the middle of the open-plan living area, great when we were alone, but with little privacy from the staff. It was much better in another villa where the kitchen was closed off from the main room by a door. Most fully staffed houses will have a chef, maid, pool guy, host, ground keeper, sometimes security, so decide in advance how much you want them around. We would often tell the staff to take the next day off, and prepare meals in advance, which they love as they still get paid.

Check Your Place for Privacy

One place we stayed was located at the bottom of a hill, so all the houses above us looked down into ours. Ask in advance, if the neighboring house is attached to yours, and if it is a rental or someone regularly lives there. Some may be right on the other side of a wall, with smokers, or have loud parties or young children. I prefer stand-alone properties. We once rented a villa when our private pool was under construction, and the owner never told us. If TV and music is important to you, then make sure your home has free fast Wi-Fi, simple controls and English channels.

Bring Cash

The best part of a private staffed rental property is that they can do all the grocery shopping for you. You select the menu items and what drinks you want. They (host, property manager, or staff) will shop, prepare and serve you three meals a day and happily provide cocktails for you at any time, depending on the attention you want. The cost of the food and drinks need to be reimbursed to the staff and they usually expect cash. We were surprised to find out that staff meals were also part of our grocery costs, and staff were expecting a tip at the end of our stay, so clarify in advance. Of course, you can give one amount to the host, or separate them if someone did something above and beyond for you. Private houses are not as cheap as an all-inclusive hotel when you add up all the costs for one couple, but they are great for a quiet vacation or for a big group.

Cruising Tips:

I have been on more than a dozen cruises and each time I came away with a different experience. People who have not cruised, have asked me what kind of ship is best to take. I have been on big ships, small all-inclusive luxury ships, party ships, ship relocations, brand new ships and everything in between. I have heard comments from friends like, *"I would feel claustrophobic"*, *"Cruising is just for old people"* or *"I would be bored."* To those who have never cruised before, I assure you, there is a cruise ship and itinerary out there that is perfect for your needs. Here is how you can find the best one for you.

Itinerary Considerations:

When choosing where you want to go, see if you will need a visa for those countries. Check where the ship stops and if you have to take a long bus ride or a tender to the areas of interests. Keep in mind, the ship can change itinerary at any time without notifying you in advance, due to weather, political unrest or ship maintenance issues. Consider safety, length of travel, comfort, connections, companions, language, culture, interests and budget.

Choose the Right Fit

Bigger ships (3000 to 5000 people) allow for more onboard adventures with more choices of dining, although specialty restaurants charge a surcharge. They all have casinos, spas and shops on board. There are games and presentations by day, shows in the evening and you may find nightclubs and late-night entertainment a lot of fun. The bigger ships have things like bowling, rock climbing, glass blowing and golf driving ranges, with some activities costing extra. These ships will have the whole gamut of guests aboard. There will be the wealthy people who book the big suites, which provide a private restaurant or bar and sometimes their own pool and deck. And there will be the guests who spend hardly anything on the inside cabins. There will usually be a lot of children aboard but the kids usually have their own area to hang out in, as well as special food. If you are social and want to meet others, young and old, and plan to do many onboard activities, then the big ships are for you. The bigger ships will have singles events for those traveling alone. The bigger ships cannot always moor right at the pier, so you may have to get on a tender to shuttle back and forth. If you are traveling with someone who has mobility issues, they may not be able to get off the ship at those ports.

Smaller, all-inclusive ships (200 to 400 people) are for a very different demographic and more personal. The guests are usually older and wealthier, some say more refined. Their rooms are mostly suites, so the price will be a lot higher. We met and got to know some very interesting people that we may not have met on the big ships, the reason being you recognize each other more often. The entertainment is limited, the nightlife usually quieter. Personalized, specialized tours, having fine food and wine and service along tranquil vistas are what these ships provide best. The benefit on this kind of cruise is that all food, most alcohol and the excursions are all included. The staff on these ships have worked their way up the ladder, so service is very good and you get to know each other better. They cater to people with mobility issues and have attentive doctors aboard in case of emergencies. So, if you want some down time to relax, this is the cruise for you.

Mid-range ships (1000 to 2000 people) can be a happy medium. They will still have a few restaurants to choose from and nightly entertainment. These are usually older ships so you may get a good deal on a cruise like this. This is particularly the case with large groups they will give you a better deal on booking a few rooms. The energy of a ship like this is dependent on what kind of guests are on board. They can be action party cruises, or a quiet relaxed cruise.

Booking last minute can be a great deal if your schedule is flexible. The cruise companies want to leave port with as many people aboard as possible. They want the bars making more drink sales, the spas giving more massages and the casino taking more chips. Book with the same cruise company for your next cruise. Many cruise lines have merged together, so booking their group of ships can give you long term advantages such as free upgrades, free perks, priority boarding, priority excursions, and priority dining options. You may even be invited to the Captain's table for dinner.

If you are a recovering alcoholic, most ships have a friends of Bill W. (A.A.) meeting nightly, so check for those that do. All ships will have a medical clinic on board. If you are traveling with infants, check that babysitters are available. If you have teenagers, check to see if they have a teen club. They are fun for the kids and a relief for parents. Ask the age of a ship and if it has undergone renovations recently. I like to take the newer ships (less than 10 years old) as the room décor is more to my liking. They also have more amenities on newer ships. More ships are catering for the single and the specialty traveler.

Choosing Your Room

The big suites should be booked well in advance. They are much more expensive than a regular room, but they are the first ones to sell out on every ship. Always book a balcony room if you can. Some of the older ships still have inside cabins with no view and little fresh air. Some rooms sleep more than two people if you are traveling with small children, and many have adjoining rooms for older children. If you plan on doing a lot of activities and not spending a lot of time in your room, then book the cheaper rooms.

Special needs: If you are traveling with people who have mobility issues, try and book a suite near the main restaurant. It can be a very long way to the other side of the ship for them. If you have someone in your group that suffers from sea sickness, book a room in the middle of the ship. If you are a smoker, you will not be able to smoke in your stateroom or on your balcony, but most ships have a designated smoking area, so try to book a room near there.

Book "Must Do" Excursions in Advance

Seasoned travelers know to do this in advance of their cruise, so they don't spend time waiting in line to book after boarding. As an option to organized excursions, you can just walk off and grab a taxi or private driver to show you around. This is what we do a lot as we don't like buses full of tourists, as it seems like there is one person who is always late getting back to the bus and making everyone wait.

An option is to team up with other people and hire your own van and tour, so you can negotiate the price with the driver. Bring local currency with you, and depending where you are sailing to, most people take either US or Euro notes. Some ports do not have a place to change money, so I usually get the local currency before I leave on my holiday at a better rate. You must always carry identification as well as your room card any time you are off the ship. You may need both to get back on. In case of emergencies, bring your insurance card, copy of your passport and a credit card with you. I have seen many people taken away by ambulance while in port so it's better to just be prepared. If you do not make it back to the ship at the time of departure you may have the chance to meet it at their next port of call. But make sure you call the cruise company immediately to let them know.

Don't Rush to Check-In

When beginning your cruise, do not try to embark early. It is always a nut-house for the first two hours. Please listen to me and do not, no matter how excited you are, head to the embarkation area early. If you wait until hour three, you will cruise (get it!) through all the check points. The first guests that get checked in cannot go to their cabins yet, as the rooms are still being serviced from the passengers who just disembarked. The early boarders will be directed to the buffet or to the bar and must wait until their room and luggage is ready. In the meantime, your luggage tagged bags (with the tags sent to you before the cruise) are on their way from the port to your room, a process that can take hours. Do not put medicine in your checked bag, just in case they misplace it. Your luggage may not be delivered to your cabin until after dinner, I suggest packing a carry-on bag for the afternoon on deck, and even dinner clothes. You may be able to bring your own luggage on, but it is a pain.

When On Board

You will have a choice of dining at the buffet, room service or the main dining room (with or without other guests at your table). You can always request another table if you are not happy with a big group or just want a quieter dinner. If you book the early seating, there will be kids at dinner. You can also book the specialty restaurants for an extra cost, and this should be done ahead of time or they may be full. We prefer to bring formal clothes for a few nights. Not everyone does, and you don't have to, but how often do you have the chance to get all dolled-up for dinner and a show?

The best lobster I had was made table-side on the cruise ship Celebrity Solstice, at their French restaurant. Every time I ordered it, they made it perfectly. They told me their secret ingredients were creamy Dijon mustard and Parmesan cheese, adding shallots, garlic and capers. Bacon was optional. They tossed in the shelled lobster tail and turned it a few times. In less than a minute it was cooked and they served it over mashed potatoes. The chef at this restaurant was a Michelin star winner, but regulations for that award state it cannot be given to a cruise ship for some reason. If you find yourself on this ship, you have to try it.

My most lobster at one sitting was when we were cruising to Alaska and first met our dinner table-mates, Ken and Michelle. The guys enjoyed their mashed potatoes, so every dinner they tried to outdo each other by ordering and consuming huge plates of potatoes. I got in on the fun on lobster night. I ended up eating ten small lobster tails because you can order as many as you like.

The drinks aboard can be very expensive, so buy a drink package if you plan on drinking a lot. The good wines in the restaurants are not included in most drink packages. The kid's bottomless drink packages is great if they like a lot of juice or pop. Don't bring your own alcohol onboard as it will be confiscated, including while in port, as you are scanned every time you come back. You may be allowed to bring very limited wine or champagne at the beginning but will likely be charged a corkage fee. Contact the Food and Beverage Manager ahead of time if you have something special, as our friends do each time. There are onboard duty free stores, but items will only be ready for pick up on your last night or the morning of your last day. The shops and the casino will be closed most days the ship is in port.

Every night you will be given the next day's activities schedule. You can do as many as you like, or none at all. I sent my uncle, aunt, and mother on a cruise to Alaska one summer. They never saw my aunt all day because she would be running from one activity to the next.

If you want to get dolled up with the help of the spa services, book early as "at sea" days are their busiest. The last full day of your cruise is when the shops put most items on sale, so be patient. Tipping can be a big part of the cost of your trip. Some cruise lines offer a standard tipping amount that you can pay before you board. If you are booking the suites, you might still feel the need to tip your butler and housekeeper more, if they have been exceptional.

On the last night of the cruise, you will be asked to pack up and leave your luggage outside your cabin with your departure tags attached. Then you can pick them up the next morning, after you clear customs. Bringing your own luggage off is your choice but it's not easy. You will be asked what time you would like to disembark. The advantage of having one of the earlier disembarkation times is that there will be plenty of taxis to get you to where you need to go. The advantage of a later time is that you can have a leisurely breakfast and enjoy the deck for a while longer. Once while traveling in the big room, we chose to be the last ones off and by then, the immigration staff had already left. We just picked up our luggage and jumped into a taxi. You can just imagine how happy that made me.

When you consider the cost and time it takes to fly and taxi into every city you visit, compared to simply cruising into their ports, you can see how much more value you receive arriving by ship. It's worth it just for the convenience of not having to pack and unpack each time you go to another place.

Less time with security, immigration control, traffic, hotels and negotiating prices, less of the un-fun things and more fun things. An inside cabin beats flying economy any day. If you think that cruising is not for you, then you have not cruised. Once you experience how comfortable and exciting it can be, you will be hooked.

Getting Tickets to Events Around the World:

Getting access to any major event is fairly easy, even for sold-out venues. Here are some tips:

You will quickly spot ticket resellers as they are the ones near the venue, asking if you are selling tickets. British scalpers usually corner the market, and travel around for the big events, so you can negotiate in English. Many travel in teams, so they may all be working with each other. The further you are from the venue, the higher the price will be. Play the scalpers off each other, *"I have a better price from that guy over there."*

Carry cash and be gutsy enough to negotiate. Keep your money in different pockets, so when you agree on a price, it doesn't look like you have a lot of cash on you. You are always taking a chance dealing with scalpers but I have never been sold a fake ticket here or overseas. One way to feel better is to photo ID the scalper with the tickets. If he refuses, don't buy from him. If a person wants you to go somewhere with them to discuss the tickets away from the venue, don't go.

When you buy from a website you will pay a premium. Retail or street brokers use tactics like advertising front row tickets for $1000, when they may not yet have them. Some are just putting out feelers to test demand. Some, will first ask you for the price range and type of seats you want before seeking out tickets, which means you may or may not get the exact ones you want. Always ask them if they already have the tickets and to show you.

Bring your own map of the venue, to see where exactly seats are located, as some sellers can mislead you about the exact location. We bought row A for one event, when there ended up being five rows ahead of us, AA, BB etc.

The soccer World Cup in Germany in 2002 was the first time a promoter insisted that buyers showed their name and matching ID on the ticket to enter the venues. Ultimately, ID matching didn't happen and was just a ploy to discourage reselling. It would be a nightmare to have checked 60,000 IDs for every game. In recent World Cups, the fan zones have turned out to be more fun and a way cheaper way to watch the game, than actually going to the stadium.

Waiting until the starting time of the event, or shortly after, gets you a better price. If tickets are scarce, be prepared to buy single tickets near each other, ideally one seat in front of the other, as singles are usually cheaper. Once in, you may even get others nearby to swap seats, or check for no-shows. Remember to pack light for events, so you can get through security faster. With sporting events, if the host country or the hometown favorite are not in the event, you can get tickets at a great price. Even if your team is not in the game, it still is an experience of a lifetime.

Travel Checklist:

Make sure you always have travel insurance, which pays out claims promptly. A well-known insurer is better, as you may have to pay upfront for medical costs.

Check the weather forecast of your destination and pack accordingly. If a major weather system is approaching your destination, be prepared to change your plans. You do not want to be stranded without a return flight home.

Make sure passports are still good for at least six more months. If you get sick or injured you may be in that country for much longer than expected and you cannot be there with an expired passport. If you have more than one passport, always enter and leave with the same passport. Border guards get very suspicious if you don't have an entry stamp when you leaving.

Double check if you, or your travel mates, need a visa for any destination or port of call.

Make sure your vaccination shots are up to date.

Always verify if your flight has any stops before your final destination.

Scan copies of your passports and credit cards, both front and back, and email them to yourself.

If you have children or significant assets, make sure your Will, Executor and Power of Attorney are all set up.

Try to be at your destination during a full moon for your long walks on the beach.

Pack your bag, then take five things out.

Bring a few small gifts or souvenirs of your country for the people you are going to meet.

Travel with carry-on luggage only whenever possible, but do not take any large bottles of liquid.

Dress nicely and politely ask the check-in person if you can get an upgrade. You will be surprised how much power the check-in people have, and sometimes how little it costs to get into a better seat.

Make sure your medicine is in your carry-on bag and is in its original packaging as it may be considered suspicious.

Medicinal liquids are in addition to the standard maximum liquids allowed.

There are great gadgets available that you can put in your luggage to track where it is.

Ideally fly direct, or use the same airline to minimize issues with connections, issues such as having to collect luggage, clearing customs or security, and having to change terminals. Before buying any duty-free alcohol while transferring flights, check you do not require a further security check as you may have to leave it behind.

Going on a long bike trek? Carry as few things as possible, especially heavy things. Carry a GPS and a satellite phone, and make sure someone knows where you are at all times. Download your maps and data in case you lose signal. Calculate riding times, roadwork and be prepared for worst-case-scenario. If you can afford it, stay in hotels or motels instead of camping, if time is a priority. Use puncture proof tires and reliable equipment. Bring sunscreen, bug spray, thermals, a rain poncho, even an umbrella or cover for those prairie thunderstorms. And always water, water.

Sally's tip is *"Always travel with Lori-Ann. She stays at the best places!"* And most importantly, if your dream is to really do an adventure like this, start making your plans now, because there will never be a more perfect time to do it!

'There was a little old lady from a small town in America who had to go to Texas. She was amazed at the size of her hotel and her suite. She went into the huge cafe and said to the waitress, who took her order for a cup of coffee, that she had never before seen anything as big as the hotel or her suite. "Everything's big in Texas ma'am," said the waitress. The coffee came in the biggest cup the old lady had ever seen. "I told you, ma'am, that everything is big in Texas," said the waitress.
On her way back to her suite, the old lady got lost in the vast corridors. She opened the door of a darkened room and fell into an enormous swimming pool. "Please!" she screamed. "Don't flush it!"

—*Anonymous*

My Top Vacation Picks and Their Sales Pitches:

Over time, some of these resorts may change ownership or quality. I receive no benefit by recommending these places, other than sharing the joy we experienced there.

Norwegian Pearl Cruise Ship
The Haven - Reserve Either One of the Two 3-Bedroom Garden Villas

"*These amazing Norwegian Pearl Villas have three separate bedrooms, and each bedroom has a luxury bath. They have a living room, dining room and incredible private garden with a hot tub. There is also a private large courtyard area. The suite includes butler and concierge service.*"
Total Approx. Size: 4252 sq. ft. Balcony Size: 1675 sq. ft.
www.ncl.com/ca/en/cruise-ship/pearl/staterooms/The-Haven

Toronto, Ontario, Canada
Ritz Carlton - Reserve the Ritz Carlton Suite (if it is just the two of you)

"*In the heart of downtown Toronto, amid sports arenas, performing arts centres and the vibrant Wellington Street scene, the sleek glass façade of The Ritz-Carlton, Toronto is a beacon of both beauty and luxury. Inside, décor invokes nature through modern materials, and is complemented by a collection of art from across Canada. The appeal goes beyond the surface with 5-star amenities.*"
www.ritzcarlton.com/en/hotels/canada/toronto/rooms-suites/the-ritz
-carlton-suite

Vernon, B.C., Canada
Sparkling Hill Resort - Reserve the Top Penthouse

"*Adorned in crystals and situated on top of a granite bluff overlooking Lake Okanagan sits Sparkling Hill Resort, a modern oasis of well-being. This is one of the premier destination spa resorts in the world. Sweeping scenes from our Mountain View and Lake View rooms allow guests to fully take in the awe-inspiring landscape of the Okanagan, while Peak Fine Restaurant serves inspired farm-to-table options, making Sparkling Hill Resort a true escape*

from the stresses of the modern world. Mr. Andreas Altmayer from Swarovski in Austria was the Chief Crystal Architect who placed and designed 3.5 million Swarovski crystals that dance within our walls."
www.sparklinghill.com/penthouse-suites

Valcartier, Québec, Canada
Hôtel de Glacé - Room Themes and Designs Change Every Year
   "Located only 4 km from the north end of Québec City, the Hôtel de Glace is a must-see attraction to discover every winter. The only Hôtel de Glace in America has seduced over a million people around the world since its opening in 2001. With huge snow vaults, crystalline ice sculptures, 44 rooms and suites, the Hôtel de Glace impresses by its dazzling decor."
www.valcartier.com/en/accommodations/ice-hotel

Santa Rosa, California, USA
Safari West - Book the Hillside King Suite at the Far End
   "Discover wildest Africa in the heart of wine country! At Safari West, every day means adventure as we journey out in search of herds of wildebeest, romping rhinos and towering giraffes. From ring-tailed lemurs to the dazzling zebra, nearly 1,000 animals from over 90 unique species roam through our 400-acre preserve."
www.safariwest.com

Cancun, Mexico
Haven Riviera, Cancun - Book the Presidential Suite
   "An oceanfront sanctuary of luxury and sophistication awaits you at Haven Riviera Cancun, an adults-only, all-inclusive resort located between Cancun and Riviera Maya. Escape to an exclusive realm of style, glamour and seclusion, where you will feel as if a tiny sliver of Mexico coastline has been reserved just for you."
www.havenresorts.com

Puerto Vallarta, Mexico
<u>Vallarta Penthouse Suite</u>
This is a private rental penthouse. It is a spectacular place right on the beach. It takes a lot to wow me, and this place did in a major way. It has huge glass walls that open up to let in the ocean breeze. It's great for groups. The lobby is stunning and is perfect for any kind of celebration. There are turtles hatching and horseback riding right at your doorstep. One of the biggest pools I have ever seen is on the ground level. Vendors on the beach cannot bother you here. Shops and restaurants are a short walk on the road. A supermarket is a couple blocks away. The low season, if you enjoy quiet time, is October. You pay extra for air-conditioning.
www.vallartapenthouse.com

Oberwesel, Germany
<u>Schönburg Hotel Castle - Reserve any river view room on the upper floor for the best view</u>
"Schönburg Castle was first mentioned in history between the years 911 and 1166. Until the 17th Century, the castle had a very changeable and martial history with many tribe and family fights. From the 12th Century, the Dukes of Schönburg ruled over the town of Oberwesel and had also the right to levy customs on the Rhine River. Schönburg Castle was one of the very few medieval castles in which after a duke's death, all of the sons became heirs to the castle and not only the oldest one, which usually was customary at that time. At the height of its power in the 14th Century, Schönburg Castle accommodated up to 250 persons of 24 families at the same time."
www.hotel-schoenburg.com

Santa Teresa, Costa Rica
<u>Latitude 10 Resort - Reserve Villa 1</u>
"Latitude 10 is located on the Nicoya Peninsula of the Pacific Coast of Costa Rica, just outside the small town of Santa Teresa. It is known worldwide for being one of the best surfing spots in Costa Rica with a variety of world-class breaks offering ideal surf conditions throughout the year. Here you can experience the diverse wildlife while you share with people from different cultures and

countries. Even though Santa Teresa is a small town, it offers a great variety of restaurants, bars, shops, activities, pristine beaches and spectacular sunsets." www.latitude10resort.com

Machu Picchu, Peru
Belmond Sanctuary Lodge - Reserve any of the view balcony suites

"Belmond Sanctuary Lodge is the only hotel located adjacent to the mystifying ancient Inca citadel. As the only Machu Picchu hotel, it offers its guests exceptionally easy access from early morning to late afternoon. This is an ideal time to explore when most of the day visitors and buses have left. Sit out on a terrace and savor Peruvian cuisine based on produce grown on the Lodge's own plot. This delightful hideaway is the perfect place to relax and unwind in the shadow of the Lost City." www.belmond.com/sanctuary-lodge-machu-picchu

Santa Cruz, Galapagos Islands, Ecuador
The Royal Palm Galapagos - Reserve any renovated villa

"This is a secluded hide-a-way nestled in the lush Miconia highland forests of Santa Cruz in the heart of the Galapagos. The Royal Palm is a spacious and exclusive 156 hectare (386 acres) private estate, only a 20-minute drive from the bustling port town of Puerto Ayora. With just eight casitas and thirteen exclusive villas, our guests can enjoy privacy, space and quiet seclusion." www.royalpalmgalapagos.com

Chiang Mai, Thailand
Dhara Dhevi Hotel - Reserve a villa with a private pool

"The luxury resort's design draws heavily from the architectural and cultural influences of the historic Lanna Kingdom. The Dhara Dhevi Chiang Mai offers some of the world's most spacious accommodations available in the world, from our beautiful setting to our acclaimed restaurants and outstanding spa." www.dharadhevi.com

Jerusalem, Israel
King David Hotel — Reserve the Royal Suite
"The King David Jerusalem Hotel, one of the world's legendary hotels, is a major landmark in a unique city. Blending the past and the refinement of the ancient world, the King David Hotel is unquestionably the most famous of all of Jerusalem's hotels.

Superbly located on an elevated site, the King David Jerusalem Hotel offers incomparable views of the walls, the minarets and the domes of the Old City. Only a 15-minute walk from the King David Jerusalem hotel lies the Old City in all of its splendor. There is a view of the entire old city." www3.danhotels.com/JerusalemHotels/KingDavidJerusalemHotel

Savusavu, Fiji
Emaho Resort — Reserve the Villa Emaho
"When you simply do not wish to be found, when you need to escape and unwind, there is no better place to disappear than Emaho Sekawa. Wake up in the morning to the sound of waves, whistling birds and magical rain forest. This unique location makes Emaho Sekawa different from any resort in Fiji. It is an ideal base camp from which to explore both ocean and rainforest, while getting to know the authentic, traditional Fiji. Experience the world's "hidden paradise" while being wrapped in luxury and romance. Emaho Sekawa is a 5-star all inclusive, private, tropical haven — Fiji's most unique resort, and the ultimate in tropical luxury."
www.emahofiji.com

Namale – Tony Robbins' Resort
"Namale's beautiful location, unique luxury accommodations, world-class dining, and array of activities and adventures make it truly unparalleled among the best Fiji resorts. Located just outside of Savusavu, Namale is one of the only Fiji 5 star resorts in the North, offering guests an absolutely unique experience focused on luxury and leisure combined with exposure to the rich local culture and natural beauty. From our unique bure design to our inventive Indo-Fijian cuisine, the Namale experience presents travelers with a truly authentically Fijian trip of a lifetime. A favorite among celebrities and high-profile guests,

Namale is honored to be among the best Fiji resorts for its exclusivity, gorgeous tropical seclusion, and array of premium offerings."
www.namalefiji.com

Vancouver Island, Canada
Clayoquot Wilderness Resort – Prefer Ensuite 1 or 2 & Mountaintop Private Helicopter Campsite
"A luxury tented safari on the edge of the world, in the heart of the glorious wild. Experience authentic luxury, bespoke adventure and restorative escape at a remote, turn-of-the-century-inspired outpost defined by great white canvas prospector tents and anticipatory attention to comfort, service, sustenance, and transformative fun. Experience luxury gone wild, truly, Vancouver Island, British Columbia, Canada"
https://wildretreat.com

Agra, India
The Oberon Amarvilas Agra – Any room facing the Taj Mahal
"Only one of the Agra hotels to offer uninterrupted views of the Taj Mahal from each of its rooms. Relive the era of Emperors and Princes with a stunning display of fountains, terraced lawns, reflection pools and pavilions. Enjoy a romantic dinner overlooking the resort's lush gardens, water bodies and the spectacular Taj Mahal in silhouette."
www.oberoihotels.com/hotels-in-agra-amarvilas-resort

Palawan, Philippines
El Nido Resorts, Lagen Island – Water Cottage
"Palawan is an archipelago of 1,780 islands on the western part of the Philippines. It has the most concentration of islands but is the most sparsely populated region in the country. Because of its scenic landscapes and high bio-diversity, Palawan is known as "The Last Ecological Frontier of the Philippines. The northern part of Palawan province is blessed with crystal-clear waters, pristine beaches, and a wealth of flora and fauna. It is here that El Nido and Taytay, home of the lovely El Nido Resorts, are located. Spectacular ancient

limestone cliffs tower over marine sanctuaries teeming with innumerable species of tropical fish and coral, as well as five species of endangered sea turtles. Lush forests abound with more than 100 species of birds. It is a truly exotic destination."
www.elnidoresorts.com

Wolgan Valley, Australia
One and Only Resort — All suites are private villas
"This is a scenic 2.5-hour drive from Sydney, located on Australia's Great Dividing Range between the Wollemi National Park and the Gardens of Stone National Park, within the World Heritage-listed Greater Blue Mountains. The resort itself only occupies one percent of its own 7,000-acre conservancy. Steep cliffs contrast with the gentle curve of the valley floor and a picturesque road winds along the river to reach the resort on the eastern end."
www.oneandonlyresorts.com/one-and-only-wolgan-valley-australia

Kangaroo Island, Australia
Southern Ocean Lodge — Reserve the Remarkable or the Osprey Suite
"Southern Ocean Lodge is Australia's first true luxury lodge, offering a unique and exclusive travel experience on Kangaroo Island in South Australia. Floating atop a secluded cliff on a rugged stretch of coast, the lodge commands peerless views of the wild Southern Ocean and pristine Kangaroo Island wilderness. Sensitive, intimate and sophisticated, Southern Ocean Lodge is a sanctuary of refined comfort and luxury, Kangaroo Island style."
www.southernoceanlodge.com.au

'Three New Zealanders and three Aussies are traveling by train to a cricket match at the World Cup in England. At the station, the three Aussies each buy a ticket and watch as the three New Zealanders buy just one ticket between them. "How are the three of you going to travel on only one ticket?" asks one of the Aussies.

"Watch and learn," answers one of the New Zealanders. They all board the train. The Aussies take their respective seats but all three New Zealanders cram into a toilet and close the door behind them. Shortly after the train has departed, the conductor comes around collecting tickets. He knocks on the toilet door and says, "Ticket please." The door opens just a crack and a single arm emerges with a ticket in hand. The conductor takes it and moves on. The Aussies see this and agree it was quite a clever idea. So after the game, they decide to copy the New Zealanders on the return trip and save some money. When they get to the station, they buy a single ticket for the return trip. To their astonishment, the New Zealanders don't buy a ticket at all!! "How are you going to travel without a ticket?" says one perplexed Aussie.

"Watch and learn," answers a New Zealander. When they board the train the three Aussies cram into a toilet and soon after the three New Zealanders cram into another nearby. The train departs. Shortly afterwards, one of the New Zealanders leaves the toilet and walks over to the toilet where the Aussies are hiding. He knocks on the door and says, "Ticket please."'

—Anonymous

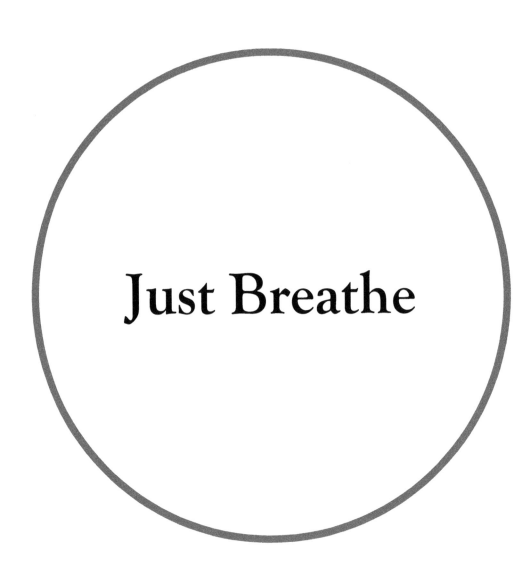

Just Breathe

MEDITATION: WHAT WORKS FOR ME

"If every eight year old was taught meditation, we would eliminate violence in the world within one generation."

The Dalai Lama

Meeting a Monk

While living in West Vancouver, a new neighbor moved in. We noticed a couple of times a week, there would be many people arriving and going over to his house. They were usually carrying a plate of food or gifts, so we just thought they had a big family or they were having Tupperware parties. Then one lovely summer day, my husband, Elvis and I were going for a walk barefoot on our street, as we often like to do. A man from the house waved and we waved back.

He came down to the street and walked with us. We had a lovely walk and chat and thought he was just a content Chinese man. He remarked that he doesn't see many people walking barefoot in Vancouver, and was pleased to see us connecting with the Earth. I told him the story about a time while walking down the street barefoot, that a snake slithered between Ralph's feet, over mine, and then between my dog's feet before disappearing into the wild grass. He smiled at this story and nodded, knowingly.

We often held block parties at our house, so we invited him and his brother, who lived with him, to the party. We all had a great time and lots of laughs. He had an easy sense of humor and laughed easily. It turned out he is a very enlightened soul, H.H. Rimay Gyalten Sogdzin Rinpoche from Tibet.

His story tells when he was born and as he grew up, he showed signs of having a pure mind. When he was old enough to talk, he told his parents that he was a reincarnated monk and wished to return to the monastery. They brought him to the place he described and he knew the moment he arrived, he was meant to be there. He was later called on by his spiritual leader to trek across Tibet and the Himalayas to Nepal alone, bringing only the clothes and shoes he wore, surviving on snow and whatever food he was offered.

At the end of his journey Rinpoche met a Canadian who knew of him, and offered his home in West Vancouver to the monk as a present. (I know, right!)

All the people that we saw coming to his house were actually bringing offerings. Rinpoche never shopped for anything. He spent his time praying and meditating with his followers and as an offering, his followers brought him what he needed, like food, eye glasses, household supplies, clothes, etc. If he didn't have food in the house, he just went without. Of course, since I heard this, I would bring him meals on the days he didn't have his meditation sessions. He often went for hikes in the woods behind our house with Ralph. Rinpoche spoke of dragons he encountered on his journey in the Tibetan mountains. He explained to us, he was meant to come to Canada to build a meditation temple here. Apparently, there are certain places on Earth that have very special energy and British Columbia is one.

He would explain to us how he has to disguise himself when he travels to China or Hong Kong because if the authorities recognized him, they may threaten him. We watched the documentary of his journey *Call It Karma* and it is just incredible. When the Dalai Lama comes to Vancouver, Rinpoche is often with him. A few years ago he chose to sell his home in West Vancouver, so he could raise money to rebuild Tibet after a big earthquake that destroyed many buildings and temples. As of now he is still working on building his temple retreat here in the Lower Mainland.

Meditation is a daily practice for me. I feel meditation helped me survive through some very hard times. The more I meditate, the clearer things in my life become. As I meditate, I see my body staying healthy. I am rarely ever sick. If I see someone in my life having a hard time, my suggestion to them is to meditate.

I am sure you have heard from more than one source that meditation is very good for the mind, body and soul. What you may not have clicked onto yet, is that it's actually the most important skill that you can acquire. The purpose of meditation is to get both sides of the brain and the body balanced. When this happens, other things in your life fall into order. You may sleep better or concentrate better. You can heal your own body, have more patience and problem solve better. You'll experience less stress on a day-to-day basis and overall lead a happier life.

Some people may mistake meditation for prayer. Prayer, for me, is when you are asking for help or an outcome. Meditation is when you clear your mind, and be still so your body is more prepared to deal with what is going on in your life. I highly suggest you teach your kids from a very young age to do this.

Some Easy & Essential Tips to Incorporate Meditation into Your Daily Routine

For self-meditation: This is the technique I use that works best for me. Take a few minutes to get your body ready for meditation. When you wake up, when you go to bed at night, while having a bath or in your parked car, the first thing you can do is:

Lie down, or lean back
Rest your arms freely by your side with your palms facing up and your fingers relaxed
Legs slightly parted with feet falling open
Close your eyes and bring your attention to your breath
Slowly breathe in through your nose as long as you can
Hold your breath as long as you can
Then exhale slowly through your mouth as long as you can, making sure all air is out
Repeat this five times

Now you are ready to start with this simple meditation:

> *Visualize white light coming in as you breathe in through the nose.*
> *Then hold your breath, while seeing the white light going all through*
> *your body.*
> *It may get held on a place in your body that needs it, so let the light*
> *stay there.*
> *Then gently blow out through the mouth, visualizing smoke exiting your*
> *mouth, pushing every bit of air out.*

The reason I use this method is I picture the part of my body that needs attention. If you have a bad back, then send the white light to your back. Imagine the pain dissolving and new, stronger parts being formed. Then blow the ashes of your pain out through your mouth. See your stronger, healthier back and imagine what life is like for you with a healthy back.

Your pain may be a headache, PMS, a cold, allergies, a sprain or anything. Visualize the white light omitting bright energy into the area of the body you are feeling discomfort. Then visualize the discomfort dissolving into ash. Then blow the ash out of your body more and more until there is no air left. Rest for a few breaths and repeat. I find that if I am focusing on the white light and then the ash, I can focus and continue longer.

If you are breathing in and your mind wanders, don't punish yourself. Become the observer. Just push the thoughts gently out of your mind and focus back on your breath. You are not trying to get rid of your thoughts, you are trying to detach from them. I have been through hypnosis sessions with different facilitators using basically this same practice. If the mind focuses on one thing it can stay calmer longer.

Zoning out is not the goal of meditation. Sometimes in meditation you get to the point of zoning out where you are almost semi-conscious. This is very similar to the state you enter just before you fall asleep; that unaware, half-awake time. Meditation is about being completely in the moment. Like a good physical exercise program, meditation takes practice. The more you do it, the easier it comes.

For beginners, my suggestion is to stay with the same method for at least twelve weeks.

I have been meditating for most of my adult life. I can get to Level 4 or 5 fairly easily, but I am looking forward to the higher levels. This is the best description I have compiled to understand the levels:

Level 1. Developing a regular schedule. We establish a practice to free ourselves from anxieties, troubles and thoughts. To do this you need to remain still. You calm your mind and breathe. In this stage, you may spend more time being distracted than being able to focus on meditating. Be patient with yourself. You may find it easier to do short meditations several times a day, rather than longer periods.

Level 2. Overcoming mind-wandering. Most of your meditation session you still have distraction, but you can sometimes hold the object of concentration for two minutes or more, before your mind wanders. During this stage, you should be concentrating on your breathing and only be trying to not let your mind wander.

Level 3. Extended Meditation. By now, the majority of your time is spent engaged with the process and you are not having to try so hard to keep your mind still.

Level 4. Transcendental consciousness where the mind is in complete silence. While you still may experience periods of agitation, you can now hold the object of meditation over longer periods of time - between five to ten minutes at one time.

Level 5. Cosmic Consciousness. You stay in the state that the mind is clear and your ego is not there. In Level 5, you can now meditate for an entire session without your concentration being disrupted.

Level 6. Unity Consciousness. In this stage, you will be able to meditate the instant you sit down. It is the point where that the heart opens up and finds beauty in everything.

Level 7. Looking inward rather than outward is this final stage. You are able to concentrate on an object of meditation for any length of time without any effort.

There Is No Time Like the Present

In my opinion, the purpose of practicing meditation throughout your life is to go to deeper levels to be able to look at life in a different light. Some say, that as they meditate, they can solve challenges easier because the mind is free. I often meditated when I came home from work. I would park the car, and just take a few minutes to unwind and cleanse my body of the stresses I may have had that day. Then I'd meditate again before I go to sleep. So right now, do me and yourself a favor. Put this book down and go to a quiet spot. Close your eyes, take in a very deep breath through your nose and hold it in as long as possible. Then slowly blow out through your mouth and push the air completely out.

Do this three times. On your next breath, breathe in white light and put that light to somewhere in your body (or someone else's if you feel they need healing light). As you hold the breath in, just focus the white energy on that area. Then as you blow out, visualize ashes being blown out because the white light has dissolved away what you no longer need in your body.

Four Simple Things to Instantly Stop Worry

When we worry about someone or something, that worry manifests itself as negative energy into the universe. You are actually harming that person, when you worry about them. When I was taught to surround myself or others with colors of light, instead of worrying, it instantly changed my life. The reason is that it makes me feel like I am actually doing something to help them, rather than feeling helpless.

> *White light is for pure energy protection*
> *Gold light is for help, and self-power*
> *Green light is for healing and prosperity*
> *Purple light is for strength*

So, if you are worried about yourself or someone else, visualize healthy, happy and safe thoughts. Clear your mind of the "worst case" scenarios, they only are destructive for everyone involved. Every time someone is sick, injured, upset or passes away, I meditate and visualize that person with these colors around them:

"White light, gold light, green light, and purple light. White light, gold light, green light, purple light. White light, gold light, green light, purple light."

This is something I try to teach everyone in my life because it is also a shield you can use for yourself or to protect others. If you are going to meet your boss, a client, going for surgery, taking a trip, giving birth or anything that is out of your comfort zone, visualizing these shields around you will make you feel more confident and strong. I have visualized these colors around my car while driving, my helicopter I am flying and even the airplane I am on. You can have more control of your own destiny by meditating with these colors or by just being mindful of using them daily.

Remember, whatever you put out into the universe comes true. If you are worrying about getting sick, you may get sick, because that's all the universe heard. If you tell yourself you will stay healthy, and see yourself in your mind's eye staying healthy, you will.

Meditate with the Masters:

My husband and I have taken sessions with different meditation gurus and have received something out of all of them. One weekend session was with a guru who was known to be able to meditate at Level 7. When we meditated with him, he would assist us to higher and higher levels.

At one full-day session, our instructor brought in spirits from the other side to assist us with our meditation. We were careful not to shake hands or touch each other while in the room as we could transfer energy. My husband and I sat in the back row. When we were meditating during the first session, I knew I was going deep. I didn't know how deep however, we were just clearing our minds. I saw and felt this powerful white energy pouring into my torso, then three faces appeared in my mind's eye. They looked like they were wearing masks with no expression. I would describe them as spirits, not human. When our facilitator asked what we experienced, I described my session as being pushed back out of my chair from their energy with images were so clear that I could draw them.

I discovered our instructor knew who they were and he was very excited they appeared to me. They were guides from the other side. I was very excited because I knew I had gone into a deeper level. Later that same day, the guru brought in an archangel named Jophiel. Apparently, we can call upon her when we are searching for something in life like love, a job, your health, and she actually appears. Most people in the room that day saw her during meditation, but they all had a different description of her. Some called her a young girl, some said they saw an older woman and it was fascinating to hear everyone's experience.

> *'The Zen Master is visiting New York City from Tibet.*
> *He goes up to a hot dog vendor and says, "Make me one*
> *with everything."*
> *The hot dog vendor fixes a hot dog and hands it to the Zen*
> *Master, who pays with a $20 bill.*
> *The vendor puts the bill in the cash box and closes it.*
> *"Where's my change?" asks the Zen Master.*
> *The vendor responds, "Change must come from within."'*
> —*Anonymous*

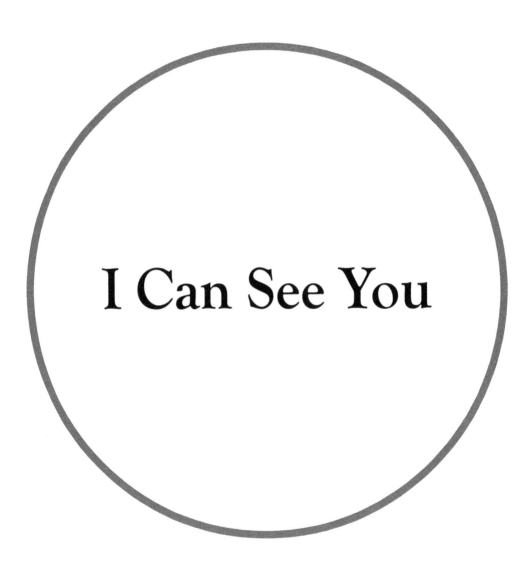

I Can See You

THE SECRET ART
OF VISUALIZING

"To accomplish great things we must first dream, then visualize, then plan...believe...act!"
                                        —*Alfred A. Montapert*

I have no idea how I adapted the technique of visualization, but as soon as I leave my house to go somewhere, I visualize the parking spot I want. Ralph and my friends just take it for granted now, when I conveniently find one. As soon as I am at the block away from Costco, someone will be pulling out of the perfect park or a space is unoccupied. Some may say this is a waste of energy just for parking spots, but it makes my life so much easier. Before I leave for the airport, I visualize an easy check-in. I spend a lot of energy visualizing a fast passage through all immigration lines. I visualize the price of things all the time, and it is amazing how often I get that price.

When Ralph and I went for a few weeks on our Santorini trip, we only booked a hotel for the first night. I kept saying to my husband that I had a certain place in mind and when I see it, I will know. We lugged our bags over the cobblestones to dozens of small hotels all over Thira. Then we came across a particular hotel. I walked through the gate and it was exactly what I had envisioned. Don't ask me where the picture in my head came from, but this was exactly it. The owner showed me two suites and the second was the one I had visualized, and I mean down to the type of bed and the view.

Call this what you will, but as everyone who has read the book *The Secret* has learned, whatever you put out to the universe, is what you get back. The important information here is that all your visualizations and your vocabulary must be in the positive vernacular. Phrases like *"I don't want to screw up"* or *"I hope this doesn't happen"* will not help you with your goals. Thoughts must always be in the affirmative form like *"I know I will do well"* or *"I know I can do this"*. If you accept whatever you put out to the universe comes back to you, then be very careful to avoid putting negative things out there.

I had a friend who was always worried about getting sick before big events. Well, you can imagine if that is what he visualizes in his mind, then that is what happens. He would constantly say, *"Oh, I hope I don't get sick."*

If the universe hears *"Get sick"* then that's what you will get.

If you say to yourself, *"I will be very healthy"* then that is what the universe hears. Ralph and I still help each other out if one of us is using the negative form of a statement.

At our annual staff retreat day, we encouraged out team to write down their personal yearly goals. We kept them individually sealed in the office safe and returned them a year later at the next retreat. I loved hearing the success stories they shared, some that were goals they thought they had forgotten and yet intuitively achieved.

Put Pictures to Your Dreams

We keep goals and bucket lists out in the open, so we regularly see them. It is amazing what opportunities can come from keeping things on your mind. I constantly suggested to all my team to put the things they are visualizing as their screen saver. It means they are constantly reminded of their goals, and it is amazing how many of them came to fruition. When we wanted to adopt a rescue Husky puppy, I had a picture of one on my computer. When we finally did find our little guy, he was ten weeks old and almost an exact match to the photo on my screen.

Take a Course on Visualizing and Anchoring

Tony Robbins is a master of reinforcement. He works with a lot of pro athletes who may be off their game and with ones who just want to be better. Presidential candidates, actors and CEOs also have found his technique has made an impact on their careers. His key is to anchor yourself in your optimum state when you are at the top of your game. Replay it in your head, relive the experience, truly feel it, listen to the reinforcing sounds were around you in that moment. What are you wearing? What are you smelling? Then create a unique physical anchor when you are in the zone. It could be a unique clap, punch in the air, a pinch, etc. The more you visualize, the clearer it becomes in your mind. The more you anchor yourself in that optimum state, the more certain you can relive and recreate that moment anytime.

Hobbies

For example, if you want to improve your golf game, recall a perfect game or swing when you were on fire. Feel the club in your hand. Smell the nature around you. Hear the sounds around you. See your swing, feel the club hit the ball. See the ball land on the fairway or right in the hole. Now how do you feel? Then reinforce your anchor. Now, repeat this over and over. Do it when you are going to sleep at night or in the morning when you are heading to work. Visualize as you are driving to the golf course, and just as you are teeing-off. Remember, anchor yourself, so your body knows what it feels like to hit that shot again. And then when you actually do hit that perfect shot, anchor yourself immediately after that, reinforcing the moment. Then go through how you felt when you hit that shot. How did you stand? How did your body feel? Think over and over about what you did to hit that shot. Perform your anchor each time for success.

Job or Client Interviews

The same thing applies if you are looking for the perfect job. Relive a time when you nailed an interview or presentation and anchor that experience. Now see your interviewer. Imagine yourself feeling confident. Imagine the handshake. What are you wearing? What are the answers to the questions? Hear them say, *"You have the job"* or *"You have the contract."* Imagine reading your contract. See your business card in your hand. See your office in your head. See your paycheck. Hear yourself tell the people in your life that you got the job. Then anchor yourself. Then repeat every time you are heading to an interview or to meet with a client.

If you are a Procrastinator

Visualize how it feels to get things done early. How do you feel when you accomplish tasks early? What do others say to you? If you are someone who is constantly late, visualize how it would feel to arrive early being calm, relaxed and excited. Trust me, I remember how the pain of being late felt, so now I am always on time, which to me, means early. Even when I know the person I am meeting is usually late, I still show up early. A friend of ours invited us over for dinner at 7pm. We showed up at 7:01, and she were still in the shower! I will send her this book.

If You Want to Lose Weight

You see yourself as your ideal size or as you once were. Imagine what it feels like to have your clothes feel loose. Imagine what other people are saying to you about your new look. Then, when you are eating something healthy that supports your goals, use your anchor. Envision thriving on the whole, natural foods that you know you should be eating. See yourself in five years, ten years and twenty years with the success you are celebrating now.

Hypnotists use this programming method all the time, NLP (Neuro-Linguistic Programming). When they put you under, they will bring you back to a time where your programming started. I was taken back to a time when I was seven years old and was sent to my dad for the summer. He and his wife had no idea how to raise kids. I was always hungry at their house, because meals were at a certain time and snacks were not permitted. As a small child, I needed food throughout the day, not just at 8am, 1pm and 7pm. So, I started hiding snacks under my mattress. I can still recall those hunger pains. So when I get stressed, I crave junk food. I am still working on getting rid of those triggers to this day.

Before You Have a Glass of Water

Our friend Rinpoche, has confirmed many things I believe about visualization and manifestation. He agrees our energy can change water molecules, cooking with love can produce better tasting food, meditation creates peace and less crime, and simply by visualizing we can improve performance. There are many scientific research studies out there that also confirm this. If you bless a glass of water before you drink it, or even put a positive sign on your water dispenser, that says for example, *"healthy, reviving and clear"*, the water can actually change its structure. I didn't believe this at first, but there is proof.

Looking for "The One"

Dating today is far more complicated than it was years ago. My Danish grandfather told me about the perfect girl he had visualized in his mind when he headed out to a dance at the local hall at the age of eighteen. He said he would even know what she would be wearing and what she would say when he asked her to dance. He told me that when he saw my grandmother, he knew she was the one.

Nowadays, you can Google what people look like. You can see what job they have and what their hobbies are. There is nothing wrong with that, but it doesn't mean they would be perfect for you.

If you are in the right time of your life that you are looking for a partner to share your love with, make a list. Don't just write down everything you want in a partner, but everything they are not. Be as specific as you can in physical and personality qualities. You may want someone who has a great sense of humor, but not that he or she is a professional comedian that works all weekend and travels a lot. You may want someone who is rich, but not someone who works 80-hour weeks or is eighty years old. Or maybe you would?

See Your Dream Home

When my husband and I were searching for our next home, I had many specific desires. I had wanted to live in a downtown penthouse for as long as I can remember. But a very specific one. It had to have a large outdoor space. There needed to be unobstructed views of both sunrise and sunset. The building had to accept pets and have three car spaces, including for my 1929 Mercedes named Fritz. It had to have air-conditioning. Ralph wanted a gym and pool. I wanted a newer building with a good strata and management. When I told my real estate agent about my requirements he probably rolled his eyes. We toured every penthouse that was for sale and none of them fitted our requirements. We put in a couple of low-ball offers just to see if we would get a deal because we would have had to do major renovations to bring it up to our standard. ***And then it happened!*** I found a listing, and called my husband and my agent to go take a look. It was 99% of all our requirements. The only thing that didn't make it perfect was that we would have a neighbor on our floor. I hadn't put that on my list because most penthouses take up the whole floor. I had to chuckle to myself because I am the one always reminding people to be as clear as possible when visualizing their dreams. As fate would have it, our neighbour did move out and it has been vacant since.

Along with meditation, visualization is a big part of my day. I visualize anything from finding that perfect dress for a party, to seeing the great weather for a special event. See it in your head, keep visual reminders everywhere. And when it happens more and more to you, you will pass this art of visualization onto everyone you care for.

> *'When John returned home from university for a vacation, he spotted a note on the refrigerator door. Written on the note were the goals his mother had set for herself:*
> *Start pottery class in September, Join running club this week.*
> *Seeing an opportunity John added "Sew John's clothes and iron his shirts"*
> *The following day, his sister added "Allow Susan to stay up later during the week",*
> *Then the dad finally added "Buy Martin a season ticket for the Toronto Blue Jays"*
> *So, the mother added one more item for herself: "Move away from the family by Thursday."'*
>
> —*Anonymous*

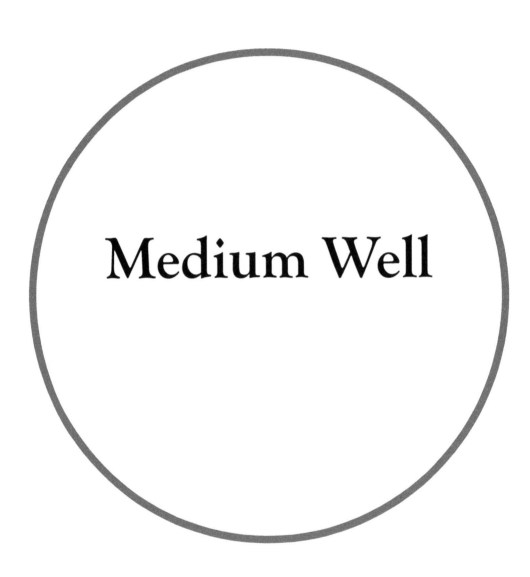

Medium Well

BEING A MEDIUM

"Millionaires don't have astrologers; billionaires do"
—*J.P. Morgan*

People who are mediums, use their intuition to communicate between spirits of those on the other side and living beings. I didn't know I was a medium until I was a teenager. I just assumed that everyone could see and hear what I did. I have attracted many people in my life with the same kind of skills. Sometimes I wish I was psychic, so I could tell what may happen in the future, but my gift is to listen to someone on the other side and convey the message. I am sure this has been a useful tool for me to have over all these years. I am also sure if I had listened harder sometimes, I wouldn't have had some of the negative experiences I endured.

Connecting with the spirit world can leave you with a feeling of peace like you have never known. I know that when it is my time to leave the earth, I will be united with my loved ones who have departed before me.

When my husband and I met, we had no idea we both had similar intuitive gifts. We were together for a long time before we started sharing stories. I knew when I met him that he had a very old and wise soul. But just because my soul is not as old, that does not mean his interpretations are clearer than mine. Sometimes we interpret a message two different ways. Sometimes we both agree 100%. I get more direct messages for other people and he frequently uses his gifts in his business life. You can only use references that you have experienced to figure out what the message is. The messenger may try to tell you about a storm, but if you have never been in a hurricane, you may not know what they are trying to convey.

I can often feel if the person I am with is a medium or a psychic. Many people just don't recognize the signs they are seeing, or know how to interpret them. Being a medium is not the same as being a psychic. I have many friends that are both. Some see clearly what "ghosts" look like, and what they are wearing. I see "cloudy, colored" images that tell me things. I can only interpret what message they are trying to tell me and for who. I also see people's auras, which are the colored energy shields around each of us. As far back as I can remember, I could see auras. I can't see animal auras, but I can sense theirs. The colors, the width and vibrancy of auras are different for each person. Some energies are barely there, and I can sometimes sense if some haven't got much time left to live. Some are non-symmetrical and they need to be balanced out by sleep, nutrition, water or de-stressing. Some people are "off" because they have been using one part of their brain and they need to be using the other part more. For example they need to use less analytical thoughts and use more creative ones.

I have had the chance to meet and have readings from some of the more renowned psychics, like Char Margolis, Silvia Brown, Ofer Cohen, Derrick Whiteskycloud and a many others from around the world. They all agree that more and more people are discovering they have an ability to communicate to and from the other side. Years ago, mediums or psychics were considered to be scam artists or even witches. It is natural to fear what we can't explain. Fortunately, more people are realizing they are using their intuition effectively, therefore accepting that these communications are real.

Some Ways You Can Work on Your Skills & Pick up on the Signs

Dreams

How many times have you woken up from a dream about someone who has already passed away? When you have dreams of the ones who have crossed over, the dreams are almost always them coming to be with you. If you lose someone, who was your shoulder to lean on, they will often still be your shoulder from the other side. Grandparents, parents, siblings, spouses and pets will still be doing their job from the other side.

Do not feel that if a loved one has not visited you that they don't care. There can be many reasons. They could be still decompressing from being on Earth, this is the process when your body dies, and your soul needs to readjust to the other side. Everyone takes a different amount of time to readjust. Many people just simply never remember their dreams to make the connection. Spirits may be visiting, but your mind may be too busy to recognize them, or they are simply not getting through to you.

I remember one dream visit very clearly. I was walking past a tourist hop-on bus and on the top level were my Danish grandparents, who had passed years before. I had a deep connection with grandfather, while my grandmother was more connected to my brother. In this dream, my grandfather got off the bus and walked with me as we caught up with what was going in my life. My grandmother just spoke from her seat at the top of the bus, *"Say hi to your brother for me."*

You Have Seen Someone or Something That No One Else Did

Once, on holiday in Hawaii at a private resort, my husband and I were sitting and reading, and I looked over at the big rocks on the beach. I saw this older, tanned, heavyset man sitting out on the rocks. Ralph must have sensed it at that exact moment, as he looked up at him also. He stayed there for maybe five seconds then disappeared. No one else on the beach seemed to have seen him. That night, I asked the manager of the resort about it and he said many others have also seen him. He was a village elder that died during a volcanic eruption many years before. He still comes by to make sure everybody is okay.

Dark Energies

Another common sign you have this skill, is when you may pick up on are dark entities. As an example, have you ever seen someone walking towards you and for some reason you get out of their way or cross the street quickly? You have just sensed what people like me, who see auras, sense. The only difference is we can actually see their aura, or colors. You may have felt their energy level or someone from the other side was protecting you from him or her.

Energies from others can be easily attached to you or people you know. One time I had my family over for lunch and everyone at the table was going through a bit of a tough time. Later that night while dreaming, I felt like I was being attacked by horrible forces. I bolted awake and ran out of the bedroom. I was shaking it was so scary. I knew instinctively that the energies came in from the family. Naively, I assumed that since they were family, that they couldn't bring negative energies with them. Many people who see auras cannot see the colors around the people they are closest to. I can't see Ralph's or my close family's auras anymore.

Electric Vibes

The opposite of sensing dark energies is when you see someone and you are just attracted to that person. They may have an electric vibe, an honest vibe, an artistic vibe or a sexual vibe. You are intuitively sensing their energy field. Some say, "Love at First Sight" is what they feel when they meet energies like these.

Another example is when you meet someone and you think you've known that person your whole life (or in another life). You probably recognize the kinship that you may have had with this person. Most likely you have known each other in a previous life. Or it could be the opposite, when you meet someone and you just don't like them, you probably didn't like them in a previous life either, but you still need to learn from each other. This is not the same as seeing their colors of their aura, but intuitive nevertheless. With work and meditation, you can grow this ability to see or sense the aura colors that surround others.

When the Phone Rings and You Were Just
Thinking About That Person

That can be a way a medium's intuition is being tuned in. I can't tell you how many times, I will call someone or send a text and they reply by saying they were just thinking about me.

When Strange Things are Happening and You are Alone

You may see a door open or shut suddenly by itself. A lamp may turn on or off by itself. This may be when someone, who is on the other side, wants to get our attention. When this happens to me, I try to immediately meditate. I ask who is doing it and I usually get an answer. When you hear stories about a place being "haunted," it is sometimes because many people have seen or felt the spirit. It doesn't necessarily mean they are evil spirits just because they startled us. But if you do feel threatened, ask them to leave.

How to Improve Your Ability to Communicate with the Other Side

Go to a professional psychic and ask them what signs you should be looking for. Ask them what the names of your guides and protectors are, and ask how to improve your skills. My friends all know that I go to psychics on a regular basis so I can be assisted along the way if I need guidance. Find a psychic that you connect with and ask them to teach you how to handle these senses. I am not saying all mediums and physics have strong skills, but I have been to many who get things bang on. If you go for a reading and it is completely off base (which has happened to me), ask them to start again. Maybe an energy was attached to you when you came into the room. At one psychic reading I had, she opened with, *"Wow, you have had a bad year!"*

I said, *"Nope. It's been one of my happiest years."* She said she couldn't get a read on me and I thanked her and left.

Ask your spirit guides, angels and protectors to come and visit at night. Some spirit guides live as energy, in the cosmic realm, or as light beings, which are very high-level spirit guides. Some spirit guides are people who have lived many former lifetimes. They have learned the lessons on Earth that they need for the other side, so they don't need to reincarnate. Spirit guides are chosen on the other side by you, when you are about to reincarnate. The guides you have chosen are to guide you through your life on Earth. Angels are not human, they may appear with a human form for some, but they have never lived a human lifetime. Many say they see a shadow out of the corner of their eye. Many say they came in human form to help them out in a life-threatening situation, which happened to me. The reason angels do not show themselves as their true from is because humans would get too startled by their appearance. Protectors could be the people in your life that have passed over. They are also the ones that people pray to, like Buddha, Jesus, or Mohammad.

The first years of life are when most people are open to seeing and hearing things from the other side. I am sure you have been around babies or toddlers when they seem to be having a conversation while alone in a room. If you have a pet or a child and they seem to be looking or talking to someone, you can ask the spirit to show themselves to you. As we get older, we are told that we are just imagining things, but we may not have been. You can ask a child who they see and as they learn to communicate, encourage them to share. Showing them pictures can help. When we are on the other side, we are all around thirty years old, so if you have your relative's younger photos, show them to your children also.

Your Messengers

A totem is your guardian spirit that comes in the form a natural object or a living being. They can come in a form of a bird, butterfly, dolphin, fish, or many other things. It is fairly easy to figure out what your totem is. Meditate on this. You will then start seeing the same thing often. It is usually the first thing that comes to your mind when you are thinking of what it could be. It could be anything from an eagle to a dragonfly to a whale. When you start seeing your totem over and over, meditate and ask yourself, *"What is the message I am needing to get?"*

My totem is a snake! Seriously, I would much rather have butterflies deliver messages to me rather than snakes! My husband's mom and his dad come to visit as hummingbirds, even on our balcony forty floors up! When I see a snake, and I see them a lot, I know that I have to pay attention to something, to be more in the present, or I could get hurt some way, etc. They show up to tell me that I am supposed to focus on that moment or that an opportunity is about be presented to me. In one 24-hour period, I saw fourteen snakes. Every channel on TV that I turned to had a snake. I was walking in the park the same day and saw two different ones. I was walking home and I saw a guy with a t-shirt with the word "snake". I finally yelled to the universe, *"Okay, I got it!"* I knew exactly what the message was and what I was supposed to do.

If you see your totem a lot, and you don't know what the message is, meditate on it.

Coming Back for a Visit

It takes a lot of energy for a spirit to shift their energetic vibrations for their presence to be felt back on earth. And it takes a whole lot more effort to move something. Once you recognize their presence, they are likely to come at that same time of day again and do the same thing.

Pay attention to the signs that only the person who has who passed would send you. They may leave coins, feathers, buttons, rocks, cards and such everywhere, but you may be too much in your head to put two and two together. My Danish grandfather loved shaping things from rocks. He was also sure there was nothing after death, a total atheist. Maybe it was because he lost his son in the prime of his life, but he was adamant there was no other side. After my grandmother died, he took it very hard. I had spent many hours talking with him. I shared my knowledge of the other side with him and as the years went on, he would say he had dreams about his wife and son. He once told me that he had a dream and they were calling him over and that they will be there when he arrives. I kept assuring him that they will be. When he finally did pass, I know they were there to greet him.

One Monday morning, a year or so after his passing, I went to work. At the front of the reception area of the school lay thirty-six polished rocks. I thought, who would leave these rocks there? I looked in the potted trees and none had these kinds of rocks. When our staff arrived, I asked who locked up Friday night and did they see these rocks? I called the cleaning company and asked them also. No one knew a thing. I went about my day and when I came home, I told Ralph this story. He immediately said, *"You know who left them, right?"* I looked at him, perplexed, and then it hit me, they were from my grandfather. I probably told him a million times, that when he dies, I want him to leave polished rocks for me and I will know he is near. So that just proves it to me. I may be a medium, but I can still get caught up with life and miss the clear signs also. We installed cameras around the school years later, and I often thought to myself, I wish I had cameras that weekend.

When Sally, who lives in New Zealand, first came to visit me, she stayed in our guest room. I asked her how she slept and she told me her bedside lights both came on in the middle of the night. That had never happened to anyone before or since.

I told her it was her father, who departed years before, saying hello. She instantly knew that was true. Her father was a prankster, so that was exactly what he would have done. He most likely did there so I could tell her, it was him. She now communicates directly with him, but he almost always pops in when the two of us are together, no matter where we are in the world.

Years later, I was alone one summer day the same bedside lamps in the guest bedroom kept coming on. I would turn them off and they would be back on when I went back an hour later. Finally, after three or four times I asked, *"Okay, who keeps doing this?"* I immediately knew, so I emailed Sally and told her that her dad was sending a message, and asked her if she knew what he was trying to say. She replied she had just checked herself into a hospital for shooting pain down her arm. She is a nurse and she knew what this could have been. She knew her dad went through me to get her to take better care of herself.

My Ukrainian grandmother comes in with a very loud burp! I am not joking! I can still picture her in her kitchen after a great meal and then she lets out this loud burp. When we spontaneously burp loudly, we always know she is with us. She was never a subtle woman.

Your Departed Loved Ones May Show up Quickly

Do not freak out if this happens to you. I have heard stories of people who have passed and come back to tell people what kind of funeral they want. They have come back to tell people where they want their ashes spread and even come back to tell someone where their valuables are hidden. I also know of situations about people going back and forth to the other side when they are about to die.

One day, the phone call came that my husband's mother had passed away. Although Ralph has a truck load of siblings, but we both felt his mom had a soft spot for him. He jumped on a plane to get home in time for the funeral. His fifteen hour flight from Vancouver to Auckland was a breeze, but his connecting flight down to Wellington was diverted to the South Island due to fog. He was getting quite anxious that he would be too late for the service, when they finally called his connecting flight and they took off. He was the only one sitting in business class. ***And then it happened!***

His mom showed up, very giddy to be in business class, something she had never experienced. She told him not to worry, he will make it on time for the funeral. She stayed for a little while and then left, with no other message. When the plane landed, he raced to his rental car and sped to the church. His family has said it was a very dramatic moment when the church doors burst open, on a dark stormy night, just as the music started and the service began.

Sometimes the Departed May Appear as One Group

As you can imagine, for a large group, their energy field would be much more obvious. On a trip to Montreal for fashion week with my mother, we took a bus tour to see the sights. At one stop, the guide pointed out an historic, wonderful cathedral and the people on the bus all flocked in to see it. My mother had spotted a Christmas store on the other side of the street, so she bolted there instead. She is obsessed with Christmas decorations. Some years she has put up more than a dozen Christmas trees with thousands of decorations, not one of the ornaments the same.

When we got back on our tour bus, everyone was raving about this church. I have been around the world looking at cathedrals, so I am kind of done with them! But the guide told us the church was planning an amazing laser show later that night. After the tour we headed back to our hotel and went for dinner. After dinner, we spontaneously decided to go to that laser show. We hailed a cab who took us the two blocks to the church. (How were we supposed to know how close it was?) There were no more twenty people there. Mom sat down in the row in front of me as the show started. *And then it happened to her!* Every one of her departed family members showed up. I had to move to the back of the church, their energy was so strong. I watched my mom's body language from where I was sitting at the back. At the end of the show, I asked her if she felt something. She had tears in her eyes and said she knew they were there. I am not sure when she changed her mind about life after death, but I know now that she can also sense them. This gives both of us comfort. I have asked her that when she does pass over to the other side, to leave me buttons when she comes to visit, so I can know it's her. I requested nice buttons, not the cheap ones.

Hoping For a Clear Message

I need to repeat this information because it is the most commonly asked question I get. Everyone takes a different amount of time when they pass over to decompress. Some can take many Earth years to decompress. Some can go quickly, like my husband's mom did. Some get reincarnated very quickly so you won't be able to get a message from them. Our time on Earth is just a blip in time to those who are on the other side. Some may take decades to live their life this time, and some might go back right away if they are ready. You will see when you are on the other side, that Earth years are no time at all over there.

You Will Not Be Given Any Messages That You Can't Handle

I have been told by many that I have made a difference in people's lives, by making them aware of their own gifts. I have had very few situations where messages from visitors on the other side, did not make sense to the person I gave it to. Many people tell me that they had been thinking a lot of their visitor who came in to give the message. Some say the messages they received have changed their relationships on Earth and their beliefs of knowing there is another side.

Some people can be apprehensive when they start working with their gifts. You may have people in your life that may think you are going loopy. But as you practice your skills, you will be surprised how clear the messages become. If you interpret a message incorrectly, do not think you don't have the skills. Interpretation is a skill that you need to work on. These messages are gifts and when they present themselves, you have to listen to them. So, next time your "spidey sense" picks up on something, act on it.

As an example, if you get a message about someone that is sick or dying, it doesn't automatically mean they will pass today. It could mean that he or she is not taking care of themselves and you need to tell them. I had a friend see one of my psychics, and he was told to get his heart checked, ASAP. He did and it was a good thing because he had blockages. He went into surgery that week!

I have had messages for waiters, salespeople, hairdressers, and countless other strangers. I have asked my spirit guides to have the spirits and messages only show up when I can concentrate on who I am supposed to give the message to. That has not happened yet, as I still get messages at all times of the day and night.

I have had total strangers tell me they really needed the message I just gave them. Once I was told to give a message to a young girl sitting near me at a restaurant. I went up to her and told her that it was not her time to pass yet. She looked at me shell shocked! I hugged her and told her things will get better, as I was sure of it. She burst into tears explaining she was planning to commit suicide that day. I sat with her a while and I know the message changed her mind. Once I had to tell a young gal to get out of a nightclub I was in, because I sensed she would get into serious trouble if she didn't.

Many years ago, I had a psychic reading with Char Margolis, a very well-known psychic/medium in North America. Within seconds, she said my entire family all came in at the same time, one guy was the particularly excited. I told her it must be my uncle. She asked if his name is Pete. It was. She explained he was so excited to talk to me, that he was jumping up and down. When I asked Pete why he hadn't visited me before this he replied (through Char) he was just watching over me. He went on to say he was on the other side with the whole family: his mom, dad and brother. He told me that they will all be waiting for my mom when she crosses over. He even said they are preparing a party for her arrival. I knew this wasn't an omen, or that my mom was passing soon because like I said, time on the other side is not like time on earth.

Funny side bar: as I am writing this chapter while cruising over the equator, someone has come to have some fun with me. The iPad I am writing on, just started writing words and deleting without my touch. When I called my mom an hour later and told her about the ghost and my iPad, she told me she had just been to the grave-site of her brother, my uncle Pete, the eternal practical joker. We both knew at that moment it was him saying hi to the both of us.

When You Want Them Out of Your Space

I have often seen spirits in my house, but if they don't create any problems, I don't try to get them to move on. When we moved downtown, I started seeing a very high-energy spirit. It turns out he goes in and out of many condos downtown, but apparently, he likes coming to our place because he enjoys our company.

If you do encounter a spirit and you don't want them around, try hanging crystals from your windows. Doing that attracts good energy and repels bad energy from entering your home or office.

Saging (also known as smudging) is one of the oldest and quickest ways to "clean out" dark energies. There are many ways and suggestions for saging. I was told you can't buy the dried bunches of sage for yourself, it should be given to you. So, just go shopping with a friend and buy one for each other. Secondly, light the dried sage and have the smoke go all over you. Then go counter clockwise around each room. Don't forget closets and balconies. When you are done, cut off the burnt sage and get rid of it by taking it far away from where you are. Do not flush it down the toilet or put in your garbage. Almost every week I would sage the school I owned. Can you imagine having up to 300 people in and out every day and the energies that could come with them?

Also, when you buy anything that is made from natural materials, they should be saged. Examples are jewelry, metals, gold, silver, rock, wood, crystals, and especially any antique piece. Think about any second-hand item, or items handed down from your family.

I once completed a big design project for friends of ours. They had just built their brand-new cottage that they will be using as an Airbnb. She asked me to help them furnish and decorate it. They were on a very tight budget, so I shopped in second-hand stores mostly. I decorated a six-bedroom house for under $15,000 and it looked like a professional designer did it. A friend who helped me, was staying with me at the cottage one weekend. We were playing a game and laughing and there may have been some wine consumed. All of a sudden, one of the six balcony chairs shot as fast as a cannon ball across the patio right in front of us. None of the other chairs moved an inch! We looked at each other in surprise, and then wham! All lights and power went out. Now we were more than a little freaked out. We slept in the same bedroom that night. And when I say slept, I mean we pulled the covers over our heads and prayed for morning to come.

How I hadn't remembered to sage the place is beyond me, as I am usually reminding others to do it when they buy used furniture. I came back there a few days later and saged the entire place more than once.

Sage Bracelets or Necklaces to Protect You

My psychic friend, Jules Stirling, has a show where she's brought to a location where spirits are known to hang out. Her producer chooses the location but tells her nothing about it. Before Jules started these shows, she called to ask if I had any suggestions to keep her safe from the dark entities. I immediately remembered a bracelet I was encouraged to buy when I was going through a tough time. The bracelet was special because only the person who mined the gems had ever touched it. The sales lady only picked it up by using a cloth, and even then, she saged it before I put it on. I don't know why the bracelet gave me such comfort, but it did, so I saged the bracelet and gave it to Jules. She wears it every time she does a reading now, putting white light around her to keep dark energy from attaching themselves to her.

Get Rid of Items

You may have just brought something into your house after which the energy of your home changed. Jules was doing a reading for a client where a very dark energy was hanging out. She walked into the bedroom of their client's house and quickly turned and bolted out. She asked the home owner if she had brought anything into the house recently. The home owner had just brought in the big antique dresser, Jules told her to get rid of it ASAP! Some entities are so attached to things that nothing can be done, short of burning it.

Helping Someone to Go All the Way

Sometimes you can convince the spirits or ghosts that have not passed over, to go to the other side and sometimes you can't. I have often tried to show spirits that they are dead by picking up items and saying something like, *"See, I can lift this, can you? Now, you are needed on the other side, go to the white light."* Sometimes I feel they get the message and sometimes they are already on the other side, but coming back for a reason. Some souls just get stuck. I hear that it isn't a great place, because they can't figure out why no one is talking to them, and that things are changing while they are not. As soon as I hear someone has passed away, I send them white light, gold light, green light, purple light to assist them to the other side.

Let Some People Go

You know people, when after you are with them, you feel exhausted or down. This may be one of the hardest things to do, but I assure you, once you stop being around their negative energy, your energy will be so lighter. If you have to see these kinds of people, then protect yourself by surrounding yourself with white light.

Move Seats

I have worked on my skills for most of my life now, and I am able to see visions of where people live, what car they drive, what their children look like, what job they do, etc. Once, I did a reading where I saw someone's desk with dark energy covering it. I could tell the dark energy was actually coming from a connecting desk. As soon as I suggested he move his desk, he said, *"I never liked that person. Some days I just didn't want to go to work and see him!"*

One reason I prefer to sit in row one on an airplane or the front row of an event, is that I see too many visions and auras and I can't concentrate or relax. When entering a restaurant, often I will not sit where the hostess has chosen, but will try to face a wall. It could be from a bad vibe, or a feeling that I will learn someone's life story from the people around.

Communicating with Animals

When my husband and I were in Greece for a few weeks, cats by the dozens would wander through our hotel. They are revered in Greece, and all locals take care of them. One day I felt a cat at my feet and I looked down and saw a Siamese kitty. Instantly I knew this cat was a messenger sent from Chop-Chop, my cat when I was a child. The cat told me he was here to look after us and he never left our villa for the entire time we were there.

I brought in my first pet psychic after our puppy, Elvis, was attacked by three other dogs and was seriously injured. They took a big chunk out of his hip. This was the second time he had been attacked, and I don't know how we got through those weeks. I have never felt so sad, angry, helpless and desperate in all my life. I now know what a parent must feel like when their child is sick.

I explained to the psychic that I just wanted to make sure that Elvis was okay, and I wanted to know if Elvis needed anything. This psychic had an instant connection with him and we got to ask him questions and get answers through her. Elvis said he was ok, and I shouldn't worry. He also conveyed that he didn't like the perfume we put on him sometimes. I told him, if he stops rolling in bear poop, I wouldn't have to put perfume on him! (He didn't do that too many times after that day). The psychic also told me not to worry as he would never have an attack on him again (and he never did). Elvis always liked to have naps in our walk-in closet so I asked the psychic about that. It turned out it was his sister, who died when she was a puppy, visited him there. She liked the quietness and darkness of the closet.

Elvis had said many times over the years (through psychics), that he just wanted to be around us for as long as he could be. But when his body was giving out on him, he was worried that there would be no one to take care of me. I told him his daddy would take care of me. He replied *"He is not a dog. How can he?"* I have been told when humans pass over, we will feel and look around the age of thirty on the other side. Animals will also be in their prime on the other side, which is what I kept telling Elvis.

And then it happened! When Elvis was fifteen human years old and while we were away for a week, he had a stroke. We came home and saw his sad eyes. Ralph lifted him upstairs to the master bed, where we all had our final last cuddles that night. In the morning, we searched and discovered the most perfect vet, Dr. Berkshire, who came over within an hour. We carried Elvis out to the deck. It was a lovely sunny day. The vet gave Elvis a relaxing injection as we were hugging and kissing him. I told him, he will be pain free and running on the other side in a few minutes. The final injection sent him peacefully to the other side. Elvis had left the building. I will always be grateful for his peaceful passing as well as the vet who helped us all through it.

Animals don't feel there is any difference living on Earth or the other side. Dying is not a big deal for them, and accept being on the other side instantly. Later that night, I knew without a shadow of a doubt that he was already back with us. He let me know, he was so happy not feeling old anymore, and that he will always be watching over us. He has come for visits whenever we travel, although he still prefers the snow to the heat, just as a Husky would. Even on the other side.

It is funny, we couldn't ever show our suitcases to him while he was alive, because he knew instantly that we were leaving him. Now, when I get the suitcases out for a trip, he comes around excitedly and can't wait to see where we are going.

Exit Points

Have you ever had near misses like a car almost hitting you? Have you had an incident where you could have drowned or had a doctor say you may die soon? These are usually the times when you could have chosen to take your exit.

We usually have seven exit opportunities. These are the times in our life when we have the option of leaving the physical realm and returning to the spirit one. Before you were born, you and your spirit guides had decided what these seven exit points would be. Remember Steve Irwin - the Crocodile Hunter from Australia? No matter how tragic, a spirit may have chosen its exit point while in the act of doing something it loves the most.

The reason we have seven exit chances, is that your spirit may feel you have already learned the lessons needed for your purpose on the other side. Sometimes life is hard and difficult to cope, but do not confuse suicide as an exit point. When we take our own life, we are not fulfilling the lessons we needed to learn, and we will be reborn to learn those lessons again.

One of my favorite stories of exiting was my friend Michelle's grandmother. Her grandparents came from Hungary to Canada with their kids, when they were young. When her grandfather passed, he was buried in Hungary. For years, Michelle had wanted to take her grandmother back to Hungary for a visit. Her grandmother had never really learned much English, so she felt a trip back home with everyone speaking Hungarian would be a nice treat for her. From the minute they checked into the airport in Vancouver, the adventure began. Because her grandmother was so fragile, Michelle asked if she could be taken to their gate by cart. Michelle was traveling with too many to fit on one cart, so the rest of them walked. When they arrived at the gate, her grandmother wasn't there. Much later, and after much panic, they finally found her at another gate. They raced onto the plane at the last minute and made their way to Hungary. I am sure Michelle thought twice about their trip at this point.

A couple of days later, when her grandmother was over jet lag, Michelle took her to the gravesite of the husband. Her grandmother seemed very happy to have traveled the long journey to be there. The next day, her grandmother took a turn for the worse and passed away. Michelle was totally devastated, feeling guilty about taking her all that way, on a trip which might have been too much for her, and with the rest of the family back in Canada not having the chance to say goodbye.

When she emailed me this story I couldn't help but smile. Her grandmother was back in her hometown where she decided it was her time to exit and to be buried beside her husband. If only we could all go out that way. I have told many people about this story and each time I feel destiny is more powerful than we think.

Prepare for Your Passing, It Will Eventually Come

It may be because I know so much about the other side, that I have no problem talking to people about death. So many families are torn apart with the passing of a loved one. Please know you will pass at some point, and your family will be much happier if you have your affairs in order, rather than being afraid to discuss them. Preparing for the crossover is like preparing for a party. There are lots to do and lots to plan. I love that some people I know have already bought their plot and have clearly laid out the instructions on what they want when they pass. But most people I talk to have not planned anything.

The first time we wrote our will, we picked up a standard form at an office supply store and filled it out ourselves. Our puppy was our whole life then, so in our will, we stated that in the event of both of us passing, Elvis would get to keep the lifestyle he was accustomed to. After our puppy passed on and we sold the business, we decided it was time to revamp our wills.

Executors and Powers of Attorney

The first thing our lawyer advised us was that the office-bought form was never a legal document without signatures of witnesses. The second was, we not only need to have executors in the event we both passed, but we also needed to have a power of attorney to pay our bills in the situation we both were incapacitated.

And then, what do we want to happen with our living will in case we are seriously and permanently injured or sick? What do we want done with our bodies after we pass? Organ donation, burial, cremation or what? It never occurred to me we needed to involve so many to help make these decisions for us, including backups in case they passed on before us.

I brought our lawyer a list of the beneficiaries, the people in our lives, as well as the charities that we would like our money to go to, when we pass. I thought about a "naughty and nice" list (like Santa's), but my lawyer chuckled and explained what a nightmare it would be for our executors to deal with all these people from around the world. So, if you haven't done these documents, or checked them in a long time, you may want to talk to a lawyer or a succession planner. Our lawyer could not believe that we didn't have a legal will in place, given the assets we had accumulated. After thinking about it, we knew how foolish it was to wait so long. Since then, we constantly remind our friends to get on it.

Make Your Last Wishes Known to Each Other

The big lesson my husband's family learned was to make sure your final wishes are put in writing, and are known by your loved ones. When his mom passed, the siblings had different thoughts of what Mum would have wanted for her burial. It turned out to be a challenging time for their big family. Before one of my grandfathers passed, I told him that all I wanted was some of his carvings he had made over the years. My brother thought talking to him about death was horrible, but I knew it actually made Grandpa proud that I wanted some of his work.

My advice is to look at your documents every five years or so, to make sure your last wishes are what you (and perhaps your family) still want.

Don't Put Things Off

I have been a regular in a nail salon since it opened twenty years ago. It was run by a brother and sister team from Vietnam and I was their first client. As their business grew, they expanded and each ran a different location. I knew both of them worked six or seven days a week while raising their children. The brother's dream was to always have a boat. He finally took possession of his boat and took it out for his first trip. They found him later that day, after he had had a heart attack and died aboard. His sister now also raises his children, and she runs both locations. I have talked with her many times about not working so hard and to enjoy her time. But she continues to say her life now is not about her, it is about all their children she is now raising.

One of my uncles and his wife used to run a small hotel, café and bar in a very small town in Saskatchewan. They, and their sons worked tirelessly cleaning the rooms, making meals and pouring drinks seven days a week. I was in my early twenties, when I offered to go up there and take over for the weekend so they could have a much needed break. I had plenty of experience running a bar and restaurant by then, and knew I could handle the small hotel for the night. I had a blast. The locals were great and the visitors didn't know any better, so everything went well.

Years later, when they had put the property up for sale, it took a while before they got a deal. When it finally did sell, they agreed to help with the transition with the new owners for a few months. Shortly after, my uncle suddenly disappeared, so everyone went looking for him, wondering where he could have gone. They finally found him in the walk-in freezer. He had had a heart attack and died, before he could enjoy any of his upcoming retirement years.

Many of us have heard stories of people dying right after they retire, but I have known too many who have died at the peak of their life. So, go get your heart checked. If a disease runs in your family, get regular checkups, listen to your own instincts, even if the doctor says you are too young to run tests for a specific reason.

I have had the unfortunate experience of finding two dead bodies. Both times were in the ocean. I was swimming one day when I lived in the Bahamas, and something large bumped into me, a corpse, that had been in the water a long time. It was a man who was fully clothed. I was a bit far from shore, but I pulled on his belt and dragged him onto the beach and called for help. The second story was very similar. I was diving with a friend and we saw something floating in the water. We swam up to it to discover it was a body. This body had been in the water much longer. The fish had had their way with it. We were too far from shore and not able to get it back on the boat, so we called the coast guard to come to our location. They told me this is a common occurrence in oceans, as undercurrents can take people out to sea very quickly.

Darwin Nominee

I have also had the sorry sight of seeing someone die very graphically. I was diving with a team in the Caribbean, when one of the guests, an American, claimed he had done many deep dives and he could handle anything. This is the location where I did some of my deepest dives, called Shark Alley, where only experienced divers should go. It was about 100 feet down to the gathering spot, so we went in teams and took our time regulating. When we all got down to the hole, the American took out a package of sardines... the rest of us just looked at each other in shock. I took off as soon as I saw the sharks heading towards him. I will leave the gory part out, but he never made it out of the ocean. Please don't be stupid when you are dealing with the wild, they will do what they can to survive.

So learn from these stories, and take time out of your busy schedule to put your affairs in order.

Ashes to Ashes

Whenever I meet a captain of a cruise ship, I always ask how many people have asked them if they can sprinkle the ashes at sea. Many. They cannot legally let you put anything in the ocean, but may inform guests when the wind is blowing at a certain time at the back on the ship.

When my puppy was put to sleep, the vet took him away to the animal crematorium. The vet said they would call us in about a week to pick up his ashes. Two days later, on an early Monday morning, the phone rang. The person said, *"Hello, Elvis is ready to come home."*

I stared into the receiver thinking, *"Oh my god, my puppy didn't die, and he must have come back to life!"* A few seconds later I figured out that the person was from the cremation company. When I went to pick his ashes up, I mentioned what my first thoughts were. They said he had been in business fifteen years, and no one had ever mentioned that.

Resting Places

We took Elvis's ashes, returned to us in a small cedar box, and went up to his favorite hiking trail where he used to sit in a stream to cool off during the hot summers. We sprinkled him there (FYI: ashes are white! We just assumed they would be dark grey). Then we found a hole in a cedar tree next to the stream that made a perfect fit for the box. We have told everyone who loved our puppy where that location is and many have visited.

We are considering various approaches for our remains. There are services that take ashes and make them into a diamond. Another takes ashes to outer space to be disbursed throughout the universe. One makes beautiful glass creations with ashes. You can have the ashes made into an hourglass, a snow globe, or a firework to blast into the night sky. Tattoo artists can create a memorial tattoo, using ashes and mixing them with ink. So why stop your bucket list at the time of your passing?

I have reminded Ralph many times that I will kick the bucket first. The long life lines on his palms as well as many psychics, have confirmed this. With my passing I know that I want a party, not a funeral. I have had the best life ever and the last thing I would want is for anyone to be sad. I will meet you on the other side, so, drink the best champagne, and have the best food, compliments of me. Oh, and a rock 'n roll band would be fun, so we can all dance.

Reincarnation

Those people that have made a big impact on your life were most likely in your previous lives in a different kind of relationship. A friend of mine was told that her husband in this life was actually her son in a past one. She totally felt that was true. Another friend feels she was wealthy in a past life as she craves a wealthy lifestyle, but has many financial challenges in this one. I have a very close friend who lost her brother while they were young. One psychic stated her youngest daughter is him, reincarnated, and she agrees.

Willie Nelson said *"I started out really young, when I was four, five, six, writing poems, before I could play an instrument. I was writing about things when I was eight or ten years old that I hadn't lived long enough to experience. That's why I also believe in reincarnation, that we were put here with ideas to pass around."*

I have been taken back to previous lives by hypnotists, and have never previously lived in a cold climate. Before I was reincarnated this time, my spirit team thought it would be interesting for me to be born in a very cold climate (winters can get lower than -40F in Saskatchewan). The funny part is as long as I can remember, I wanted out of Saskatchewan and to travel to hot countries. I was also a man in many of my past lives, apparently a pilot in World War One. I was shot down over enemy lines and ended up escaping from capture. Maybe that is why I love flying a helicopter so much. We all experience both genders. I died giving birth one lifetime, which may be part of the reason I didn't want children in this one.

My husband and I were at our local fair one summer, where a hypnotist entertainer was performing. He called for a few volunteers to come up on stage, and I went up and he put us under. The first thing he did was hypnotically convince us that we were in the Arctic. We cuddled each other on stage to try to warm ourselves. I felt very uncomfortable. He then told us we were on a hot sandy beach. Apparently all the others started fanning themselves, taking garments off. I just sat in my chair leaning back enjoying the heat with a smile on my face. He later hypnotized me to be Dolly Parton, singing *Nine to Five*, which I did with some flair apparently. But after the show was over, I was shivering for hours, and didn't fully warm up till I got home and had a long hot bath, proving I am happier in warm conditions. Maybe that's why I have been having hot flashes while going through menopause…for some eighteen years!

How Many Lifetimes Do We Get?

I am sure you have met someone that you think is wise beyond their years. It could be a toddler or a 100-year-old. They just seemed to have life figured out. The purpose of us having to live many lives on Earth, is to get the knowledge for the work we will need to help others on the other side. Our purpose on the other side will be a joy, not a burden.

The magic number seems to be fifty-six lifetimes. Those are the wisest souls who have learned so many lessons, over so many lifetimes. I believe Ralph to be around fifty lifetimes old. He just seems to understand what someone else is going through, and shows compassion easily. The only way he could have this ability is to have experienced many situations in previous lifetimes. A close relative of mine, must have lived only a few lives, as life seems very challenging for him. He is learning many lessons this lifetime, both good and bad. The premise behind this is not just how hard life is, but how many lessons we must learn, or experience. When we experience things, we can understand and feel more compassion towards other souls.

No matter how hard or wonderful your life is, we are all still learning the lessons that we need to learn in order to do our job on the other side. When you see someone famous or wealthy and think to yourself that you wish you had their life, remember it is their destiny in this lifetime, and to deal with all that comes with that position, good and bad. Right now, my life is amazing. I truly feel I am the most blessed soul on Earth. But I am still here, so I must have more lessons to learn, and more to experience.

Using Your Skills

We are all in the process of change and growth. If you work on developing your skills, it can be an asset in every part of your day. Using your "sixth sense" takes many forms. Doctors may not know why they can diagnose a patient on sight. Stockbrokers and investors may not be aware of where their hunches are coming from. Coaches may not know why they put someone in the game. But the one thing they all have in common is their intuition. So, practice honing your skills, trust that they will eventually come. Believe in yourself. Use your intuitive skills for when your ***"And then it happened"*** moments present themselves, so you can be better prepared.

And finally, always use your gifts for the greater good of all.

> *'A Green Bay Packer fan was enjoying himself at the game in a packed Lambeau Field, until he noticed an empty seat down in front. He asked the guy next to it if he knew whose seat it was.*
>
> *The guy said, "Yes, that's my wife's seat. We have never missed a game since the Lombardi days, but now my wife is dead."*
>
> *The fan offered his sympathy and said it was really too bad he couldn't find some relative to give the ticket to so they could enjoy the game together...*
>
> *"Oh no," the guy said, "they're all at the funeral."'*
>
> —*Anonymous*

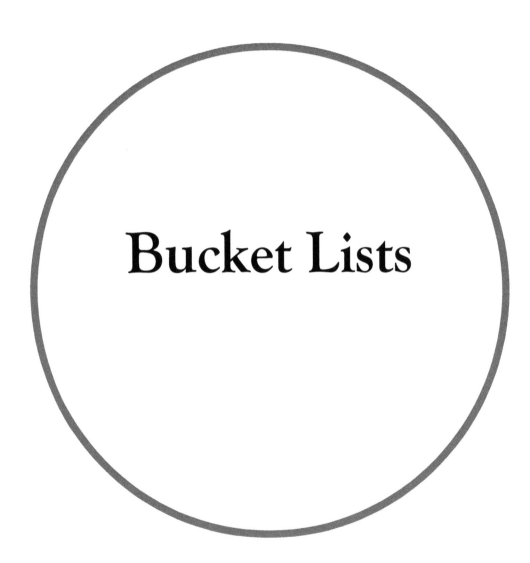

Bucket Lists

KEEP ADDING TO
YOUR BUCKET LIST

*"And in the end, it's not the years in your life that count.
It's the life in your years"*

—*Abraham Lincoln*

I have been making goal lists since I was young. The more you put your goals out to the universe the more things you will accomplish. Make it your screen saver. It could be a picture, an abbreviation or a full description. I have made wish boards, wish books and even have sent them to myself on a postcard. If you are making a list, make it with different areas of life and different degrees of difficulty. Life is all about choices. When was the last time, you did something for the first time? Here are some you may want to add to your list.

THINGS I HAVE CHECKED OFF MY BUCKET LIST

Learn to ride a horse
See a salmon run
Blow glass
Make pottery
Take my whole family on vacation
Skydive
Climb the Eiffel Tower
Repel down a waterfall
Fly in a Learjet
Travel to 100 countries
Own a penthouse
Meet Richard Branson
Meet royalty
Meet Bill Clinton
Be on a TV show
Show my house in a magazine
Ride in a gondola in Venice
Put on my own charity art show
Join a board of a charity
Polar bear plunge
Start my own charity
Go on safari in Africa
Visit Machu Picchu
Visit the Taj Mahal with no tourists around
Sleep at an Ice Hotel
Feed a baby elephant

Stay in a castle
Float in the Dead Sea
Fly First Class
See the Mona Lisa
Learn how to box
Reach my DTM in Toastmasters
Learn to fly a helicopter
Swim with sea turtles
Write a book
Learn to scuba dive
Hear the Pope speak at the Vatican
Fire walk
Make someone's dream come true
Put together a book of my father-in-law's poetry
Go to the Galapagos
Walk Copacabana Beach
Stay at a glass bottom cabana over the ocean
Arrange a flash mob
Meet Oprah
Meet Michael Buble
Pay off all my debts
Become a millionaire
Learn to ski downhill
Learn to ride a motorbike
Meet Wayne Gretzky
Do random acts of kindness at least once a week
Watch an Indy race live
Sit in the first row of an NBA game
Wine taste in Napa Valley
Walk nude on a beach
Go to the Olympics
See Niagara Falls
Forgive my dad
See Stonehenge
Go on a dog sled ride
Release baby turtles in the ocean

Dive in the Great Barrier Reef
Learn to make soap
Be in a parade
Present flowers to the winning horse
Go to the French Open
Visit the Dom Perignon vineyard
Sit in the front row of a concert
Marry a man smarter than me
Bathe an elephant
Visit the Great Pyramids
Be nominated for a business woman award
Fly in a hot air balloon
Visit a live volcano
Pay off my mortgage
Go to Tahiti
Be financially independent
Own my own business
Learn different languages
Speak in front of 10,000 people
Learn to sing
Learn to make sushi
Learn to cross-country ski
Buy my own car
Climb Mount Kilimanjaro
Beat Cancer
Learn how to fix a car engine
Dye my hair red
Mentor young entrepreneurs

THINGS STILL ON MY BUCKET LIST

Write a blog on Caesar salads
Be a guest judge on Dancing with the Stars
Go to outer space with Virgin Atlantic
Meet the Queen (now that I have seen her bedroom and bathroom)
Meet the Dalai Lama
Go to Scotland and rent an entire castle
Have my penthouse on the cover of a magazine
Fly first class on Air Emirates in the Bedroom Suite
Have Michael Buble over for dinner
Travel on a private jet around the world
Host an event where all rescue animals are adopted out in all SPCA's
in Vancouver
Do Monaco in style
Build our own retirement community
Go to Richard Branson's private island
Serve on a pet rescue board
Laugh everyday
Stay happily married to Ralph forever
Have a famous artist perform at my place for dinner guests
Invent something that helps people as they are aging
Be a Key Note speaker in another country
Bike the Rhine in Germany
Buy a driver-less car
Sleep in an underwater hotel
Act in a Hollywood movie
Go to the South Pole

Be a guest on the Ellen DeGeneres show
Do a two-minute plank exercise
Go back to a size 10
Travel while promoting my book with my husband
Design a wine label
Have my cocktail that I invented, go viral
Go to a worldwide movie premier
Have my book on a Best Sellers list
Go to the Oscars and then Elton John's after-party (which is booked for 2019)
See a total eclipse of the sun
Meet a Pope
Meet the Obamas
Catch and cuddle a lamb
Go to Antarctica
Be in the Guinness Book of World Records (working on right now)
Go to Mardi Gras
Find a bra that fits and is comfortable
Be in the delivery room for a birth
Visit the White House
Learn Sign Language
Die with no regrets

EPILOGUE

I feel very fortunate to have all the adventures and experiences that I have had so far. There are some that I would like to forget, but I know it was my destiny to learn life lessons, so I will be better prepared for my job on the other side.

I want to say thank you to each and every person I have met from every corner of the world. I am the person I am today because of all the incredible experiences I have had with all of you. And to the people I haven't met yet, I can't wait to meet you!

And the biggest thanks of all goes to my mother, for loving me through the good times and bad. For all the fights, my brother and I had, that drove you crazy. For putting up with me at the age fifteen, when I knew every single thing in the world and would not listen to you. For not locking me in my room when I broke curfew. For not stopping me, but worrying about me when I traveled the world. And thank you for all the sappy emails you send me. I love you so much! You are my hero for raising two challenging kids and not running away from home (like you so often threatened)!

What I hope readers get out of my stories is that they can recognize your ***"And then it happened"*** moments when it comes along, and have courage and take the leap.

Life is a jumble of possibilities intended to round out your character. You don't always have to sit and think about doing something when an opportunity comes along. Sometimes the universe just hands you an opportunity that will change your direction in life. And please, celebrate each and every event with those that you love. Do not wait till the end.

I highly recommend to all of you to write a book when you are ready. While writing, I learned so much about myself and what I should be doing in my life. I can't believe I didn't do this sooner, but then again, I wasn't ready for it until now.

And finally, be open to listening to your totems and your spirit guides for the messages they are sending you. Meditate as often as you can, before you go to sleep and when you wake up, and let the universe know you are ready for your messages. Follow your own instincts and take some risks. If something scares you a little, but excites you a lot, you are on the right path. And remember, the only difference between an adventure and an ordeal is how you look at it.

Sending all of you white light.
Cheers,
Lori-Ann Keenan

'An elderly lady was at her doctor's office for her annual exams. When the doctor was finishing up, he asked the lady if she had any other concerns. The lady responded, "Yes, just one. My husband can't seem to get it up anymore."
The doctor replied with, "Well you know there is a pill for that now?" The lady explained that her husband takes so many pills as it is, and he won't want to take another one. The doctor then said, "All you have to do is crush it up in his morning coffee, and then see what happens." The lady decided to give it a shot.

A few weeks later the lady was back at her doctors for the results of her exams. When the doctor came in the room he excitedly asked, "So, how did it go?"
The lady replied, "Oh doctor, it was just terrible!" The doctor was shocked and ask why. The lady explained "Well, I did just as you suggested. One morning I crushed up the pill in his morning coffee, 20 minutes later he grabbed me, threw me on the table and made mad passionately love to me for 45 minutes!"
The doctor said "Well that's great!"
She replied, "No, it is just awful, we can't go back to Starbucks anymore!"'

—Anonymous

INDEX

About the Author

Whether flying helicopters or reading auras, Lori-Ann Keenan is a living, breathing testament to full-spectrum living. An accomplished business person, speaker, interior designer, philanthropist and artist, she is a master of manifestation who has studied the masters of success.

An expert in creating a life of adventure throughout her many years as a successful entrepreneur, Lori-Ann, together with her husband, have followed the principles of manifestation to create a life that most only dream of. Her adventurous and courageous stories are a testament to her unshakable passion for life, her deep caring for others, and her belief that whatever you can dream you can do.

While her professional contributions are many, those who are friends with Lori-Ann, believe that her defining characteristics are generosity, humor and an undying sense of fun, adventure and romance. Mentoring or public speaking, Lori-Ann greets people the same way she greets everyone each day, with enthusiasm and reverence.

Lori-Ann will always encourage you to dream big, believe in yourself and celebrate often. She will be ready to provide you with a helping hand and the kick in the butt that you might need to follow her lead and be ready for your "And then it happened" life-changing moments.

CPSIA information can be obtained
at www.ICGtesting.com
Printed in the USA
LVHW042131140219
607627LV00002B/4